EXPECTATIONS
IN
ECONOMIC
THEORY

EXPECTATIONS IN ECONOMIC THEORY

S. A. Ożga

Routledge
Taylor & Francis Group

LONDON AND NEW YORK

First published 1975 by Transaction Publishers

Published 2017 by Routledge
2 Park Square, Milton Park, Abingdon, Oxon OX14 4RN
711 Third Avenue, New York, NY 10017, USA

Routledge is an imprint of the Taylor & Francis Group, an informa business

Library of Congress Catalog Number: 2007026448

Library of Congress Cataloging-in-Publication Data

Ozga, S. A. (S.Andrew)
    Expectations in economic theory / S.A. Ozga.
        p. cm.
    Previously published: Chicago : Aldine Pub. Co., [1965].
    Includes bibliographical references and index.
    ISBN 978-0-202-36155-0
        1. Economic forecasting. I. Title.
HB3730.09   2007

330.1-dc22

ISBN 13: 978-0-202-36155-0 (pbk)
ISBN 13: 978-1-138-52324-1 (hbk)
ISBN 13: 978-0-203-79257-5 (ebk)

2007026448

DOI: 10.4324/9780203792575

Contents

Preface

SOME parts of this book were originally written as lecture notes for a graduate course on Risk, Uncertainty, and Expectations which I gave at the London School of Economics in 1961–63. Few of those who attended the course would, however, be able to identify the respective sections. For the text has been then extensively revised and expanded, and new sections have been added to cover the field. More stress has also been laid on methodological considerations which are pertinent to all attempts to introduce the notion of expectations into economic theory. They throw more light on the sense and usefulness of those attempts than any technical analysis of their formal properties might do. In spite of these extensions and alterations, the text remains, however, in the field of what may be called general economics. No special knowledge of any particular chapter of it is required to follow the argument.

Much credit (and responsibility) for what this book is like goes to those students who, by their presence at the lectures and the interest in the subject, created a suitable atmosphere for it to be written. The final text owes also a great deal to valuable comments of Professors E. H. Phelps Brown, J. E. Meade and G. L. S. Shackle who very generously gave their time to read the first draft and suggested many modifications and improvements.

London School of Economics　　　　　　　　S. A. OŻGA
June 1965

9

AN INTRODUCTION ON METHOD
AND SCOPE

In a study of expectations it is impossible not to become involved in methodological considerations. It is better, therefore, to make all the necessary resolutions right at the beginning and once for all, rather than to have to deal with them over and over again in asides and digressions. This is not a book of methodology. Not very much, therefore, can be said in it about why these – rather than other methodological resolutions – have been made. A few words of explanation must, however, be given about what these resolutions are and what limitations they impose on the nature and the scope of the analysis with which it is concerned.

The book deals with economic theory. The first resolution which must be made, is thus about what kind of a theory it is with which it is to be concerned. The word theory may mean many things; it may mean a hypothesis put forward as an explanation of something, an idea, or a notion. In a normative sense it may mean a recommendation, a rule, or principle to be followed. In science it usually means a system of hypotheses to be accepted as an explanation of certain facts, a set of general laws, and principles. It is also used to distinguish the general principles and methods of a subject from the practice of it.

The theory with which the present book is concerned is that of science. In very general terms it may be defined as a system of hypotheses, one following from another, which permits us to derive from known facts predictions of other facts. Theory of gravitation permits us – for instance – to derive from the fact that an apple detached itself from the branch of a tree, the prediction that the apple lies on the ground. If the knowledge of the fact which we predict is important for us, in the sense that it permits us to achieve better the objectives we pursue, the

13

theory may have a practical value. If the facts we predict are already known, the theory may still have an explanatory value. Explanation derives from prediction. For to explain a fact, the theory must predict it. The relation, however, is not the other way round. Prediction may not be explanation. If, for instance, the future population of a country is estimated by extrapolating its past trends, the estimate is a prediction and not an explanation. For a theory to explain a fact, the prediction must be derived from hypotheses which predict other facts as well. The fact, for instance, that an apple lies on the ground is explained by the theory of gravitation, not because the latter fits this particular fact but because it fits many other facts. It is always possible to find a formula which fits some facts. To become a theory and explain them it must also fit other facts.

The hypotheses in a theory are about the world in which we live. They are, however, not about the world as it is but only about some formal representation of it. An object, for instance, cannot be identified in any other way than by its characteristics, such as weight, colour, or temperature. We do not know what the object is. What we may know is only some of these characteristics. A formal representation of the object is a description of these characteristics. What characteristics are relevant and what is the form of the description, depends on the context of the theory. Irrespective, however, of what the case may be, the description is always in terms of an operation, by means of which the characteristics are supposed to be ascertained. The weight is what we ascertain when we weigh an object, the colour is what we perceive when we look at it, and the temperature is what we see on the thermometer. The same applies to facts about sensations or states of mind. A formal representation of fear or pain, for instance, is a description of what we feel or what we do when we experience them.

Any formal representation of the world must always be arbitrary. It depends on the choice of the operations in terms of which its characteristics are defined. What we call the weight of an object may, for instance, be ascertained either by using scales or by asking ourselves what we experience when we take the object in the hand. In the former case the description is in tons or pounds, in the latter it is in terms of heavy or light. Although the word 'weight' is used in either case, the description is in fact different. What we call colour can be ascertained, not only by looking at the object, but also by measuring the length of the light waves when light is refracted from it. The description may thus be in terms of red, green, blue, as well as in terms of some measure of length. Temperature may be ascertained in centigrade by using a thermometer, or as hot or cold by touching the object by hand. Similarly, the formal representation of pain or fear may be either, a description of what we feel when we experience it, or a description of our wincing, shrieking, or running away. What is behind the formal representation is the matter of one's beliefs, of interpretation. We may believe that when a person winces, he or she experiences the same sensation as we do when we say that we are in pain. A theory, however, does not go as far as that. If wincing is the formal representation of pain, the theory stops at that. It is about a formal representation of the world, and not about what we believe that this representation represents.

It follows that only those terms can be used in the text of a theory for which an operation is provided as a definition. They are what the theory is about. The operations which define them need not necessarily be performed. They may require special conditions of an experiment which – owing to technical, social or other obstacles – can never be satisfied. What the terms describe can then never be ascertained. But none the less, the terms may be meaningful and the theory useful; it may contain hypotheses about what the terms are likely to be, which not only fit a certain class of facts, but also predict and explain others. A hypothesis, for instance, that all bodies fall faster the longer they fall would explain the fact that apples falling from taller trees are usually more often broken than those which fall from lower trees, and a term describing speed as a measure of the distance travelled per unit of time would be meaningful, even if no experiments could have ever been performed which would enable us to say what this measure actually is.

The choice of the operations which define the terms of a theory is arbitrary. Methodology of science lays down some general conditions which an operation must satisfy to be accepted as scientific. But even on this very general level, the status of certain types of operations is not quite clear. This applies particularly to the operation of introspection. The subjectivist view is that if introspection were ruled out, all scientific investigation of what we actually experience would become impossible. The behaviourists maintain that introspection is not a scientific operation, because the results of it cannot be either confirmed or refuted by anybody except by the person who is the subject of it. According, therefore, to whether the former or the latter view is accepted, the formal representation of the world may or may not include characteristics to be ascertained by introspection.

If we adopt the attitude of a behaviourist, and reject introspection as an operation by means of which terms in a scientific theory can be ascertained, this does not necessarily mean that we have to reject it also as an operation in terms of which they can be defined. As has been pointed out in the preceding paragraph, the terms which introspection defines may appear in a theory as theoretical terms. Hypotheses may be put forward as to how they relate to other terms; and if these lead to useful predictions, the theory in which the terms appear may be useful as well; although the latter does not provide then for any operation which would be acceptable to a behaviourist as a means by which we could either ascertain what these terms are, or test directly whether the hypotheses about them are true.

The following example may help to clarify the nature of the controversy, and the attitude towards it which is adopted in this book. Suppose that the fact which we want to explain is that of people carrying umbrellas during the rain. This can be done by means of a hypothesis that people want to protect themselves against the rain. The hypothesis fits not only the fact of people carrying umbrellas, but also other facts; such as, houses having roofs even in a very hot climate, of people standing under the trees when it is raining heavily, etc. The same, however, may also be achieved by means of a hypothesis that people carry their umbrellas because they like the rhythmic sound of rain drops falling upon them. This hypothesis, too, fits other facts. People like rhythmic sounds in music, and often fall into rhythm when they do noisy work.

To decide which of these two hypotheses to accept, and which to reject, a behaviourist would try to derive from them predictions of other facts – other than those of people carrying umbrellas – and to confront them with what actually takes place. He would probably say that if people were attracted by the rhythmic sound of rain drops falling on their umbrellas, they

16

would tend to go out in greater numbers when it is raining than they do otherwise; and that this is not what actually takes place. He might even devise an experiment. He might build a hall with artificial rain to see if people would go there with their umbrellas to enjoy the sound of it. An introspectionist, on the other hand, would settle the matter with much less ado. He would dismiss the hypothesis on the ground that we all know by introspection that we carry umbrellas to protect ourselves against the rain, and not to listen to it. And, even if the behaviourist's hall turned out to be overcrowded with people carrying their umbrellas, he would not be easily convinced that he was wrong. He would rather dispute the validity of the experiment by pointing out that if people went there, it was not to listen to the artificial rain but to have fun out of being together in rather unusual conditions.

In the present book we do not take sides in the dispute. The attitude we adopt in it is that of an opportunist. In the study of expectations there are not many occasions to perform experiments, and not many known facts with which predictions can be confronted. Unless, therefore, behaviouristic tests are supplemented by an appeal to introspection, not much can be said about the relative merits of the hypotheses proposed. A behaviouristic test is always preferable, and therefore, whenever there is a possibility of it, it must not be left unexplored. As not many possibilities of such tests exist, it may be also worthwhile to subject some of the hypotheses to a test by introspection, a plausibility test as we will call it to underline its lower status. Do we think that we ourselves would behave in the particular circumstances as the hypothesis says that we should? Or, do we experience what it says that we should experience? The answer is usually indecisive, but it may throw some light on how well the respective theory would fit the facts if it could be confronted with them. For, a plausible theory or hypothesis means in this case that the theory or the hypothesis is thought fit to survive a behaviouristic test if it could be subjected to it. How much significance is to be attached to such plausibility tests is for the reader to decide. If he happens to be a strict behaviourist, he would probably dismiss them altogether as not scientific. But one wonders how much of the present-day theory of economics and of social sciences in general he would have to dismiss as well.

17

These methodological resolutions affect the character and the scope of the analysis which is the subject matter of this book. The analysis consists mainly in sorting out the operations which determine the sense of the hypotheses proposed, in subjecting their results to plausibility tests, and in confronting predictions derived from them with the behaviour actually observed. Predictions are of two kinds. A theory which explains human behaviour may attempt to predict what, in particular circumstances, a particular man would do; or it may predict some features of human behaviour in general. For instance, in a theory explaining why people carry umbrellas the prediction may be about a particular man doing this or about more people carrying umbrellas when it is raining more. Different hypotheses are then required to make the prediction. In the first case, the hypothesis must be about how much the respective man is annoyed by various amounts of rain. In the second case, the prediction can be derived from the hypothesis that people are more annoyed, the more rain there is; there is no need to make any assertions about how much they are annoyed by any particular amount of it. We will see that hypotheses about expectations which have been introduced in various forms into economic theory, lead usually to predictions of this latter type.

The interpretation of the theory, as a scientific theory which predicts and explains excludes from the investigation all normative considerations. The literature on uncertainty and expectations has both a normative and a descriptive aspect, one often intermingled with the other in the same scheme of thought. The insistence on the descriptive character of the theory requires, therefore, that more stress has to be laid sometimes on the incidental aspects of an argument, than on those for the sake of which it was originally invented. Nothing at all can be said about such otherwise important developments as decision theory, forecasting, and operational research. The admission of the plausibility test, on the other hand, brings within the scope of the investigation considerations of which many a scientist would not approve. They seem, however, to be so pertinent to this particular field that they can hardly be left out altogether.

PART ONE

FORMALIZATION OF EXPECTATIONS

THE subject matter of this book is the analysis of expectations as an element in economic theory. Before, however, anything can be said about them from this particular point of view, a few words of explanation must be given about what expectations actually are, how they are related to our behaviour in general, and in terms of what meaningful operations the characteristics which constitute their formal representation can be defined. This is the topic for the first three chapters. The discussion exceeds the limits of few words. It will, however, become apparent in the course of it that the notion of an expectation is too complex to be defined in one sentence or analysed in one paragraph. Much unnecessary confusion has in fact arisen in the literature from not enough attention having sometimes been paid to the actual sense of the words used. The time spent on these preliminaries may not, therefore, be wasted. Although on first impression the subject may not seem to be quite in the field of economics proper.

The first chapter deals with expectations in the most general sense. Its purpose is to introduce the elementary notions of evidence, prospect and subject of expectations, of outcomes, their weights in the prospects, of possible states of the world, and of pay-offs to be derived from them. An attempt is also made in it to establish a formal connection between expectations and behaviour. The analysis, however, is conceptual only. It singles out the elements of a more complex structure, and lays them bare for further investigation. It does not give any clue yet to how they work.

The second and the third chapters deal with the relations between these elements. The possible logical relations between them are analysed in the second chapter; those which derive from subjective factors in the third. It is here that the main excursions are made into fields which are only loosely connected with economics proper. For most of the discussion of logical relations turns around the question of what elements in the prospect are implied in the evidence, and what significance is to be attached to probability as the weight of an outcome in the prospect. In the discussion of the subjective factors the stress is laid on the elucidation of the nature of the operations in terms of which their formal representation can be defined and ascertained.

1

The Nature of Expectations

THIS introductory chapter deals with expectations in a descriptive way. Their meaning, and some of the elementary notions involved in them, are brought into focus to facilitate their subsequent formalization. The stress, however, is laid on using suitable words to describe them, rather than on giving these words a content which would suit any particular theory.

(1.1) Expecting, Forecasting, and Programming

(1.1.1) For the purpose of theoretical analysis it is convenient to distinguish between (i) expectations proper, (ii) forecasts, and (iii) programmes. *Expectations proper* are attitudes, dispositions, or states of mind which determine our behaviour, or at least accompany it. They may be the actual thinking of individuals, if the expectations are those of individual persons; or they may be the attitudes of groups of persons, if the expectations are those of whole groups. It does not matter whether the thinking is imaginative or in the form of a disposition to action. Stopping the car before an obstruction implies thinking even if it is not fully brought to our mind what we are doing.[1]

Expectations proper must be ascertained either directly by introspection or they may be derived from the observation of our behaviour. If we expect rain today, we experience something that we may be able to identify by introspection as an expectation of rain. Or we may simply take an umbrella when going out, and our expectation of rain can be derived from the observation of what we do. In the former case, expectations are ascertained directly through something that is comparable to our senses. In

[1] On the nature of thinking see H. H. Price, *Thinking and Experience*, 2nd ed., Hutchinson (London, 1962).

the latter, we need a theory which supplies a connection between the expectations and the behaviour. In the case of the expectation of rain, the theory is that we do not want to ruin our clothes or catch cold by exposing ourselves to rain, that an umbrella protects us from this, and that, therefore, our taking the umbrella goes usually together with the expectation of rain

(1.1.2) A *forecast* is an explicit formulation of one's view of the future. It may be a BBC weather forecast, our saying to somebody – or even to ourselves – that it is going to rain today or some other statement about what is going to happen; and it may come from an individual person or from a group of persons, as an informal utterance or as an official document.

The feature which distinguishes a forecast from an expectation proper is that it takes a definite form and it can be directly observed and ascertained. Even if it is not communicated to anybody, it is in the form of a statement in words, and it is only in this particular form that it can be observed. Its formal representation can, therefore, be only a description of the form in which it occurs.

(1.1.3) A *programme* is an explicit formulation of one's intention to do something in the future. It too may take the form of an informal utterance made by an individual person, or of a plan or budget of a whole group of persons. As in the case of a forecast, the relevant person or group of persons state explicitly their views about what is going to happen in the future. A programme, however, differs from a forecast in that it implies a resolution to act in a certain way and to make the future conform to it. In the case of a forecast, the person who makes it is in the position of an observer who looks at the world around him and tells other people how it will behave. In the case of a programme, the person is a part of that world and behaves himself.

The same statement or document may be seen both as a forecast and as a programme. We may, for instance, say that we will take the umbrella today. This is our resolution, a programme. At the same time, however, we may think that what we are saying is going to happen; because we usually take the umbrella when we want to. Thus, we are also making a forecast.

(1.1.4) Programmes and forecasts are facts which may be regarded as instances of our behaviour. It is, therefore, legitimate to speak of them as being prompted or accompanied by expecta-

24

ions proper. Our expectations of rain may lead to our taking he umbrella, as well as to our expressing the intention, or making a forecast, that we will do so. A theory is, therefore, required to establish a connection between forecasts and programmes on one hand, and expectations proper on the other.

The simplest theory that might be thought of is that forecasts and programmes are a formal representation of expectations proper. If, for instance, we say that it is going to rain today, we are supposed to hold at the same time an expectation of rain which we describe in the words which we say. To make a plausibility test of the theory, we might try to find out by introspection whether what we say about rain corresponds in fact to what we ourselves identify as an expectation of rain. It is possible that it does not correspond to it, because some people either deliberately lie or at least do not speak their minds. To make a behaviouristic test of the theory we might also try to find out whether the theory predicts correctly the forecasts and programmes we make. If, for instance, our programme is to take the umbrella, but at the same time we make a forecast that we will not take it because we usually are absent-minded and forget to do so, our expectation proper cannot be identified with both the programme and the forecast.

(1.1.5) Quite a different question is whether expectations proper can be formalized as explicit statements in words. It may be argued that the experience which we identify as an expectation of rain, is not affected by our saying, or not saying, to ourselves or to somebody else that it is going to rain. Expectations proper may, therefore, be considered as if they were always explicit statements in words. If we take the umbrella, we behave so as if we were saying or at least thinking in words that it is going to rain.

This is, in fact, the attitude which we adopt in this book. Whatever the details of the formal representation of expectations may be, they are supposed to be always given in words, or in symbols which are defined in words. Whether they are the same words as those which are used in a programme or in a forecast is a matter for the theory to decide. Even, however, if they are the same, they are not a programme or a forecast. They are a formal representation of an expectation proper.

(1.1.6) It must be clear by now that the crucial terms of any

25

theory of expectations are expectations proper. Programmes and forecasts are only facts, forms of behaviour, which a suitable theory may predict and explain by means of a hypothesis about expectations proper. Whenever, therefore, in the course of our discussion the word expectations is used without qualification, it is supposed to mean expectations proper. Only if it is thought necessary to stress the fact that a particular statement is not a formal representation of an expectation proper, but a forecast or a programme, will the latter be substituted for it. [1]

(1.2) The Evidence and the Individual

(1.2.1) Three elements are usually involved in an expectation: (i) the individual, (ii) the evidence, and (iii) the prospect. The individual is who expects. The evidence is what the individual knows. And the prospect is the individual's view of what is going to happen. [2] If, for instance, we look at dark clouds and say that it is going to rain today, we are the individual, the dark clouds we see are the evidence, and the view that it is going to rain today is the prospect. [3]

(1.2.2) Consider first the element of the *evidence*. It may be formalized as a set of statements which provide explicit answers to questions about the conditions which give rise to the prospect. In the example of our expectation of rain the questions would be: what clouds are there in the sky?, what is the direction of the wind?, etc. The answers that the clouds are dark, the wind is from the south-west, and so on, are the evidence.

We rarely, if ever, formulate the evidence in words: and even

[1] From the point of view of what they are about, expectations have been classified by Modigliani and Cohen, *The Role of Anticipations and Plans in Economic Behaviour and their Use in Economic Analysis and Forecasting*, University of Illinois Bulletin (1961), into anticipations, decisions, and plans. Anticipations are about the behaviour of the world; and decisions and plans are about the behaviour of those who expect. Decisions are definite and, if feasible, are always implemented. Plans are subject to revision. Thus, if they are stated explicitly, anticipations are forecasts, and decisions and plans are programmes.

[2] Compare N. Georgescu-Roegen, The Nature of Expectations and Uncertainty, in Mary J. Bowman (ed.), *Expectations, Uncertainty and Business Behaviour*, Social Science Research Council (New York, 1958).

[3] Georgescu-Roegen used the word prediction to describe what we call prospect. The latter, however, seems to be more in line with how these words are used in the literature. We will reserve, therefore, the word prediction to describe the facts which a theory enables us to predict.

if we formulate it, the formulation is never complete. The evidence is never fully brought to the surface of the mind. We do not know exactly what questions to ask. We have certain general notions and habits of thought which affect our expectations, but we are never fully conscious of what they are. We also know facts but do not formulate this knowledge in words. If, for instance, we look at dark clouds and take an umbrella, we very rarely say to ourselves that there are clouds in the sky.

If, however, the evidence is to be an element of a theory, it must be identified somehow. For the sake of this identification it must, therefore, be described in words. The question to which it provides answers may not be asked, and the answers may not be given, but the knowledge, or lack of knowledge, of particular facts can be identified only as an explicit answer, or lack of answer, to a question about those facts.

(1.2.3) The *individual* transforms the evidence into the prospect; or – as it may sometimes be more convenient to say – is the agent through whom the evidence is transformed into the prospect. It need not be an individual in the strict sense of this word. It may be a group of persons, a board, or a committee of experts, who all of them together arrive at a particular prospect or decide on a course of action which implies a prospect.

Theory of expectations in economics has little to say on how this transformation is made. The actual process of expecting is in the nature of inference, of throwing up hypotheses which are subsequently accepted or rejected. It takes place in one's mind. If, for instance, we look at dark clouds, a hypothesis comes to our mind that there will be rain today, and we accept it as a prospect. Or, if we only take the umbrella and do not formulate the hypothesis in words, we act as if we did so.

In the expectations of groups of people, a part of the process of transformation of the evidence into a prospect may take the form of following some rules of procedure, a majority vote for instance. A part of the process is then revealed to us in the actual proceedings. This is, however, only a very insignificant part. The actual transformation of the evidence takes place in the minds of the members of the group, both spontaneously and under the impact of the debate. The rules of procedure apply only to the aggregation of individual expectations into those of the group.

(1.2.4) What questions may the evidence be supposed to

answer? If a theory is used to derive a prospect from it, the questions are supplied by the context of the theory. If, for instance, the theory is that rain depends on the state of the clouds, the questions about clouds are relevant. If the theory is that rain depends on the direction of the wind, the relevant questions are about the direction of the wind.

In the majority of cases, however, no theories are available from which prospects could be derived. And if they are available, they are often subject to reservations. It is, therefore, impossible to say once and for all, which questions are relevant to a particular prospect. At present, political events are thought to be irrelevant to the prospect of rain, but it is by no means impossible that a connection between them will be discovered later on, and they will become relevant. If a method is invented to produce rain, some political parties may be more inclined to use it than others.

It may be useful, none the less, to speak of the evidence as of a set of answers to relevant questions *in abstracto*, without pretending that all of them can be always identified. For, in some cases, the relevant questions may be so clearly separated from the irrelevant ones that it would be too pedantic not to concentrate on the former only to simplify the exposition. There is, for instance, little doubt that which face of a die will turn up when the die is thrown on a table depends solely on the properties of the die and on the way in which it is thrown.

(1.2.5) The questions asked may be of two types: about particular events, and about connections between possible events. An example of the first type is, 'what clouds are there in the sky or what is the direction of the wind?' That of the second type is, 'what is the connection between the state of the clouds, or the direction of the wind now, and the weather tomorrow?' Questions of the first type may be called *factual* questions: those of the second type *theoretical* questions. The answers to factual questions are statements about instances of events: those to theoretical questions are generalizations about connections between events.

With respect to factual questions, it is assumed throughout this book that if an answer to any of them is supposed to be known, it is known in an absolute sense. The individual considers the particular statement about an event as either true or false.

This applies both to physical and to mental events. The difference is only that in the case of physical events, the knowledge may be acquired by observation and is accessible to everybody; and in the case of mental events, it is acquired by introspection and is accessible to those only who are the subject of it.

Answers to theoretical questions are never known in an absolute sense. A generalization is a hypothesis which may be disproved by further observations. Even, therefore, if it has not been disproved yet, it can be accepted with reservations only. These are greater or smaller, according to how well the generalization fits the instances about which it generalizes. If, for instance, it has been observed that rain has always followed after dark clouds, a generalization that dark clouds are followed by rain is accepted with little reservation. If the connection has been observed in some cases only, the reservations are much greater.

(1.2.6) Very little is said in this book about the nature of these reservations. In very general terms, they indicate the degree to which a hypothesis is acceptable as a basis for the prediction of instances of events to which it refers. This is, however, about all we can say about it here. The problem is that of inductive logic, and there is no way in which its solution could be made an integral part of a theory.

This has important consequences for the formalization of the evidence. For, if answers to theoretical questions were included in it, the formalization would have to provide for a representation of the reservations attached to them. And if the latter was not available, the evidence could not be formalized. To get rid of this difficulty we will, therefore, regard the evidence as consisting of answers to factual questions only. A set of such answers is the required formal representation of it. As all answers are supposed to be true, the problem of the reservations with respect to the evidence does not arise. Theoretical questions may be asked in the course of the process of the transformation of the evidence, and the answers given to them may affect the prospect. But they do not appear in either of them. If, for instance, we look at dark clouds and expect rain, the evidence in our expectation is supposed to consist of statements about a very large number of instances of dark clouds having been followed by rain; and the formulation of the generalization that dark clouds are usually followed by rain is a part of the process in the course of which the evidence is transformed into the prospect. All uncertainty about the future originates thus in this process of transformation. The formalization outlined in this paragraph does not allow for any uncertainty about the evidence.

(1.2.7) As there is no limit to factual questions which may be relevant to a particular prospect, it is always possible to extend the evidence by adding to it answers to questions which have not been answered before. The evidence might be called *absolute* if this process were completed. Then the evidence would contain answers to all relevant questions which it is possible to ask. The answers, which in the particular circumstances the individual actually knows, may be called the *actual* evidence.

(1.3) The Prospect

(1.3.1) The prospect is a certain view of the future. If we expect rain today, our view of the future is that it will be raining within the next few hours. What we expect is usually called an outcome. Rain today is thus an outcome in the prospect of rain. As in the case of the evidence, we very rarely describe the outcomes explicitly in words. But if they are terms in a theory, their formal representation must be in words.

(1.3.2) The outcomes are never without reservations. The actual evidence is never absolute; and even if it were absolute, there might be some indeterminacy in the world, which would make the knowledge of the future impossible. Thus to each outcome there is always attached a certain *weight* which qualifies it to a greater or smaller extent.

The fact that a weight is attached to the outcome may be made explicit by means of a modal form of the prospect. If we expect rain, we may say that it will be probably raining today, or that it may be raining today. But even if we do not make it explicit, the weight is always there. We often forget about it. We may be so certain of rain today that we may not want to qualify the prospect at all. But if we were pressed hard, we would probably admit that the possibility of a mistake always exists. In principle, all future is uncertain.

(1.3.3) The nature of the weight of an outcome will be discussed later on. It may, however, be pointed out at this stage that whatever it may be, the very fact that a qualification is attached to each outcome implies that a prospect contains always more than one of them. If we cannot be absolutely certain that it will be raining today, we must also consider the possibility that it will not be raining. 'Rain today' and 'no rain today' are then two outcomes in the prospect of rain. The greater weight is attached to the outcome of rain relatively to that of no rain, the more likely we are to say that it will rain today and to take the umbrella.

The number of outcomes in the prospect depends on what is the subject of the expectation. If it is simply rain, there are two outcomes only : rain and no rain. But if the subject of the expectation is the amount of rain, the number of outcomes is infinite. Any number of inches may then be an outcome in the respective prospect.

(1.3.4) In theoretical analysis it is often convenient to neglect some outcomes in cases in which their number is very large or infinite. Only integral numbers of inches may be, for instance, considered, or only those the weights of which exceed a certain minimum. An extreme case is that of a 'sure prospect'. The prospect contains then one outcome only, and a full weight is attached to it. In principle the prospect cannot be a sure prospect if it is to be complete. But it may be deliberately given this form to simplify its formal representation in a theory. The usefulness of the simplification depends then on the usefulness of the theory.

In verbal exposition the prospect is often stated in an incomplete, sure-prospect form to make the argument more readable. Outcomes are also referred to as absent, or not included, in the prospect if their weights are so small that they can be neglected. Extensive use is made of these simplifications in the remaining parts of this book. It must, however, be remembered that whenever this is done the existence of the neglected outcomes is always taken into account. The statement that we expect rain today means that the outcome of no rain appears in the prospect with a very small weight. It is not meant not to exist.[1]

(1.3.5) As time goes by, what was the future becomes the past, and what was expected becomes known. The event which actually

[1] The procedure is quite arbitrary. It has nothing to do with the principle of neglecting small probabilities which was used by Buffon to resolve St Petersburg paradox. For criticism and references see K. J. Arrow, Alternative Approaches to the Theory of Choice in Risk-Taking Situations, *Econometrica*, **19**, October (1951), p. 414.

occurs may then be called the *result*. We will speak of what ha happened as that a particular result has *occurred*. And if the result is one of the outcomes in a prospect, we will say that the particular outcome has *come off*. Thus, if it rains today, it is the outcome of rain that has come off.

Which outcome comes off may depend on (i) how the world happens to behave, and on (ii) how the individual decides to behave. If the subject of the expectation is the weather, the behaviour of the world only is relevant. Whatever the individual may decide to do, rain will come or not come just the same. If, however, the subject of the expectation is whether rain will or will not ruin the individual's clothes, what actually happens may also depend on whether the individual decides to take, or not to take, the umbrella. If the outcome of his clothes not being ruined comes off, this may be due to the fact that there was no rain, as well as to the fact that he had the umbrella to protect himself against it.

In the analysis of possible connections between expectations and behaviour it is useful to distinguish between these two cases. To stress the fact that a particular outcome is supposed to come off as a result of the behaviour of the world, we will often call it a possible *state of the world*. The outcome which actually comes off, that is to say the result which occurs, will then be called the actual state of the world. If the result depends also on the behaviour of the individual, we will speak of a 'possible' and 'actual' outcome.

(1.4) The Subject of Expectations

(1.4.1) The *subject* of an expectation is what the prospect is about. In more precise terms, it is a function which determines the description of an event. The outcomes are then the values which the function may assume. In the example of the expectation of rain, the subject is a description of the event of rain. It may be in terms of rain or no rain. The outcomes of rain, and of no rain, are then the possible values of the function which determines this description. Or the description may be in terms of the amount of rain, measured in inches for instance; and then the possible values of the function which determines it are the outcomes of the possible amounts of rain. In economics, the subject of an expectation is usually something that pertains to our economic affairs. It may be the prices of some goods or services, profits from alternative investments, incomes, etc. Prices, profits, and incomes describe then the expected events.

An event in this case need not necessarily be a single instance of rain or of a price. It may be a whole series of them. It may be, for instance, a sequence of prices over all days of a year or a sequence of days with rain and with no rain. We will speak in such cases of *repetitive events*.

(1.4.2) If the outcome is a possible state of the world, the processes and the conditions on which the result depends may be called a *mechanism*. Thus in the expectation of rain, the mechanism is the clouds moving, the wind blowing, the air rising or falling, etc. They determine the characteristics of the event which will occur. The event may be described in various ways. The same mechanism may thus determine the result in expectations on different subjects. The subjects, however, are then related one to another. For they describe the same event. It is impossible for the respective mechanism to work so that the outcome of no rain comes off in the expectation on one subject and that of two inches of rain in that on the other.

(1.4.3) Our actual behaviour may depend on several expectations, each of them on a different subject. Suppose, for instance, that a businessman makes an estimate of the price at which he expects to sell his products and of the costs which he expects to incur. The output which he decides to produce depends then on both these expectations.

In situations like this it is often convenient to distinguish between (i) primary and (ii) secondary expectations. *Primary expectations* are those in which there are no other expectations between the evidence and the prediction. We look at the clouds and think that rain will come. Or a businessman looks at the reports from the markets and concludes that the prices of his products will increase. Whether the prospect is intuitive, derived by calculation, or implied, is quite irrelevant. What is important, is that it follows directly from the evidence and not from any other prospect. *Secondary expectations* are those in which the prospect is arrived at by steps, a different expectation being involved in each step. The prospect of having our clothes ruined by rain may, for instance, be derived from the evidence of dark

33

clouds through the expectation of rain. And the businessman's expectation of large profits may be derived from the evidence of the reports from the market through his expectations of high prices and low costs. The expectations through which the secondary expectations are derived may be called *intermediate expectations*.

(1.4.4) Expectations on different subjects may be held simultaneously without any of them being intermediate to any other. A trivial example of expectations on different subjects being held simultaneously, but independently one from the other, is that of expectations of profits and of having one's clothes ruined by rain. Even, however, if the expectations are on such subjects as profits and prices, they may be independent one from another. A businessman, for instance, may expect on the ground of the reports from the markets that the price of his product will increase, and at the same time he may expect on the ground of his general feel of the situation that better times are ahead and that his profits will increase. The latter expectation need not be derived through the former. Both may be primary; and if they are secondary, they may be derived through still other expectations.

(1.4.5) If the subjects of expectations are related, the question may arise whether the expectations referring to them are consistent one with another. The businessman's profits are the difference between the revenue which he obtains from the sale of the product, and the costs of that product. If, therefore, he would expect the revenue to decrease, the costs to increase, and the profits to increase, he would be inconsistent in his expectations.

The most general criterion of consistency of expectations is that they satisfy the relations which are supposed to obtain between their subjects. If they do, the prospect in one of them may be derived from that in the other. If, for instance, we expect dark clouds this evening, and dark clouds in the evening go always together with rain the following day, we may derive from the prospect of dark clouds this evening the prospect of rain tomorrow. And if the businessman expects that his revenue will increase and his costs decrease, he may derive from this the prospect that his profits will increase. In other words, even if the expectations are held independently one from the other, the

34

prospects in them must be so related one to another as they would be if one of them was intermediate to the other.

If this criterion is not satisfied, two types of inconsistency may arise. The connection between the subjects of the expectations may be in virtue of a theory, as in the case of the state of the clouds in the evening and the weather tomorrow. The inconsistency may then be called a *theoretical inconsistency*. The other type is that in which the connection between the subjects is implied in their meaning, as in the case of a businessman's expectations of profits. It may be called a *logical inconsistency*. The first type has no meaning outside the context of the theory which supplies the connection. Nothing, therefore, can be said about it until more is known about the latter. The second is simply bad logic. The forms in which it may arise will be discussed in Chapter 2.

(1.4.6) The subject of expectations may be either (i) a description of a *physical event*, such as the amount of rain or the output of cars from a factory, or it may be (ii) a description of a *mental event*, such as the pleasure one expects to derive from having a car. In either case the event expected is directly accessible to the observer. The difference is only that in the case of physical events the observer may be anybody; and in the case of mental events the observer can be that person only who experiences them.

The same events may be expected to occur at different points of time. Strictly speaking the descriptions of their characteristics represent then different subjects. But we will find it more convenient to refer to them as if they were the same subjects. Thus the expectation of rain this afternoon is on the same subject as that of rain tomorrow. The subject is only at a different point of time.

(1.4.7) Expectations may themselves be subjects of expectations. In the morning we may expect rain tomorrow, and we may also expect that in the evening we will be expecting rain tomorrow. The expectation which we will hold in the evening is then the subject of the expectation which we hold in the morning.

To avoid clumsy repetition we will call expectations which themselves are subjects of expectations *conditional expectations*. They are conditional in the sense that they are not expectations actually held but only outcomes in a prospect of them, which may or may not come off. The evidence, the prospects, the outcomes, and the weights which appear in such expectations may then be called *conditional evidence, conditional prospect, conditional outcomes,* and *conditional weights.* Thus the expectation of rain tomorrow, which we expect to hold this evening, is a conditional expectation; the evidence of dark clouds in the evening and the prospect of rain tomorrow which we think we may see and expect this evening are a conditional evidence and a conditional prospect; and the outcome of rain and its weight in that prospect are a conditional outcome and a conditional weight.[1]

(1.4.8) Expectations of this kind may be related to other expectations in the following ways. (i) An expectation of a future expectation and an expectation of a future event (the expectation of one's expectation of rain, for instance, and the expectation of the rain itself) may be held at the same time and in virtue of the same evidence. (ii) The subject of the conditional expectation and the subject of the expectation which is held at the moment (the rain, for instance, which is the subject of the expectation which is expected and the rain which itself is expected) may be the same or related one to the other. And, (iii) the result of the expectation on an earlier subject (the rain in the evening, for instance) may be a part of the conditional evidence in the conditional expectation on a later subject (of rain tomorrow, for instance). The existence of such relations gives rise to problems of clarification and revision of expectations, which will be discussed in (1.6) and then in (2.6) and (3.7).

(1.4.9) An expectation must be further distinguished from a belief in the existence of a relation. A relation is not an event and cannot be the subject of an expectation. If a businessman expects a particular supply of a product, or a particular price of it, the supply and the price are subjects of his expectations. But if he believes that a certain relation will obtain between them, his belief is not an expectation and the relation is not the subject of it. The businessman's belief could be a subject of an expectation if the latter were about whether he will, or will not, believe in something. We may, for instance, expect that in a month's time he will believe that a particular relation between supply and

[1] Compare F. Modigliani and K. J. Cohen, *The Role of Anticipations and Plans in Economic Behaviour and their Use in Economic Analysis and Forecasting,* University of Illinois Bulletin (1961), pp. 81–2.

price will hold in two months' time. The subject of our expectation would then be his belief. We may also expect to find a certain relation to be satisfied by something that will occur. The businessman, for instance, may expect that over a particular period of time there will be a certain negative correlation between the supply and the price of his product. The subject of his expectation is then a particular measure of this correlation. But a relation as such cannot occur; and a belief in its existence cannot, therefore, be an expectation.

On the other hand, if the individual believes that a certain relation obtains between the subjects of different expectations and is not inconsistent in his expectations, the prospects in the latter must satisfy the relation. If, for instance, the businessman expects that the supply of a product will be large, and the demand for it small, he must expect at the same time that its price will be low.

(1.5) The Time Dimension

(1.5.1) Expectations stretch over time. If they are held at present, the evidence is about the past and the prospect about the future. To avoid misunderstanding it may, therefore, be useful to have special terms to denote the points or periods of time to which these elements refer.

(1.5.2) The time at which the expectation is held may be called the *time of the expectation*. If we expect now that rain will come tomorrow, now is the time of the expectation of rain. It is the time at which the evidence is transformed into a particular prospect.

It is possible, and very common indeed, that the same expectations are held over long periods of time. A businessman, for instance, may expect the price of his product to be higher next year than it was last year, and he may stick to this opinion over the whole present year. This does not mean that the time of the expectation in this case is the whole present year. The position is rather that as time goes by, the time of the expectation moves forward. New experience is added to the evidence, and the future to which the expectation refers becomes less distant. In fact, therefore, new expectations arise as time goes by. It may happen that the prospects in them remain the same. The expectations, however, are different at every successive point of time.

(1.5.3) The time to which the prospect refers may be called the *time of the subject*. If we expect rain tomorrow, tomorrow is the time of the subject of the expectation. If a businessman expects that the price of his product will be higher next year than it was last year, the time of the subject is next year.

The length of the time of the subject and its exact position in relation to the time of the expectation depends on what is the subject of the expectation. If the subject is the price in a particular transaction, its time is the time of that transaction. If the subject is the average price over a month or over a year, its time is that particular month or that particular year. It may be closer to, or further away from, the time of the expectation according to whether the month or the year is closer to, or further away from, the time at which the expectation is held.

(1.5.4) If we think that the rain which we have now will continue over the whole day, the time of the subject follows immediately the time of the expectation. But this need not be always so. We may be thinking today that it will be raining tomorrow. The rest of today must then go by before the time of the subject begins. For lack of a better word the time which is in-between the time of the expectation and time of the subject may be called the *time in-between*. As in the case of the time of the subject its length depends on what is the subject of the expectation.

(1.5.5) As time goes by, the time of the expectation on a particular subject moves onwards; the time of the subject becomes closer and closer to it; and the time in-between shorter and shorter. In addition to expectations on that subject we may, however, hold also expectations in which the time of the subject comes sooner and the results of which become known before the time of the subject of the others arrives. And if they are relevant to the latter, they may become a part of the latter's evidence. The answers to questions about some of the events in the latter's time in-between, which were previously unknown, become gradually revealed by facts, and in the light of this new evidence the latter expectations may change.

In some cases we will find it convenient to distinguish between two kinds of changes. One may be called *clarification* and the other *revision* of expectations. We will speak of clarification of expectations if the new evidence contains an answer to a question which could not have been answered before. If the new evidence gives a different answer to a question than the former evidence did, the expectation is revised.

Suppose, for instance, that we attach more or less equal weights to the outcomes of rain and of no rain tomorrow because we do not know what will be the state of the clouds this evening. If then we see that the clouds are dark and in the light of this additional evidence we give more weight to the outcome of rain and less to that of no rain than we did before, our expectation is clarified. If, however, we originally expected a fine day tomorrow because the barometer was pointing that way, and when we saw the dark clouds in the evening and the barometer not moving we discovered that it was out of order, the resulting change in our expectations would be that of revision.

(1.5.6) The process of the adjustment of expectations may be continuous. As time goes by, the evidence changes continuously as more and more facts become known, and the prospect may also be changing continuously. In analysis it may, however, be useful to specify clearly the time at which a particular change takes place. It may be called the *time of adjustment*. It is in fact the time of a new expectation, because new evidence is then transformed into a new prospect. But it is often convenient to speak in such cases of adjustment, to stress the fact that the subject of the expectation remains the same.

The exact position of the time of adjustment may be anywhere during the time in-between of the original expectation. It itself may be the subject of an expectation. If, for instance, we expect in the morning that there will be rain at night, we may also expect that we will adjust this expectation in the light of the information we may receive during the day. And if we admit the possibility of doing this on the ground of the state of the clouds which we may see any time, the adjustment may in fact take place any time as well. The prospect in our expectation of that time may then contain a large, even an infinite number of outcomes.

(1.5.7) It is possible to argue that, as the outcome in a prospect exists only in the individual's imagination, all elements of an expectation are located at the same point of time, at that point at which the transformation of the evidence into the prospect takes place. This is in fact the position which Professor Shackle has taken in his last book.[1] The individual's behaviour is ex-plained there as an adjustment to what happens in his imagina-tion. Those courses of action are regarded as the most desirable which give rise to prospects most pleasant to contemplate.

In the analysis which is the subject matter of this book, the time dimension describes the position in time of the individual contemplating the prospect, and of an outcome coming off as they can be objectively ascertained by an observer and as they are seen by the individual who expects. These are in fact two different operations, and the concepts of time they describe are different as well. It is assumed, however, that no confusion can arise in the analysis from having objective and subjective time running parallel one to the other, and from interpreting the time dimension according to how the context of the theory requires.

(1.6) Consistency, Clarification, and Revision

(1.6.1) The possibility of conditional expectations and of the relations mentioned in (1.4.8) gives rise to the following prob-lems. The fact that the expectation of an expectation and the expectation on the subject of the conditional expectation in the former are held at the same time, and in virtue of the same evid-ence raises the question of whether the prospects in them are consistent one with the other. Can we, for instance, expect that there will be rain tomorrow and that in the evening we will be expecting a fine day tomorrow? The possibility of the prospect being affected by results in the time in-between raises the ques-tion of the adjustment of expectations. How are we going to change our expectation of what will happen tomorrow when we discover what has happened this evening?

No general answers can be given to these questions. The criterion of consistency and the rules according to which expect-ations may be adjusted depend on the subject of the expectation and on its formal representation. The following examples, how-ever, may help to see better the difficulties which are involved.

(1.6.2) Suppose that at time t_o a businessman is interested in profits which he will have at time t_s. What these profits are going to be depends to a large extent on the result of the General

[1] G. L. S. Shackle, *Decision, Order and Time in Human Affairs*, Cambridge University Press (1961).

Election which will become known at time t_k between t_o and t_s. At t_o the businessman may then hold three different expectations: (i) an expectation of profits at t_s, (ii) an expectation of his own expectation of these profits which he will hold at t_k, and (iii) an expectation of the results of the General Election. All the relations mentioned in (1.4.8) are then present. All the three expectations are held in virtue of the evidence which is available at t_o. The subject of (i) is the same as that of the conditional expectation in (ii). And the result of (iii) is expected to be the evidence in the conditional expectation which is the subject of (ii).

If the prospects which are the outcomes in the prospect of (ii) were sure prospects, the question of consistency would not raise any difficulties. The prospect in (ii) would then have as many outcomes of sure prospects of profits as there are outcomes of the possible results of the General Election. Their weights would be those of the outcomes of the election results in (iii). And the outcomes of profits in (i) would be the sure prospects of profits in (ii).

But if the conditional prospects in (ii) are multi-outcome prospects, no simple rules of consistency can be established. The outcomes in (i) must then be the same as those in the conditional prospects in (ii). For otherwise the former could not be derived from the latter. But the weights attached to the outcomes of profits in (i) will be different from those of the outcomes of the election results in (iii). A criterion of consistency must, therefore, imply some formal representation of these weights and the discussion of it must be postponed until more is said about what this formal representation may be.

(1.6.3) Adjustment of expectations, when an answer is obtained to a question which could not have been answered before, has been called *clarification*. An extreme case of it is that of one of the outcomes in the prospect coming off when the time of the subject arrives. At the time of the expectation several outcomes are considered; and then the expectation is clarified when one of the outcomes becomes the actual result. We may call this case *clarification by result*.

This is an extreme case because clarification then takes place instantaneously when the result becomes known. Generally this is not so. Clarification usually takes place not at a particular point of time but over the whole period between the time of the original expectation and the time of the subject. Events on which the result depends become known gradually, and in the light of this new knowledge new more precise prospects are arrived at. As the time of the subject approaches we usually know with increasing certainty what the result will be, and ultimately we know exactly what it is.

This raises the question of what changes in the prospect occur when new knowledge is added to the evidence. In the case of clarification by result the time of the subject has already arrived, and one of the outcomes in the prospect has become the actual result. Suppose, however, that the time of the subject has not arrived yet. What do we mean by clarification in that case?

(1.6.4) As in the case of consistency of expectations, a precise answer requires a definite formal representation of expectations. A change in the prospect means in this case a change in the weights of different outcomes. The weights must, therefore, be formalized if any meaning is to be attached to a change in them. One point, however, is quite general. Whatever the formal representation of the weights, clarification of an expectation before the time of its subject arrives may always be regarded as a clarification by result of the expectation of a conditional expectation on that subject. And then, the change in the prospect in the former depends solely on what change in it is consistent with the particular changes in the latter.

The point may be made clear by means of the example given in (1.6.2). At t_o a businessman holds an expectation of profits which he will have at t_s, an expectation of the election results at t_k, and an expectation of his own expectation of profits at t_s which he will hold at t_k. The prospect in this last expectation consists of as many outcomes of the future expectations of profits as there are outcomes in the prospect of the election result. When the time of the General Election arrives, the expectation of the election results and that of the conditional expectation of profits become clarified by result. The expectation of profits must then change as well. The prospect in it must become consistent with the clarification by result of the expectation of the conditional expectation of profits. In other words, the outcome which has come off in the latter becomes the new prospect in the former.

(1.6.5) It follows that as clarification of an expectation proceeds, no new outcomes can appear in the successive prospects. For if the businessman is consistent in his expectations, he cannot regard the particular outcome of profits as possible in his expectation of the expectation of profits, and as impossible in his expectation of profits themselves. Some outcomes may drop out from the prospects as clarification proceeds. The businessman, for instance, might think that zero profits would be possible only if the Labour Party was to win the election. And if then the Conservative Party has won, he may no longer include the outcome of zero profits in the prospect he contemplates.

This is all we can say about clarification of expectations in general. As clarification proceeds the weights of some outcomes may become so small that the outcomes may be completely neglected and drop out from the prospect. No new outcomes can appear in it. The number of outcomes in the prospect cannot, therefore, increase. It can decrease only until gradually it becomes equal to one when the expectation is clarified by result. What happens to the weights of the outcomes which have not dropped out yet we cannot say. The answer depends on what is their formal representation.

(1.6.6) There cannot be any revision of expectations in the example given above. The only change in the evidence which takes place in it is that when the result of the General Election becomes known an answer is given to a question which could not have been answered before. Suppose, however, that the example is changed so that profits in it depend not on the result of the General Election but on some conditions which can only be guessed in a very general sense. It may then be argued that some answers to questions about these conditions are a part of the evidence which is implied in the prospects of profits at all points of time. The results of profits before t_s may, therefore, throw some light on whether these answers are right or wrong. If profits at some time t_k before t_s turn out to be according to expectation, the answers must have been right, and the expectation of profits at t_s is clarified only. If they turn out to be different from what was expected, the answers must have been wrong, they are replaced by others, and the expectation of profits at t_s is revised.

The criterion of whether the expectation of profits at some future date is, or is not, revised is in this case the fact that the expectation of profits at some earlier date has not, or has been, confirmed by the actual result. It is quite unambiguous if the prospect in the latter expectation is a sure prospect. For the expectation is then confirmed by the result if this sure prospect comes off. If, however, several outcomes appear in the prospect and then one of them comes off, it is impossible to say in any general sense that the respective expectation has or has not been confirmed. The answer depends on which outcome and with what weight has come off. Furthermore, if there are many outcomes in the prospect, the revision may take the form of the revision of the weights only, the outcomes remaining the same. As in the case of consistency and of clarification, a more general discussion of the problem of the revision of expectations requires, therefore, a formal representation of weights of outcomes and must be postponed until the respective representation is decided upon.

(1.7) Strategies and Pay-Offs

(1.7.1) We have already pointed out before that which outcome will ultimately come off may depend on the behaviour of the world as well as on that of the individual who expects. And we decided then to call the outcome a possible state of the world if the behaviour of the world only is relevant, and a possible outcome if the behaviour of the individual is relevant too. The distinction is quite fundamental for any theory in which a connection is supposed to exist between expectations and behaviour. It may, therefore, be useful to set up already at this stage a model of a prospect in which both types of outcomes are involved.

(1.7.2) Suppose that there are n possible states of the world, $W_1, W_2 \ldots W_n$. What they are depends on the subject of the expectation. If, for instance, the subject of the expectation is the weather tomorrow, the possible states of the world are a cold, windy and rainy day, a cold and windy but dry day, a mild calm and muggy day, and so on. The more exact is the description, the greater is the number of possible states of the world, different one from another.

Suppose further that the individual may behave in m different ways which in one sense or another are relevant to the theory in which this model is used. Let us denote them by $S_1, S_2 \ldots S_m$.

The individual may, for instance, take the umbrella or leave it at home. If this is the behaviour which the theory is meant to explain, $m = 2$, and there are only two S's, S_1 and S_2. Which of them the individual decides to adopt is quite irrelevant to which state of the world will come off. This is a part of the definition of a state of the world. As long, therefore, as the subject of the expectation is the state of the weather, the behaviour of the individual does not affect the prospect.

The individual's behaviour may, however, affect the prospect of what is going to happen in the state of the world which comes off. If for instance, the individual does not take the umbrella, his clothes will be ruined by rain if the outcome of the latter comes off. If thus in addition to the expectation of how the world will behave the individual holds also expectations about what will happen to him if he himself behaves in a certain way, the prospect in the latter case must consist of sets of n possible outcomes, each set corresponding to each different way in which he may decide to behave. Let us denote these outcomes by a_{ij} where i is the way in which the individual may decide to behave and j is the state of the world which may come off. It is not necessary for a_{ij} to be different for all j's. If, for instance, W_k denotes rain with thunder and W_s rain without thunder, a_{ik} and a_{is} may both denote the individual's clothes being ruined by rain.

(1.7.3) The relation between the possible states of the world, the ways in which the individual may behave, and the possible outcomes is summarized in Table 1.7.3a. The columns of the matrix represent the n possible states of the world; the rows represent the m ways in which the individual may behave; and the elements in the body of the table the possible outcomes. If the possible states of the world were rain and no rain, and the possible ways of behaviour were to take the umbrella and not to take it, the matrix of possible outcomes would look as in Table 1.7.3b.

Table 1.7.3a

	W_1	W_2	...	W_n
S_1	a_{11}	a_{12}	...	a_{1n}
S_2	a_{21}	a_{22}	...	a_{2n}
.....				
S_m	a_{m1}	a_{m2}	...	a_{mn}

Table 1.7.3b

	Rain	No rain
Umbrella taken	Clothes dry and the umbrella in hand	Clothes dry and the umbrella on the arm
Umbrella left at home	Clothes ruined by rain and both hands free	Clothes dry and both hands free

The possible states of the world and the ways in which the individual may behave are sometimes described in continuous variables. Suppose, for instance, that the price of a businessman's product depends on the level of national income and on the output the businessman decides to produce. The possible states of the world may then be described in terms of the possible levels of national income; the behaviour of the businessman may be described in terms of the output he decides to produce; and the possible outcomes are the price he obtains for his product. The relation cannot then be represented as a matrix. The price in that case is a continuous function of the level of national income and of the volume of output.

(1.7.4) In the remaining chapters of this book the ways in which an individual may behave will be called *strategies*. The term has been borrowed from the theory of games. It describes everything that the individual may do during the period in-between, a separate act or a series of acts, which affect the outcome. If, for instance, the subject of the expectation is what is going to happen to his clothes when he goes out, the strategy which the individual may choose is not only that he takes the umbrella but also that he opens it up if the rain comes, closes it again if the wind happens to be too strong to hold it steady, and so on.

(1.7.5) Behaviour can be explained by expectations only if the individual is interested in what outcome ultimately comes off. The explanation is then teleological. We behave in a particular way because we want to obtain or avoid what we expect. We do not want our clothes to be ruined by rain. We take, therefore, the umbrella when we expect rain.

To distinguish the possible outcomes in which the individual may be interested from those which are irrelevant to his behaviour, we will call the former *pay-offs*. To have our clothes ruined by rain is a possible pay-off from the strategy of having left the umbrella at home. We attach a certain value to this particular outcome, a negative one in this case, and we take this value into account when we decide which strategy to choose.

In economics, the pay-offs are usually expressed either in money or in utility. These will, therefore, be the two cases with which we will be mainly concerned in this book. All real pay-offs, such as having our clothes ruined by rain or having to carry an umbrella, will be reduced there either to a monetary measure, to what our loss or discomfort is worth in money; or they will be reduced to a utility measure, a degree to which they are desirable or undesirable. How this degree is to be ascertained depends on the context of the theory. More, therefore, will have to be said about it later on. At the moment it will suffice to bear in mind that if any connection is to be established between behaviour and expectations, the expected pay-offs must express the individual's valuations of the outcomes to which they refer.

(1.7.6) A matrix of pay-offs will be used in this book as a standard form of a prospect to which the individual is supposed to adjust his behaviour. The actual content of the prospect will depend on what is the subject of the expectation and what behaviour it is supposed to explain. It will, therefore, vary as our discussion moves from one hypothesis to another. But in all cases with which we may be dealing, an attempt will be made to put the prospect in this form.

The first question in this discussion is, what is the formal representation of the terms involved? As far as the strategies and the states of the world are concerned, the answer is that their formal representations are descriptions in words of what may happen and what the individual may do. The same applies to the evidence from which the prospect is derived. This matter has been settled already in (1.2) and (1.3). The answer, however, is much less straightforward if the question is about pay-offs and about the weights of outcomes in the prospect. If the hypothesis applies to pay-offs in utility, the theory must provide for an operation in terms of which utility is defined. And if the outcomes in the prospect are weighted, an operation is also required to define the weights.

The second question is what connection is supposed to exist between the terms of the theory. This is the actual content of its hypotheses. For expectations to be a term in a theory two connections must in fact be established; one between the evidence and the prospect, and the other between the prospect and the behaviour. The analysis of expectations as we have it in economics is usually concerned with the second relation. This, therefore, will be the main topic of this book. In the remaining chapters of this introductory part we will, however, consider also the first relation.

2

Logical Relations in Expectations

THE relations with which we will be concerned in this chapter are those between the evidence and the prospect. The question is whether, and in what cases, the evidence in an expectation can be interpreted as a premise and the prospect as a conclusion. The element of the individual is then suppressed. The transformation of the evidence into the prospect is the matter of logic, quite independent of who holds the expectation.

Much attention is given in this analysis to the problem of the formalization of probability weights. No attempt, however, is made to discuss any of the finer points of the probability theory. In particular, the argument does not exceed the limits of discreet probability measures. The stress is on the sense of the propositions considered, and not on their technical precision.

The analysis of logical relations between the evidence and the prospect does not presuppose that in actual life prospects in expectations are really independent of the individuals who hold them. We know that this is usually not so. The actual evidence is never absolute and its implications are never wholly perceived. Even, therefore, if the prospects were implied in the evidence, this would not mean that in the actual process of expecting the implication would be fully realized. Furthermore, the prospect is the result of a process which takes place in the individual's mind and is determined by the individual's attitudes and dispositions.

In the analysis of logical relations these subjective factors are completely neglected. The analysis deals with those aspects of the prospect only which are wholly determined by the evidence. The evidence is supposed to be quite unambiguous and its implications clearly perceived. The formalization of weights which emerges from the analysis is thus completely objective. The element of the individual does not play any part in it.

(2.1) Deductive Relations and the Degree of Confirmation

(2.1.1) The principal rule of deductive logic is that of a *syllogism*. The premise is a general statement (such as 'all men are mortal'), and a particular statement (such as 'Socrates is a man'), and the conclusion is that 'Socrates is mortal'. The conclusion is implied in the evidence. If we say that all men are mortal and that Socrates is a man, we say in fact that Socrates is mortal too.

A precise formulation of the deductive relation in the above example is that *if* all men are mortal and Socrates is a man, *then* Socrates is mortal. A syllogism does not say anything about whether the premise is true. It only says that there is a certain relation between what is meant by the premise and what is meant by the conclusion. The latter is implied in the former.

(2.1.2) The question now arises whether the relation between the evidence and the prospect in an expectation can be a deductive relation. Suppose, for instance, that Socrates is a living person. His possible death might thus be a subject of an expectation. The fact that he is a man and that other men who have lived have not survived longer than a limited number of years would be the evidence. The conclusion that Socrates will die would be the prospect.

The prospect in this case is not implied in the evidence. What is missing is the generalization that all men are mortal. It could be formulated in the course of the transformation of the evidence into the prospect. But it is not a part of the evidence. It is an answer to a theoretical question, and our formal representation of the evidence contains answers to factual questions only. The resolution to formalize the evidence in this way precludes in fact the possibility of any deductive relations between the prospect and the evidence. For, if the evidence is about the past and the prospect about the future, no statement in the latter can be implied in the former.

(2.1.3) In a deductive relation one conclusion only is implied in the premise. If the premise is that all men are mortal and that Socrates is a man, there is no other conclusion than that Socrates is also mortal. And if the conclusion is a possible outcome and the premise a generalization arrived at in the course of the process of expecting, one only outcome is implied in that generalization.

50

This does not mean that the prospect is a sure prospect. The problem of the weight remains because the generalization is never without reservations. The possibility of its not being true is always present. The outcome that Socrates will not die cannot, therefore, be excluded either.

(2.1.4) Suppose now that we know that Socrates is a man and that so far none of the men of whom we have heard has survived longer than a limited number of years. If no deductive relations obtain between these facts and the prospect of Socrates' possible death, how can the latter be derived from them? The question is not about how we arrive at the particular outcome in the sense of becoming aware of it. The fact of the outcomes being thought of is the result of a creative effort and does not derive from the evidence.[1] Our question is one of logic only. A certain evidence is available. Certain outcomes are thought of. What logical relation obtains between them?

The relation is that of the *degree of confirmation.* An outcome cannot be implied in the evidence; it can only be confirmed by it to a greater or smaller degree. The degree of confirmation is a relation in this case because it has no meaning without the elements of the possible outcome and of the evidence to which it refers. To say that an outcome is confirmed *per se* does not make sense. As it is impossible to say that something is above without referring to what is below, it is impossible to say that something is confirmed without referring to that by which it is confirmed. It is only in relation to some evidence that the degree of confirmation of an outcome acquires a meaning.

The relation is logical because it must be intuitively perceived. It cannot be established by observation. Even if it happens that in spite of the evidence of dark clouds the rain has not come, it remains true that with the evidence as it was the outcome of rain was confirmed by it. As in the case of a deductive relation, the relation of the degree of confirmation is concerned solely with what the outcome and the evidence mean. It is not concerned with any events which actually take place.

(2.1.5) With respect to the form of the relation we may distinguish between a *comparative* concept of the degree of con-

---

[1] Compare Shackle's distinction between unexpected and counter-expected events. G. L. S. Shackle, The Logic of Surprise, *Economica,* **XX,** May (1953), pp. 112-7.

firmation and a *quantitative* one. In the comparative case the relation says merely that one outcome is more confirmed by a particular evidence than some other. The relation is one of ranking only. Nothing is said about how much more is the former outcome confirmed than the latter. In the quantitative case the degree of confirmation is given a numerical measure. It is possible to say then not only that one outcome is more confirmed by the evidence than some other but also how much more it is confirmed by it.

It is by no means necessary for even the comparative concept to apply to all possible pairs of evidence as the premise and of outcome as the conclusion. Keynes thought of the relation between them as being of the same kind as the relation of similarity.[1] Things may be similar one to another, but it may not make much sense to speak of two of them as being more similar one to the other than some other two. It is impossible, for instance, to compare the degree of similarity between two books, one bound in red calf and one in blue calf, with that between two others, one bound in red calf and one in red morocco. Nor may it be possible to compare the degree to which the outcome of rain is confirmed by the evidence of dark clouds with the degree to which the outcome of an increase in the price of a product is confirmed by the evidence that an increase in it was observed in the past months. Even if they are comparable in a subjective sense, that is to say even if we are prepared to bet on one rather than on the other, they need not be comparable in the logical sense. Comparison means in this case ranking along a one-dimensional scale; and both similarity and confirmation may turn out to be multi-dimensional relations, not reducible by any rules of logic to a one-dimensional form.

(2.1.6) The question, what form the relation of the degree of confirmation may take, must be distinguished from that in what form it can be perceived. It is by no means certain that it can be perceived at all. What we perceive depends not only on the nature of things to be perceived but also on our faculties of perception. As there are people who are not able to perceive many deductive relations, so it would not be surprising if there were also people who are not able to perceive the relations of the degree of confirmation.

[1] J. M. Keynes, *A Treatise on Probability*, Macmillan (London, 1921), p. 36.

(2.2) Classical Probability and the Principle of Insufficient Reason

(2.2.1) The concept of the degree of confirmation was implied already in the classical interpretation of probability by Bernoulli and Laplace. Keynes was the first to make it explicit.[1] He defined probability as the degree of rational belief in a particular outcome which it is logical to hold in virtue of a particular evidence. The term 'degree of confirmation' was introduced by Carnap[2] to avoid the psychological connotations of the word 'belief'.[3]

(2.2.2) According to the classical interpretation probability is the ratio of favourable to all possible cases if all of them are equally likely. If, for instance, we contemplate a toss with a die, the six possible cases are the six positions in which the die may come to rest. If the die is as we call it 'true', all of them are equally likely. The case of an ace is favourable to the outcome of an ace, one out of six possible and equally likely cases. The probability of the outcome of an ace is thus one-sixth. Similarly, if we draw a ball from an urn containing equal numbers of white and black balls, the probability of the outcome that a white ball will be drawn is one-half.

Cases in this context are outcomes as well. They are outcomes in a prospect which satisfies the condition that all outcomes in it are equally likely. In the example of a toss with a true die, equally likely cases are the outcomes in the prospect of the actual position in which the die may come to rest. And in the example of a ball being drawn from an urn, they are the outcomes in the prospect of which ball will be drawn. We will see later on that it is convenient to have a special word to denote outcomes which satisfy the condition of equal likelihood. The word 'case' does not perhaps convey by itself the idea of outcome. But it may be accepted for historical reasons. The classical definition of probability has always been put in this way.

If cases are equally likely, then treated as outcomes they are also equally probable. If all the six positions in which a die may come to rest are equally likely, the probabilities of the outcomes

[1] *A Treatise on Probability, op. cit.*, p. 4.
[2] R. Carnap, *The Logical Foundations of Probability*, The University of Chicago Press (1950).
[3] See also H. Jeffreys, *Theory of Probability*, 2nd ed., Clarendon Press (Oxford, 1948), p. 15.

that it will come to rest in these positions is 1/6 for each of them. The word 'likely' as distinct from 'probable' has been introduced to stress the fact that equally likely cases are equally likely in some *a priori* sense; whereas equally probable outcomes are equally probable in the sense that the ratio of favourable to all possible and equally likely cases, is the same for them.

(2.2.3) Probability in the classical sense is a property of the mechanism on the working of which the result depends. In the example of throwing a die or of drawing balls from an urn the mechanism is the throwing of the particular die or the drawing of a ball from the particular urn. It determines the event the description of which is the subject of the expectation: that one out of six faces of the die will turn up or that one out of an equal number of white and of black balls will be drawn.

The properties of the mechanism are such that if the description of the event is in terms of the actual result (in terms of the actual position of the die, for instance, or of the actual ball being drawn), the outcomes in the respective prospect are cases which are equally likely. Probability of an outcome in the prospect on a subject of a different description but determined by the same mechanism (of an odd result in the toss with the die, for instance, or of a white ball being drawn from the urn) is then the ratio of the number of cases which are favourable to the number of all those which are equally likely. If, therefore, the mechanism is there and all its properties can be ascertained by inspection, the probabilities of all outcomes in the prospects on all subjects which are determined by it are also there and can also be ascertained by inspection.

(2.2.4) The logical rule on the ground of which cases in the classical interpretation of probability are described as equally likely is the so-called Principle of Insufficient Reason. It was originally formulated by Bernoulli. Keynes gave it the name of the Principle of Indifference. In very general terms it says that cases are equally likely if there is no reason to suppose that one is more likely than another.[1]

[1] For criticisms see J. M. Keynes, *A Treatise on Probability, op. cit.*, Chapter IV, p. 48; K. J. Arrow, Alternative Approaches to the Theory of Choice in Risk-Taking Situations, *op. cit.*; E. Nagel, Principles of the Theory of Probability, *International Encyclopedia of Unified Science*, I, No. 6, The University of Chicago Press (1939); L. J. Savage, *The Foundations of Statistics*, Chapman & Hall (London, 1954), pp. 63–7.

(2.2.5) In this general form the Principle of Insufficient Reason is subject to the following criticisms. Suppose that we do not know anything about the colour of a book. We may then argue that we do not know either that the book is red or that it is not red. The probability of the tautology that the book is either red or not red is one. For whatever the equally likely cases might be and whatever their number, all of them would have to be favourable cases; whatever the colour of the book might be, it would have to be always either red or not red; the ratio of favourable to all possible cases would have to be one to one. The probability of the results that the book turns out to be red and that it turns out not to be red is then one-half each, because on the ground of the Principle of Insufficient Reason these results represent equally likely cases, and the probability ratio for either of them is one-half. The same argument may be applied to the results that the book is blue or not blue, green or not green, and so on. Thus probability of one-half would have to be attached not only to the result that the book is red, but also that it is blue, green, yellow, and so on. And the probability of the tautology that the book is of some colour would then become not one but the sum of so many one-halfs as there are colours we may only think of.

Furthermore, the Principle of Insufficient Reason may not apply to cases which are described in terms of arbitrary measures. The quantity of a particular substance in space may, for instance, be measured either by its volume or by its density – the reciprocal of volume. If the possible range of the volume is then divided into equal intervals, these will correspond to non-equal intervals of density. Equal intervals of volume from 1 to 2 and from 2 to 3 correspond, for instance, to not equal intervals of density of 1 to $\frac{1}{2}$ and $\frac{1}{2}$ to $\frac{1}{3}$. If, therefore, we would say on the ground of the Principle of Insufficient Reason that the volume of a substance is equally likely to be either in the interval from 1 to 2 or in that from 2 to 3 ; and that its density is equally likely to be in the interval from 1 to $\frac{2}{3}$ as in that of $\frac{2}{3}$ to $\frac{1}{3}$, the two statements would be inconsistent one with the other.

Similar considerations apply to the so-called geometrical probability. If, for instance, we draw a line at random through a particular point on the circumference of a circle and divide the range of possible angles at which it can be drawn into equal intervals, these will not correspond to equal intervals of the

55

length of the line within the circle. Thus the positions of the line which are equally likely if the Principle of Insufficient Reason is applied to the possible angle of the line are not equally likely if it is applied to the possible length of it.

(2.2.6) These difficulties do not arise if the Principle of Insufficient Reason is interpreted as that the outcomes of the respective results are equally confirmed by the evidence. For this can be the case only if there is no statement in the evidence which would apply to one of them and not to the other. The measure of probability depends then on the form of the language in which the evidence is expressed.[1] But this is true of all logical relations.

The following example[2] may help to see the point. Suppose that an urn contains equal numbers of white and of black balls, all of them of the same size, made of the same material, put into the urn at the same time and mixed together, etc. Everything that the evidence says about the white balls in the urn applies also to the black balls. The outcome that the first ball drawn from the urn will be a white ball is then equally confirmed by the evidence as that it will be a black ball. If, however, the evidence is that the drawing is made by magnet, and that the white balls are made of iron and the black balls of tin, some statements in the evidence apply to the white balls only and some others to the black balls. The statement, for instance, that the ball is made of iron and that it is strongly attracted by a magnet applies to white balls only, and the statement that the ball is made of tin and is not very strongly attracted by a magnet applies to the black balls. The outcomes that the first ball drawn from the urn will be white and that it will be black are then not equally confirmed by the evidence.

In the example given before, the outcomes that the book will turn out to be red and that it will turn out to be not red are not equally confirmed by the evidence because the statements that the book may be blue, yellow or green applies to not red books but not to red ones. The same may be said of the outcomes that the volume of a substance will turn out to be between 1 and 2 and between 2 and 3. They are not equally confirmed by the evidence because what is said about one interval does not apply to the other. The former, for instance, corresponds to the interval

---

[1] J. K. Arrow, *op. cit.*, *Econometrica* (1951), p. 413.
[2] Given by Keynes, *A Treatise on Probability*, *op. cit.*, pp. 53–4.

of density of 1 to $\frac{1}{2}$ and the latter to that of $\frac{1}{2}$ to $\frac{1}{3}$. Also the two equal intervals of the possible angles at which the line may be drawn in the geometrical example correspond to different intervals of the possible lengths of the line. The Principle of Insufficient Reason applies, however, to the results of a toss with a 'true' coin or with a 'true' die if each of the possible positions in which the coin or the die may come to rest is taken as a separate outcome.

(2.2.7) The outcomes to which the Principle of Insufficient Reason applies are equally confirmed by the evidence, and the classical probability is a numerical measure of the degree to which they are confirmed by it. Like all numerical measures it is arbitrary. For there is nothing natural in the measure of the degree of confirmation to be a positive rational number not greater than one, and in the measure of the degree of confirmation of a tautology to be equal to one. This follows, however, from the classical definition. The axiom of addition (that the probability measure of the outcome that either one or the other of two possible and mutually exclusive results comes off is equal to the sum of the probability measures of the outcomes of either of these two results taken separately) and the axiom of multiplication (that the probability measure of the outcome that both one and the other of some independent[1] results comes off is the product of the probability measures of the outcomes of either of these two results taken separately) are implied in it. If the probability measure of an ace in a toss with a die is $\frac{1}{6}$ and the probability measure of a six is also $\frac{1}{6}$, the probability measure of either an ace or a six is $\frac{2}{6}$ and the probability measure of an ace in the first toss and a six in the second toss is $\frac{1}{36}$.

(2.2.8) The formalization of the weights of outcomes in a prospect could follow the lines indicated in this section in those cases only to which the Principle of Insufficient Reason actually applies. Games of chance, such as tossing coins, playing dice, roulette, lotteries, etc., are typical examples. The mechanism on the working of which the result depends is in those cases sufficiently simple for the equally confirmed outcomes to be identified. The situation is then usually described as one of *risk*. Whoever might be confronted with it, an observer or the player

[1] Results are independent if the probability of one of them coming off is independent of whether the other result has or has not come off.

57

himself, could easily determine in an objective sense what the classical probability measures of the particular outcome actually are. These may thus be accepted as a formal representation of the weights of the respective outcomes in the prospect of the result. The operation in terms of which they are defined is the inspection of the physical characteristics of the mechanism.

This formalization of the weight is not possible in cases in which the mechanism is so complicated that equally confirmed outcomes cannot be identified. Their probability measures cannot then be ascertained in an objective sense. It is, for instance, impossible to derive from the evidence of past trends of prices any objectively acceptable conclusions as to which outcomes in a prospect of future prices are equally confirmed by it. An element of personal judgement cannot then be completely disposed of, and the situation is usually described as one of *uncertainty*.

The distinction between uncertainty and risk is very often referred to in economic theory. But no formal representation of expectations has been suggested so far, in which risk and uncertainty could be identified each of them separately. Pure risk arises in those situations in which we cannot formulate any further questions in the evidence which, if answered, would make us change the probability weights which we have already attached to different outcomes. Pure uncertainty arises when none of the questions which we can formulate have been answered. Different hypotheses are often suggested to explain behaviour in either of these two situations. In fact, however, the elements of uncertainty and of risk combine always one with the other, and there is no way in which they could be separated. [1]

(2.2.9) The fact that a greater probability weight is attached to a particular outcome than to some other does not necessarily mean that the individual will be more concerned in his behaviour with pay-offs from the former than with those from the latter.

---

[1] For a more detailed analysis of the distinction between uncertainty and risk see F. R. Knight, *Risk, Uncertainty and Profits*, Houghton Mifflin Company, Boston and New York (1921); M. Shubik, Information, Risk, Ignorance and Indeterminacy, *Quarterly Journal of Economics*, LXVIII, November (1954); pp. 629–40. D. Ellsberg, Risk, Ambiguity, and the Savage Axioms, *Quarterly Journal of Economics*, LXXV, November (1961), pp. 643–69; and, W. Fellner, Distortion of Subjective Probabilities as a Reaction to Uncertainty, *Quarterly Journal of Economics*, LXXV, November (1961), pp. 670–85.

What connection is supposed to exist between the prospect and the individual's behaviour depends on the actual context of the theory. It is possible that no connection between behaviour and a particular representation of the prospect can be established at all. That a particular formalization of the weight is possible does not mean yet that it is also useful.

(2.3) The Frequency-Distribution Interpretation

(2.3.1) The interpretation of probability as a measure of the degree of confirmation has also been criticised on the ground that cases in which it is possible to identify outcomes equally confirmed by the evidence are rather rare. In general, probability in the classical sense cannot be ascertained by means of the operation in terms of which it is defined. The probability of death of an Englishman of a particular age cannot, for instance, be derived from the available evidence by means of the Principle of Insufficient Reason. The fact that there may be rules of logic which we cannot perceive is not of much help either. If we do not know how long people live and how often they die at each particular age, we simply do not know what the probability of their death actually is.

The constructive part of the criticism is that if we know how long people live and how often they die, the relative frequencies of death and survival are the probabilities of the two outcomes. If, for instance, at a particular age and in particular circumstances 5% of men die and 95% survive, the probability of death is $\frac{1}{20}$ and that of survival is $\frac{19}{20}$. In this interpretation probability is no longer a measure of the logical relation of the degree of confirmation. It is a fact to be ascertained by observation.

(2.3.2) In this crude form the notion of probability as frequency distribution is subject to the objection that it itself is only probable. The fact that a certain frequency distribution has been found in a particular series of observations does not mean yet that in another series the same frequency would obtain. The particular frequency distribution is only one of many others which too could have been observed. It is, therefore, a probability which is only probable and just happened to be the case in that particular instance.

(2.3.3) In the course of its subsequent development the notion of probability as frequency distribution has been clarified and refined so as to meet this objection.[1] The respective interpretation is as follows. Probability presupposes randomness. This means that there is no law or formula which would enable us to predict what is going to happen. The numbers on the milestones we meet on the road do not come up at random; but the numbers of the cars we meet do. For there is a formula which governs the sequence of the former; and no formula governs the sequence of the latter. Subject to this condition, the probability of a particular outcome has been defined as the limit which its frequency is supposed to approach as the number of observations becomes greater and greater. If, for instance, we toss a coin once, the frequency distribution is one for the result which has actually occurred and zero for the other. If we increase the number of tosses both results tend to come up. And as the number of tosses becomes greater and greater, the frequency distribution of the results may be expected to approach closer and closer one-half for heads and one-half for tails. It may happen that the limit is not one-half because the coin is loaded. As long, however, as it exists, it is the probability of the respective outcome.

(2.3.4) The interpretation of probability as the limit which the frequency distribution tends to approach may be criticized on the ground that no clear indication is given in it of the sense in which it is a limit and in which the actual frequency distribution tends to approach it. In mathematics, a function is said to have a limit if it is possible to make its dependent variable approach a certain value as closely as we like by making its independent variable sufficiently large. In $y = 1 + 1/x$, for instance, we can make y approach unity as closely as we like if we only increase sufficiently x. Unity is thus the limit of y in the function $y = 1 + 1/x$. In the frequency interpretation of probability this is not so. We cannot make the actual frequency distribution approach the limit as closely as we like by increasing the number of observations.

[1] See E. Nagel, Principles of the Theory of Probability, *op. cit.*, p. 18; R. von Mises, *Probability, Statistics and Truth*, Allen & Unwin (London, 1957); H. Reichenbach, *The Theory of Probability*, University of California Press (1949).

The following example may help to see the point.[1] Suppose that when we increase the number of tosses with a particular coin we observe the frequency distribution of heads and tails approaching closer and closer one-half and one-half. One-half seems thus to be the limit. Suppose, however, that we want to approach it within the distance of 2% of its value by making the number of tosses sufficiently large. This would be possible only if there existed a certain sufficiently large number of tosses which would satisfy the condition that the actual proportion of heads in it cannot be less than 49% and cannot be more than 51%. Let the minimum number of tosses which satisfies this condition be 1000. Suppose that if we toss the coin so many times, the actual number of heads cannot be less than 490 and cannot be more than 510. If we toss the coin less than 1000 times, the number of heads might deviate from the limit of one-half by more than 2%. But if 1000 of tosses is reached, this is no longer possible.

Suppose now that in a particular series of 1000 tosses the number of heads happened to be exactly 510 and that we decide then to make one more toss. The result of this 1001st toss would have then to be a tail. For otherwise the limit of one-half of tosses would be exceeded by more than 2%. Either, therefore, there is some law which determines the result of the 1001st toss, and the results do not satisfy the condition of randomness. Or the 1000 tosses are not enough to approach the limit within the distance of 2%. The same argument, however, would apply to any other number of tosses which we might think of as both necessary and sufficient to approach the limit within a particular distance. As long, therefore, as the results come up at random, the limit cannot be interpreted as the frequency distribution which could be approached as closely as we like by making the number of observations sufficiently large. The concept of a limit as it is used in mathematics does not apply to this case.

(2.3.5) Probability in the sense of frequency distribution is supposed to be an empirical fact. Von Mises, for instance, maintained that the records of the casino in Monte Carlo, of births and deaths, and other statistical data, point quite clearly to the

[1] Compare also N. Georgescu-Roegen, The Nature of Expectations and Uncertainty, *Expectations, Uncertainty and Business Decisions*, Mary Jean Bowman (ed.), *op. cit.*, pp. 13–16.

existence of limits to which the respective distributions converge. The fact that in principle we might not be able to approach them as closely as we like by increasing the number of observations does not matter much. For the available record of observations permits us to ascertain with a reasonable degree of accuracy what they actually are.

This, however, does not dispose of the difficulty. If the results satisfy the condition of randomness, any record of observations is only one of many possible results. If, for instance, we make a series of tosses with a coin, any sequence of heads and tails is possible, even one of all heads throughout. There is, therefore, nothing particular about the sequence which happened to be the case. If it points to a limit, the limit has no other significance than that it is the limit of that sequence. Another sequence of observations might point to a different limit. We are thus back at where we were in (2.3.2). Probability as a limit to which the frequency distributions converge in the series actually observed is only a probability which is probable and just happened to be the case.

(2.4) *Frequency Distribution and the Classical Probability Measure*

(2.4.1) The ambiguity as to what the frequency-distribution probability actually is may be disposed of in two ways. One is to define probability, not as a limit which the frequency distribution of results tends to approach, but as the actual frequency distribution; different in different series of observations. Consider, for instance, a series of tosses with a coin which we intend to make. The probability of heads and of tails may be defined as the frequency distribution of these two results in that particular series. In order to find out what this distribution is likely to be we may make a sample of tosses and argue that the actual distribution in the sample is an indication of what the distribution in the whole series will be. The larger the sample the more closely will the distribution in it approach the distribution in the series. In a sense the latter may, therefore, be regarded as a limit which the former tends to approach. But the probability is not the limit. It is the actual frequency distribution in the series.

In this case the ambiguity is disposed of at the cost of depriving the word probability of any other meaning than that of the frequency distribution in a particular series of observations. It is simply another name for the distribution of actual results. It is doubtful if anything more than confusion can be gained from using two different words to describe the same thing. The word probability will not, therefore, be used here in this sense.

(2.4.2) The other way in which we can get rid of the difficulty is to define probability as the classical measure of the degree of confirmation and to accept the frequency distribution of actual results as an indication of what this measure is likely to be. Suppose, for instance, that we are interested in the probability of death at the age of thirty. We cannot deduce it from the available evidence by identifying the states of the world which are equally confirmed by it and segregating them into those which have the characteristic of somebody's death at thirty and those which have it not. The mechanism on which death and survival depend is too complicated and its working too obscure for this to be possible. But we may none the less define the probability of death as the proportion of the states of the world with the respective characteristics and try to find out what this proportion is by means of a theory, without identifying either the mechanism or the states of the world.

(2.4.3) The theory may be as follows. Suppose that the mechanism on the working of which the results depend remains unchanged over a long series of observations. Then whatever the actual properties of the mechanism might be and whatever characteristics the states of the world might have which are equally confirmed by the description of the mechanism, the same states of the world are equally confirmed by it at every instance of its working. If, for instance, a die is and remains true over a long series of tosses, the states of the world of the six positions in which it may come to rest are equally confirmed by the description of the die's properties at every point of time at which the die happens to be used. Similarly, if the conditions determining the activity of bacteria, human resistance, and other factors on which death and survival depend are such that n unspecified states of the world are equally confirmed by a description of these conditions, then irrespective of what this description actually is, the same states of the world are equally confirmed by it at every point of time at which the conditions remain the same.

63

Furthermore, not only the n states of the world which may come off at a particular point of time are equally confirmed by the description of the mechanism, but so are also all the possible sequences of them. For if there is nothing in the evidence that applies to one state of the world and not to some other at a point of time, there cannot be anything in it either that would apply to one sequence of them and not to that of some other. If, for instance, a die is and remains true, not only the states of the world of its coming to rest in each of the six possible positions are equally confirmed by the evidence that it is true, but so are also the states of the world of its coming to rest in any of the possible sequences of those six positions over a series of tosses.

(2.4.4) This has the following consequences. If probability is interpreted as the classical measure of the degree of confirmation, the probability that an event will occur which has a particular characteristic may be denoted by m/n, where m is the number of the equally likely cases with that characteristic, and n is the total number of equally likely cases. It can be shown that the frequency distribution of events with that characteristic in the outcomes of sequences of events are then close to m/n in a large proportion of them. If, for instance, we contemplate a series of tosses with a true coin, m/n for heads is one-half, and the number of heads is close to one-half of all tosses in the series in a large proportion of sequences of heads and tails which in the series may occur.

The longer is the series, the larger is the number of possible sequences of events with the particular characteristics which may occur in it, and the greater is the proportion of those sequences in which the frequency distribution approaches m/n within a particular distance. If, for instance, we contemplate two tosses with a coin, the frequency distribution of heads or of tails in one-half of the possible sequences is not smaller than $\frac{1}{4}$ and not greater than $\frac{3}{4}$; if we contemplated three tosses, the frequency distribution in three-quarters of the possible sequences would be within these limits; and if four tosses were to be made, seven-eighths of the possible sequences would satisfy this condition. Similarly, if in the example of the probability of death the ratio of the number of outcomes with that characteristic to the number of all those which are equally confirmed by the evidence is m/n, the ratio of the former to the latter in a sequence of outcomes approaches m/n closer and closer in a greater and greater proportion of such sequences the longer the sequences are. The relation is often described as the Law of Large Numbers. It is a logical relation between the possible frequency distributions of outcomes in a sequence of events and the total number of outcomes in the sequence. It does not say anything about the frequency distribution in the sequence which actually comes off.

The argument may then be put into reverse. If the frequency distributions of results with a particular characteristic in the observations which have been made cluster around some value m/n, the results are likely to be coming from a mechanism which produces these distributions in greater numbers than others. In other words the properties of the mechanism must be such that m/n is also the ratio of the outcomes with that characteristic to all outcomes that are equally confirmed by those properties' description. Along these lines the classical measure of probability might thus be inferred from the observation of frequency distribution.

(2.4.5) The argument begs the question of what is the logic of inference in the reverse part of it. For the conclusion that the properties of the mechanism are such that m/n is the relevant measure of probability is not implied in the fact that frequency distributions close to m/n have actually been observed. The sequences might have been just those in which the frequency distribution is much different from the classical measure of probability of outcomes out of which the sequences consist. As there are comparatively few such sequences in relation to the number of those in which the frequency distribution is close to m/n, it may be argued that it would be very unlikely if exactly those were to come off. But it is by no means impossible that this actually has been the case.

No attempt is made here to analyse this question. The inference is accepted as valid if the record of observations is sufficiently clear. How many observations have to be made, how long the sequences of results have to be, and how closely and uniformly the respective frequency distributions have to approach the required value for this condition to be satisfied cannot be determined on any *a priori* grounds. There must always be some degree of arbitrariness in the conclusion. But there are cases (in insurance, for instance) in which the degree of arbitrariness is so small that it may be neglected.

(2.4.6) This leads us to the following formalization of the weights of an outcome. If the record of past observations points unambiguously to a certain typical value of the frequency distribution of results with a particular characteristic, there is a strong presumption that the classical measure of probability of an outcome with that characteristic is equal to that typical value of frequency distribution. The probability measure equal to that distribution may thus be accepted as the formal representation of the weight of the outcome that the result which comes off will have the respective characteristic.

If the limit in Von Mises's and Reichenbach's interpretation of probability were identified with what we have called here a typical frequency distribution, the formalization suggested in this paragraph would be that of probability in the sense of a limit which the frequency distribution tends to approach. As it has been put here it differs from the frequency distribution interpretation in that it relies not on the existence of some probability limit which a long series of observations of frequency distributions might help us to discover, but on a consensus of opinion as to what the typical frequency distribution actually is. If the consensus of opinion is sufficiently clear for the typical frequency distribution which emerges from it to have an objective value, the formalization suggested in this paragraph is possible, quite irrespective of what is the meaning of the limit which the actual frequency distribution is supposed to approach.

The interpretation of the probability weights as the classical ratios of favourable to all equally likely cases may not be acceptable to those who insist on the frequency interpretation on grounds of principle. In the limited context of this book the matter, however, is not particularly important. The classical interpretation has been chosen here for the sake of convenience only. With a certain amount of effort the argument could be redrafted so that it would also suit the frequency interpretation. But it would then be more difficult to read; and as the actual formalization of the weight would remain the same (determined by the same operation) very little in fact would be gained by this procedure.

(2.5) Consistency of Probability Weights

(2.5.1) It has been pointed out in (1.4.5) that if subjects of expectations are related, the respective prospects may not be consistent one with another. The inconsistency may be theoretical if the subjects are related in virtue of a theory and logical if they are related in virtue of what they mean. The present section deals with logical consistency in that special case in which the weights of outcomes are formalized as probability weights.

In general, if a number of outcomes is equally confirmed by the evidence, the probability weights of the outcomes that events will occur which have the required characteristics must conform to the rules of probability calculus. Probability weights of the outcomes with either one or some other of mutually exclusive characteristics are equal to the sum of the probability weights of the outcomes with these characteristics taken separately; and probability weights of the outcomes with several independent characteristics are equal to the products of the probability weights of the outcomes with those characteristics taken separately. For instance, the probability weight of the outcome that the result of a toss with a die will be an even number is the sum of the probability weights of the outcomes of two, four and six; and the probability weight of the outcome that the result will be both even and greater than two is the product of the probability weights of the outcomes that it will be even and that it will be greater than two. [1]

In the remaining paragraphs of this section those general rules are applied to a case in which the subjects of the expectations are the characteristics of some future events as well as the individual's own expectations of these characteristics which he will hold at some date during the former expectations' period in-between. The relations between the probability weights in the respective prospects are fairly obvious. As, however, expectations of one's own expectations play an important part in some of the theories

---

[1] The two probabilities are independent one of the other because the probability of the result being even is $\frac{1}{2}$ irrespective of whether all six possible outcomes are considered or only those four which are greater than two, and the probability of the result being greater than two is $\frac{2}{3}$ irrespective of whether all or even outcomes only are considered.

which will be discussed later on, it may be useful to state them explicitly.

(2.5.2) The following example may be used to simplify the exposition. Suppose that as in (1.6.2) a businessman is interested in the amount of profits which he will earn at t_s and that one of the factors which may affect the level of those profits will be the results of the General Election to be held at t_k before t_s. At present, that is to say at t_o, the businessman may hold the following expectations: (i) the expectation of profits at t_s, (ii) the expectation of his own expectation of profits which he will hold when the results of the General Election become known, and (iii) the expectation of the results of the General Election at t_k. Suppose that the General Election is the only event before t_s which may affect the level of his profits. The only information, therefore, which will be added during that period to the evidence in the expectations of profits is that about the results of the election.

Suppose further that the outcomes in these three expectations are as follows : in the case of the expectation of profits there are five outcomes ; -2, -1, 0, 1, and 2. The reason why no other outcomes are considered may be that round figures only are taken into account and that the weights of the outcomes of profits and of losses outside the range of -2 to 2 are so low, that the respective outcomes may be neglected. In the case of the expectation of the results of the General Election there are two outcomes only. The winning party may be either the Conservative Party or the Labour Party.

The third case, that of the businessman's expectation of his own expectations, is more complicated. The prospect in it consists there of outcomes of his expectations of profits. As the General Election is supposed to be the only event which may affect these expectations there can be only two outcomes in that prospect. One refers to the case in which the information that the Conservative Party has won the election becomes a part of the evidence. The other refers to the case in which the information that the Labour Party has won the election becomes a part of the evidence. The prospects in these two outcomes of expectations are the outcomes of the five levels of profits with such weights attached to them as the businessman would regard as relevant if he knew that the elections have been won by the

Conservative Party in the first case, and by the Labour Party in the second case. Which of these two outcomes comes off depends on which party wins the election. The businessman will, therefore, attach to them the same weights as he does to the outcomes of the Conservative and of the Labour Party winning the election in his expectation of the results of the election.

(2.5.3) Suppose now that all weights in these expectations are probability weights and that they are as in Table 2.5.3. The five numbers in the first column are the five outcomes of profits. The weights which the businessman would attach to the different levels of profits in the two outcomes of his expectation of profits are shown in the second and the third column of the table. The weights of the two outcomes of the result of the election in his expectation of that result are either 0·5 and 0·5 or 0·375 and 0·625. And the weights which he attaches to different levels of profits with the results of the election still unknown are those in the fourth and the fifth column of the table.

Table 2.5.3

Profits	Conservative Party	Labour Party	Result unknown and the probability weights 0·5 and 0·5	Result unknown and the probability weights 0·375 and 0·625
(1)	(2)	(3)	(4)	(5)
−2	0·1	0·3	0·2	0·225
−1	0·2	0·4	0·3	0·325
0	0·4	0·2	0·3	0·275
1	0·2	0·1	0·15	0·1375
2	0·1	0	0·05	0·0375

The question is now whether and in what sense the prospects summarized in the table are consistent one with another. They are related through the fact that the evidence is the same in all of them. The time of the expectation is the same and so is, therefore, what the individual knows.

(2.5.4) The fact that the weight is a probability weight implies that there are some states of the world which are equally confirmed by the evidence and that they can be segregated into groups according to whether they have or have not the particular characteristics. This must, therefore, apply also to the weights in our example. The fact that the weight of 0·5 or 0·375 is attached to the outcome of the Conservative Party winning the election means that if all equally confirmed future states of the world were segregated into two parts according to whether they have or have not the characteristic that the Conservative Party has won the election, the number of those in the first part would be 0·5 or 0·375 of the total number of all of them. The weights in the second and in the third column imply the segregation of the possible states of the world into more parts. The two former parts, that is to say the states of the world in which the Conservative Party or the Labour Party has won the election, are subdivided each into five parts according to what is the level of profits in them. The weight 0·1 at the top of the second column, for instance, means that the number of the states of the world in which both the Conservative Party has won the election and the level of profits is −2, is one-tenth of all the states of the world which are equally confirmed by the evidence and in which the Conservative Party has won the election. The same applies to the weights in the last two columns of the table. They say that if all the equally confirmed states of the world are segregated into five parts according to whether profits are −2, −1, and so on, the ratios of their numbers in each part to the total number of such states is 0·2, 0·3, and so on; or 0·225, 0·325, and so on.

(2.5.5) The point is now that if the weights are interpreted in this way, they are not independent one from another. For if we know how the particular states of the world are distributed between those in which the Conservative Party has won the election and those in which the Labour Party has won; and how they are distributed in either of these two parts between those in which profits are −2, −1, and so on; we can derive from these data the distribution of the states of the world between those in which profits are −2, −1, and so on, irrespective of who wins the election. The proportion of the states of the world in which profits are −2 is simply the respective proportion in the part in which the Conservative Party has won the election, multiplied by the proportion of the latter in the total number of

70

the states of the world, plus the proportion of the states of the world in which profits are -2 and the Labour Party has won, multiplied by the proportion of all the states of the world in which the Labour Party has won the election. In our example, the weight $0\cdot2$ at the top of the fourth column is equal to $0\cdot1$ multiplied by $0\cdot5$ plus $0\cdot3$ multiplied by $0\cdot5$, and the weight $0\cdot225$ at the top of the fifth column is equal to $0\cdot1$ multiplied by $0\cdot375$ plus $0\cdot3$ multiplied by $0\cdot625$.

This is the condition which the expectations in our example must satisfy if they are to be consistent one with another. In general the condition is that if the weights of outcomes are formalized as probability weights the rules of probability calculus apply to them. For it is according to the rules of probability calculus that in the above example the weights of the outcomes of the different levels of profits are derived from the weights of the outcomes of the two election results and of the combined outcomes of both profits and the election results. The weights in the fourth column in Table 2.5.3 are simply the mean values of the weights in the second and the third column.

If the conditions of probability calculus are not satisfied, the individual is inconsistent in his expectations in the sense that the states of the world which he regards as equally confirmed by the evidence when he holds an expectation on one subject are not equally confirmed to him when in virtue of the same evidence he holds an expectation on some other subject. If in our example the weights in the last two columns were different, it would not be possible to segregate the same states of the world into parts so as to make them fit all the probability weights in the table. Either the states of the world would have to have different characteristics in different expectations, or different states of the world would have to be accepted as equally confirmed by the same evidence.

(2.5.6) The criteria of consistency explained in this section apply to all expectations in which weights of outcomes are formalized as probability weights. If this is not the case, no equally confirmed states of the world are implied in the weights, and the question whether the same or different equally confirmed states of the world are implied in expectations on different subjects does not arise.

71

(2.6) Adjustment of Probability Weights

(2.6.1) If the weights of outcomes are formalized as classical probabilities, some progress can also be made in the analysis of the adjustment of expectations. It has been pointed out in (1.5.5) and (1.6.6) that expectations are clarified if the evidence is amplified by answers to questions which could not have been answered before; that they are revised if a different answer is given to a question than was given before; and that the result of an expectation on the same subject at an earlier time may throw some light on whether one or the other is actually the case. Expectations of profits at some later time may, for instance, be revised as a result of the fact that profits at some earlier time have turned out to be different from what was expected.

In the preliminary discussion of this topic in (1.6.6) the general criterion that expectations with a later time of the subject become revised if the expectations with an earlier time of the subject are not confirmed by the actual results was found inadequate because if several outcomes appeared in a prospect and one of them came off, it was impossible to say on the ground of this fact alone whether the respective expectation was or was not confirmed. The weight of the outcome must be considered too. The discussion had, therefore, to be postponed until more has been said about the nature of the weight and its possible formal representation.

Now we are in a better position to follow up this line. We cannot say anything about the distinction between clarification and revision. For there is no logical criterion of whether an expectation is or is not confirmed by the actual result if the prospect in it consists of several outcomes and one of them comes off. But if the weights are formalized as classical probabilities, a logical rule may be established for the adjustment of these weights.

(2.6.2) The point may be explained on an example. Suppose that we are asked to experiment with a true die the sides of which are marked with heads and tails, but we are not allowed to inspect the die. In particular we are not allowed to see how many sides of it are marked with heads and how many with tails. All we are told is that at least one side is marked with heads and at least one with tails. There may thus be five outcomes in the ƿrospect of the number of sides which are marked with heads: ʜat of one side, of two sides, of three, of four, and of five. As ᴀll of them are equally confirmed by the evidence, the same ƿrobability weight (that of 1/5) is attached to each of them. In ᴛable (2.6.2) H denotes the five hypotheses listed in the first ꜩolumn and P(H) the five equal probability weights of ⅕.

The third and the fourth columns contain the weights of the ꝋutcomes of heads and tails which appear in the expectations which themselves are outcomes in expectations. There are five outcomes of such expectations, each corresponding to a different ʜypothesis in the first column. The weights of the outcomes of ʜeads and tails in them are shown in the respective columns. In ᴛhe expectation, for instance, which would come off if the first ʜypothesis happened to be true the outcome of heads appears with the probability weight of 1/6 and that of tails with 5/6.

The probability weights in the fifth and sixth columns are those of the outcomes in an expectation on a combined subject,

Table 2.6.2

H	P(H)	P(h/H)	P(t/H)	P(h, H)	P(t, H)
(1)	(2)	(3)	(4)	(5)	(6)
1 Heads	1/5	1/6	5/6	1/30	1/6
2 Heads	1/5	1/3	2/3	1/15	2/15
3 Heads	1/5	1/2	1/2	1/10	1/10
4 Heads	1/5	2/3	1/3	2/15	1/15
5 Heads	1/5	5/6	1/6	1/6	1/30
	1			1/2	1/2

$P(H/h')$ $P(h'',H,h')$ $P(t'',H,h')$ $P(H/h',h'')$ $P(H/h',t'')$

(1)	(7)	(8)	(9)	(10)	(11)
1 Heads	1/15	1/90	1/18	1/55	1/7
2 Heads	2/15	2/45	4/45	4/55	8/35
3 Heads	1/5	1/10	1/10	9/55	9/35
4 Heads	4/15	8/45	4/45	16/55	8/35
5 Heads	1/3	5/18	1/18	5/11	1/7
	1	55/90	35/90	1	1

that of both a particular hypothesis being true and of heads or tails coming off at the first toss. They are derived from the former columns in accordance with the rules of probability calculus. There are ten possible combinations of five hypotheses and two results of the first toss, and the probability weight of each of them is the product of the probability weights of the hypotheses and of the results taken separately. Thus 1/30 at the top of the fifth column is the product of 1/5 at the top of the second column and 1/6 at the top of the third column. The totals of the weights in the fifth and the sixth columns are the probability weights of the outcomes of heads and of tails in the expectation of the result of the first toss, both equal to $\frac{1}{2}$.

(2.6.3) Suppose now that we make the first toss and heads come off. How are we going to adjust our expectations in the light of this result?

The fact that heads have come off means that column (6) does not apply. The numbers of the states of the world which are now equally confirmed by the evidence and have the characteristics listed in the first column have turned out to be related one to another as in column (5). This column represents now not one-half of the possible and equally confirmed states of the world, but all of them. If, therefore, we multiply the probability weights in it by 2, we obtain the adjusted weights of the outcomes of the five hypotheses in our expectation of the actual properties of the die. These adjusted weights are shown in column (7). In the light of the result that heads have come off at the first toss the weights attached to the outcomes that the die has four or five sides marked with heads have been increased and those of the outcomes that only one or two sides are marked with heads have been reduced.

The adjusted weights of the combined outcomes may further be derived from column (7) in place of (2) and from columns (3) and (4) as in the former case. They are shown in columns (8) and (9). The adjusted weights of heads and tails in the expectation of the next toss are now 55/90 and 35/90 respectively. In the light of the fact that heads have come off at the first toss it is more probable that they will also come off at the second toss.

(2.6.4) We may experiment in this way with the die on and on by making further and further tosses and adjusting the weights in the light of each successive result. If, for instance, at the second toss heads come off again, the adjusted weights of the hypotheses will become as in column (10). The weights of the outcomes that many sides of the die are marked with heads will increase still further and those of the other will decrease. If at the second toss tails come off, the adjusted weights will be as in column (11). The weights of the hypotheses in the middle will now be greater and those on the extremes smaller than they were originally.

It can be shown in fact that the adjusted weights follow the frequency distribution of results in the successive tosses. The closer this frequency distribution approaches $\frac{1}{2}$ for heads and $\frac{1}{2}$ for tails, the greater becomes the weight of the hypothesis that three sides of the die are marked with heads and three sides with tails, and the closer to $\frac{1}{2}$ and $\frac{1}{2}$ are the adjusted probability weights of heads and of tails at the next toss. If the frequency distribution approaches 1/6 for heads and 5/6 for tails, the probability weight of the hypothesis that only one side of the die is marked with heads becomes dominant, and the adjusted weights of heads and tails approach 1/6 and 5/6.

(2.6.5) The above rules are those of the Bayes' theorem.[1] The relevant formula is

$$P(H/x) = \frac{P(x/H) \cdot P(H)}{P(x)}$$

where $P(H/x)$ is the *a posteriori* probability of the hypothesis H (when the result x is already known), $P(x/H)$ is the conditional probability of x if H is true, $P(H)$ is the *a priori* probability of H, and $P(x)$ the *a priori* probability of x. In the example discussed in the preceding paragraphs H is a particular hypothesis about how many sides of the die are marked with heads and x is the result of the first toss, of the first and second toss, and so on.

The formula does not apply to the case discussed in (1.6.2) and (2.5.2) because the results of the General Election on which the businessman's profits depend are supposed to be known as soon as the election is over, and the *a posteriori* probability of the hypothesis that the Conservative Party or that the Labour Party has won is supposed to become at once equal to unity or

[1] For a more general discussion see H. Jeffreys *Theory of Probability, op.cit.*, p. 38. Compare also J. Marschak, Probability in the Social Sciences, *Mathematical Thinking in the Social Sciences*. P. F. Lazarsfeld (ed.), The Free Press, Glencoe (Illinois, 1954), pp. 181–5.

to zero. The expectation of profits is then clarified by result. The formula could apply to the case discussed in (1.6.6) if the conditions on which the level of profits depends could be identified and the conditional probabilities of profits ascertained. If, for instance, the businessman is supplying meat products, his profits depend on what proportion of the population is vegetarian. If then the conditional probability weights of the outcomes of particular levels of profits could be ascertained for all possible proportions of the population being vegetarian, the adjustment of the probability weights of the various outcomes of profits would have to be in accordance with the Bayes' theorem.

(2.6.6) The conclusions derived from Bayes' formula apply to all those cases in which the results of expectations on the same subject at successive dates depend on the working of a mechanism whose properties are unknown but supposed to remain constant. It is then logical for the adjustment of expectations to take the form of the probability weights of outcomes approaching more and more the actual frequency distribution of results which have been observed. If, for instance, the general conditions on which profits depend remain unchanged, it is logical for the businessman to adjust the weights of the outcomes of the various levels of profits in accordance with the frequency distribution of those levels of profits in the past.

This supplies a logical rule for the frequency distribution of results to be accepted as an indication of probability weights in the classical sense, and for the formalization of the weight of an outcome in general as a classical probability to be derived from the observed frequency distribution. The rule does not tell us what the classical probability actually is because at any stage of the process of adjustment the *a posteriori* probability weights depend not only on the frequency distribution of results which have been observed but also on *a priori* probability weights with which the process began. It tells us only that whatever these *a priori* probabilities might have been the *a posteriori* weights approach closer and closer the actual frequency distribution the more and more of results have been observed. It is, therefore, logical to accept the latter as an indication of what the former may be, but not as a measure of what it actually is. The reservations which have been made with respect to the reverse part of the argument in (2.4.5) remain valid.

(2.6.7) So do the objections to the interpretation of probability as frequency distribution which have been made in (2.3.4) and (2.3.5). Bayes' formula makes sense only if some significance is attached to *a priori* probability measures, before any frequency distributions have been observed. Furthermore, the rule that it is logical to go on adjusting the probability weights so that they tend to approach more and more the observed frequency distributions does not change the fact that the latter are the frequency distributions in particular series of observations only. Other series of observations might have led to different frequency distributions. If, therefore, the probability weights were identified with frequency distributions, they would be only different names for them and would not add anything to what the latter describe.

3

Subjective Factors in Expectations

In the analysis of logical relations in expectations the element of the individual is suppressed. The prospect is completely determined by the evidence. In fact, however, the prospect is arrived at by an individual and is influenced by his general attitudes and dispositions. The analysis of logical relations must, therefore, be supplemented with a study of subjective factors which affect expectations in addition to and sometimes even against the rules of logic.

All psychologism in economics has always been looked upon with suspicion. Doubts have been expressed whether it is consistent with the scientific character of the discipline. Various devices have, therefore, been applied to by-pass the question of the formation of expectations altogether and to go from the evidence straight to the prospect. They will be studied in the second part of this book. Some effort, however, has also been made to incorporate the study of the formation of expectations into economics proper, or to use in it hypotheses and conceptual framework which have been developed outside its field. The present chapter has been written with an eye on this latter approach. It gives a brief outline of some elementary notions and procedures which have to be described and explained if the hypotheses discussed in the later chapters are to be understood.

(3.1) Perception in Expectations

(3.1.1) In the first chapter of this book the evidence was formalized as a set of answers to questions about the past. A distinction was also made between the absolute and the actual evidence. The former was supposed to contain answers to all questions which could be formulated. The latter contained those answers

78

only which in the particular conditions the individual actually knew.

In the actual practice of expecting few questions are formulated, and the answers to them – even if they are implicitly known – are never fully brought to one's mind. The whole evidence is usually perceived in a very vague way, some elements in it being completely overlooked, others distorted or misunderstood. Even, therefore, if it would be possible to derive the prospect from the evidence in some objective sense, the prospect might be influenced by the individual's perceptions. It is in fact very difficult to say what is the actual evidence. It depends on what is perceived. The evidence which is perceived by one individual may be quite different from that which is perceived by some other even if both of them happen to be confronted with the same facts.

Furthermore, the outcomes in a prospect are hypotheses which do not follow automatically from the evidence. They must be first thought of by the individual. In a way they too must, therefore, be perceived as a possibility. Even, therefore, if the individuals had the same perceptions of the evidence, they might think of different outcomes and arrive at different prospects.

(3.1.2) Very little is known about the process in the course of which the evidence is perceived and the outcomes thought of. The economist has not got much to go on in this case even if he is prepared to ask for assistance from outside his field. The only case in fact in which such assistance has been asked for and accepted is that of certain features of economic behaviour being explained by means of the hypotheses of Gestalt psychology.[1]

The basic principle of Gestalt psychology is that our perceptions of the world around us are not those of individual elements which are combined into a whole but of a whole which gives a meaning to the elements. If we look at a drawing, we do not perceive every line in it. We perceive the picture of a man into which the lines combine, and the lines only so far as they are relevant to our perception of the man. If some lines are removed from the drawing, this may have no effect on our perception of the man. We may even not notice that the lines have been removed.

[1] G. Katona, *Psychological Analysis of Economic Behaviour*, McGraw-Hill (New York, 1951).

79

Furthermore, the same elements may be seen either as one whole or as some other according to our inner attitudes and dispositions. If the drawing of a man is not very clear, we may need some time to perceive him; or we may also perceive something else if we look at it in a different way.

(3.1.3) Applied to expectations the principle of Gestalt psychology explains why the same evidence may be seen by different people in a different way. The elements out of which it consists (that is to say the answers to the questions which might have been asked) may be seen by them as parts of different wholes.

One may go even further than that. The outcomes, the weights attached to them, and the answers to theoretical questions which may be asked in the course of the transformation of the evidence into the prospect, may be treated as parts of the whole which the individual perceives. What is perceived is then not only the evidence but also the prospect. Both combine into a meaningful whole. To expect, means then to see that whole. And as different people may see the same elements as parts of different wholes, so they may also see the same elements in the evidence as parts of different wholes of expectations. They may combine them with different answers to theoretical questions, different outcomes and different weights attached to them.

(3.1.4) Gestalt psychology does not permit us to determine what expectations will be held in particular circumstances. It does not tell us anything about how people perceive nor what they perceive. Applied to expectations it explains only some general facts about them, independent of their actual content.

The facts are (i) that different individuals may arrive at different prospects even if they are confronted with the same evidence, and (ii) that prospects in expectations of the same individual may not change in response to a change in the evidence or may change in a discontinuous way. Both facts are important from the point of view of the analysis of our behaviour. For they lead to the conclusion that if the behaviour of an individual is determined by his expectations, it cannot be predicted on the ground of the inspection of the evidence only. The factors which determine the individual's perceptions must also be taken into account. It is impossible to establish a connection between the evidence and the prospect even with respect to one particular individual with all his personal characteristics accepted as data. For in some circumstances, a change in the evidence may not lead to any change in the prospect because no change has occurred in the individual's perceptions. In others, the effect on the prospect may be out of proportion to the change in the evidence because the individual perceives now quite a different whole and quite a different prospect makes this whole meaningful. In what circumstances one, and in what the other, response is likely to occur depends on what factors govern the individual's perceptions.

(3.1.5) In view of the above it is useful to distinguish between two types of behaviour: (i) habitual, and (ii) non-habitual behaviour. *Habitual* behaviour is determined by expectations in which either there is no reorganization of the whole into which the elements of the evidence and of the prospect combine, or the reorganization takes place more or less automatically along already familiar lines and results in a different but also already familiar whole. *Non-habitual* behaviour is determined by expectations in which the reorganization results in a new, unfamiliar whole. If we notice, for instance, a change in the state of the clouds, we may dismiss it as irrelevant to the prospect of rain; we may adjust the prospect more or less automatically from that of fine weather to that of rain and take the umbrella; or we may perceive in the state of the clouds something that suggests a thunder-storm and stay at home.

The distinction may also be interpreted as one between habitual and non-habitual decisions, or habitual or non-habitual expectations. The criterion of the distinction is always the same: whether a particular expectation, decision or behaviour implies, or does not imply, a reorganization of the elements of the evidence and of the prospect into a new, unfamiliar whole.[1]

(3.1.6) The distinction may be also used as a criterion to separate (in principle at least) those forms of our behaviour about which it is possible to formulate empirical generalizations without any previous study of our perceptions from those which cannot be generalized in this way. If we see the present evidence

[1] Compare G. Katona, *op. cit.* H. A. Simon, The Role of Expectations in an Adaptive or Behaviouristic Model, *Expectations, Uncertainty and Business Behaviour*, Mary Jean Bowman (ed.), *op. cit.*, pp. 49–58; and A. D. Roy, The Empirical Testing of Alternative Theories of Uncertainty, *Uncertainty and Business Decisions*, C. F. Carter, G. P. Meredith and G. L. S. Shackle (eds.), Liverpool University Press (1957), p. 76.

as a part of the same whole that we saw before when we happened to be confronted with it in the past, the prospect and our behaviour is also the same, and a generalization is valid. The study of the prospects at which we arrived in the past is then relevant to the prospects at which we are going to arrive in the future. If, however, our expectations are non-habitual, no similar wholes could have been perceived in the past even if the same evidence was available then. Even, therefore, if we knew at what prospects we arrived in the past, we still would not be able to say anything about those at which we are going to arrive in the future.

It has been already pointed out that in the present state of our knowledge we cannot say in advance when a reorganization of the elements of the evidence and of the prospect into a new whole will and when it will not take place. The distinction between habitual and non-habitual expectations could, therefore, be a basis for a qualification only. We hope to be able to formulate a theory which would enable us to say what prospects the individual combines with a particular evidence if his expectations are habitual. But we must also take into account the possibility that what we say may not apply because the expectation may turn out to be non-habitual.

(3.2) Formalization of Expectations by Introspection

(3.2.1) Gestalt psychology does not tell us anything about what expectations are held in what circumstances. It gives us an explanation of the general fact that different expectations may be held in the same circumstances. The actual content of expectations is, however, outside its scope.

In the remaining sections of this chapter we will be concerned with the formalization of the content of expectations. In particular an attempt will be made there to take into account the subjective factors on which expectations depend. The crux of the matter is how the weights of the outcomes and the pay-offs from them are to be formalized if they are to play their part in a theory. The outcomes themselves and the evidence are statements in words about the actual or possible events. The weights, however, and the pay-offs may be anything. They may be numbers, rankings, or descriptions of feelings and attitudes,

82

according to how we decide to define them in the formal scheme of the theory.

(3.2.2) To be a part of a theory, the weights and pay-offs must be formalized in terms of some operation. This may simply be introspection. Many would reject the procedure straightaway as not scientific. We have, however, decided to approach it with an open mind. The only question, therefore, that is relevant here is how far it can go. The minimum requirements are that it must provide an indication whether a particular pay-off is or is not desirable or a particular outcome relevant. Otherwise it would be of no use at all. If in our example of the expectation of rain the individual could not even tell us that he takes or does not take into account the outcome of rain, we would not be able to say anything about the prospect at which he arrives. And if he could not tell us that he would like or would not like to have his clothes ruined by rain, we would not be able to say anything about his behaviour. There is little doubt that these minimum requirements can easily be satisfied. But can introspection go further than that? Can the pay-offs and the weights be ranked by introspection? Or can numerical measures be attached to them?

(3.2.3) That pay-offs can be ranked according to how desirable they are is usually accepted as granted. The ranking of weights, however, requires some explanation. The question arises according to what criteria they are to be ranked. In Chapter 1 the weight was described in very general terms, as an indication of the qualification of the outcome. In the analysis of probability weights in Chapter 2 it was formalized as a property of the mechanism on the working of which the result depends. It was supposed to be ascertained by inspection of the mechanism or derived from the observed frequency distribution. The question of words in which the nature of the weight was to be described did not then arise. But if an individual is asked to rank the weights by intuition he must be told what he is expected to rank, and the words may then become important.

In the operations which are discussed in the present section the ranking is supposed to be that of some subjective qualifiers of the outcomes – of the degrees to which the individual believes that they will come off, or of the intensities of surprise which he would experience if they come off. The choice of the actual words may affect the ranking. It is, for instance, possible that the notion of the intensity of surprise is clear to the individual, but that of the degree of belief is not clear. At this stage, however, we will only take note of this possibility. The argument will proceed as if it did not arise. The ranking of weights by intuition will be regarded as uniquely determined, quite irrespective of in what terms they are described.

No exception is likely to be made to the possibility of such ranking in principle. The doubts we might have refer more to the degree of its precision than to our ability to do it at all. In fact we do such ranking of possible outcomes in nearly every minute of our life: when we say that rain is more probable than hail; that we would be more surprised if the General Election were held next year than we would be if it was postponed; and so on. It seems, therefore, that in principle at least we are able to do it. Some doubts may only remain as to with how good results.

(3.2.4) More difficult is the question whether introspection can go as far as to enable us to attach numerical measures to subjective pay-offs and weights. The first reaction is likely to be negative. We cannot ascertain by introspection any numerical measures because we do not feel or see any numbers when we think of pay-offs as desirable or of outcomes as qualified. But in fact the matter is not as simple as that. Although we may not feel or see any numbers we none the less may be able to arrive at them indirectly if we ask ourselves the proper questions.

A question which we may be able to answer and which may lead to a numerical measure of subjective pay-offs or of the weights of outcomes is how the differences in their desiredness or in the qualifications attached to them compare one with another. We may, for instance, feel that not only we prefer sunshine to rain and rain to hail, but that we also much more prefer sunshine to rain than rain to hail. Or we may not only feel that sunshine is more probable, likely, or less surprising than rain and that rain is more probable, likely or less surprising than hail, but we may also feel that sunshine is much more so in relation to rain than rain is in relation to hail. If we are able to do that, that is to say if we are able to rank not only the subjective pay-offs and weights themselves but also the differences between them, we may derive from the rankings of the latter numerical measures of the former.

(3.2.5) The procedure is as follows. To provide for a scale of the desiredness of pay-offs or of the weights of outcomes, take two arbitrary numbers as measures of these characteristics in two arbitrary outcomes. Zero, for instance, may be taken as the measure of the desiredness of a zero monetary pay-off and unity as that of one thousand pounds. Or zero may be taken as the measure of the weight of an outcome which is regarded as virtually impossible and unity as the measure of the weight of an outcome which is absolutely certain. These arbitrary numbers provide for the origin and the unit of the scale. They are like the boiling point and the freezing point on the Celsius scale of temperature.

Having established the scale we may then place other outcomes on it according to how we rank the differences between the subjective pay-offs from them and from those at the two extremes of the scale, or according to how we rank the differences between the weights to be attached to them. If, for instance, we find an outcome with a subjective pay-off which is so much greater than that at the bottom of the scale as it is less than that at the top of the scale, the numerical measure of the subjective pay-off from it is 0·5. Similarly, if we find an outcome which we regard as so much more probable, likely or less surprising than that at the bottom of the scale as the prospect at the top of the scale is more probable, likely or less surprising than the one we have found, the numerical measure of the subjective weight of the latter is 0·5. If then we find an outcome with a subjective pay-off or a weight which is exactly in the middle between those of the outcome at the top of the scale and that we found before, the numerical measure of the pay-off from it or of its weight is 0·75. And so on, all outcomes may be given numerical measures of subjective pay-offs and of weights by following the rule that if the pay-off or the weight of an outcome is ranked by the individual exactly in the middle between those of some other two outcomes, the numerical measure of that pay-off or weight is exactly in the middle between the numerical measures of those other two.

(3.2.6) The operation described in the above paragraph is often referred to as the *Jevonsian operation*.[1] It may be criticized on

[1] See D. Ellsberg, Classic and Current Notions of Measurable Utility, *Economic Journal*, **LXIV**, September (1954); and S. A. Ożga, Utility and Probability: A Simplified Rendering, *Economic Journal*, **LXVI**, September (1956) p. 421.

the ground that it relies on introspection which is not a scientific operation. Furthermore, the question still remains, whether introspection can really go as far as to enable us to rank not only pay-offs and weights but also the differences in them. The individual may, for instance, be subjected to the following consistency test. When he has decided upon outcomes with numerical measures of pay-offs or of weights of 0·25 and 0·75, he may be asked to choose an outcome which is exactly in the middle between them. It is by no means certain that he would then choose the same outcome which he chose before as being in the middle between zero and unity.

If, however, we approach the methodological question with an open mind and do not rule out the possibility of the individual passing successfully the consistency test, the Jevonsian operation may lead to the following formalization of the prospect. The outcomes are descriptions in words of the events which may occur. The subjective pay-offs from them are numerical measures of the desiredness of these events, arrived at through ranking of the differences in them. And the weights of the outcomes are numerical measures of the qualifications with which they appear in the prospect. The measures may be called utility and subjective probability. The actual words, however, in which they are described are not important. Their significance is determined by the operation in terms of which they are defined.

Whether this formalization is possible depends on whether the individual is consistent in his ranking of differences and on whether the theory of which it is a part is useful. There are no physical obstacles to ranking of differences in subjective pay-offs and in weights. The question is only whether it leads to any useful predictions of facts.

(3.2.7) An alternative operation which could enable us to determine the numerical measures of subjective pay-offs and of weights of outcomes by introspection, is to construct a scale of pay-offs and weights on the ground of the individual's feelings and attitudes which he experienced in the past; and to ask him then to place on it the outcomes he contemplates now, according to how the feelings and attitudes to which they give rise compare to those which he experienced before. It may, for instance, be explained to the individual that the numbers from 0 to 0·1 on the scale correspond to his experience of being more or less satisfied

86

with the pay-off or of being a little surprised that the outcome has come off ; those from 0·1 to 0·2 correspond to his being pleased with the pay-off or of being very surprised; those further up along the scale to being very pleased, happy, delighted, or startled, astonished ; and so on up to unity at the top. The individual may then be asked to arrange the outcomes along that scale according to which of these adjectives provides the right description of his actual feelings and attitudes. The operation is in fact the same as that of teachers putting numerical marks on their students' essays. It may, therefore, be called a *marking operation.*[1]

The question whether a formalization of expectations by means of a marking operation is possible is again one of consistency and of usefulness. Everybody who is asked to give numerical measures of his subjective pay-offs from outcomes and of weights can produce some numbers. The question is only whether he is consistent in his marks and what they mean. As they refer to what happens in the individual's mind nobody can say how well they correspond to the facts. The only way to test the result is to test the theory in which these numbers appear.

(3.2.8) The operations described in this section imply introspection. To determine the individual's rankings of the differences in subjective pay-offs and in weights or to ascertain the numerical measures at which he would arrive by marking, one has to ask him what they are. This is the main point in all the methodological objections to introspection. The data which introspection enables us to obtain cannot be checked by anybody except by the person who is both the subject and the object of it.

As has been already explained in the introduction, this does not mean yet that the data are meaningless. They are defined in terms of operations which can be performed. Even, therefore, if objections are raised against them being accepted as empirical, they still may be included into a theory as theoretical terms; hypotheses may be formulated as to how they are related to terms which can be objectively observed. It may, for instance, be postulated that the subjective pay-offs defined by the Jevonsian operation satisfy the condition of the diminishing marginal

[1] The operation has been suggested by Professor Popper. See J. W. N. Watkins, Decisions and Uncertainty, C. F. Carter, J. P. Meredith and G. L. S. Shackle (eds.), *Uncertainty and Business Decisions, op. cit.* (1957), p. 119.

utility; or that the weights defined by marking are identical with classical probability weights in those cases to which the latter apply. They obviously need not be. The subjective weights need not even add up to unity. But if the theory of which these hypotheses are a part leads to useful predictions, they may be accepted as useful as well.

(3.3) The Gambling Operation

(3.3.1) The alternative to introspection is observation of the individual's behaviour. Thus if introspection is rejected on methodological grounds or the theory which implies introspection turns out not to be useful, the subjective pay-offs and the weights of outcomes must be formalized so as to make it possible to derive their numerical measures from the individual's behaviour. The theory must then provide for the respective operation.

The operation which is usually considered in this connection is that of the individual being confronted with strategies, the pay-offs from which are uncertain and asked to choose between them. The individual may, for instance, be confronted with an uncertain outcome and asked to stake a particular sum of money to win another sum of money as a prize if the outcome comes off. The product of the numerical measures of the subjective pay-off from the prize and of the weight of the outcome may then be regarded as the measure of the subjective pay-off from the gamble. If the individual accepts the gamble, the measure of the latter is revealed to be greater to him than the measure of not having to pay the stake. If he rejects the offer, the former is less than the latter. And if he is indifferent whether to gamble or not to gamble, the two are equal one to the other.

We will call this operation a *gambling operation*. It has been used to determine utility in the modern versions of Bernoulli's theory of moral expectation. Ramsey[1] made the first steps, and his ideas were subsequently developed by Von Neumann and Morgenstern,[2] de Finetti[3] and Savage.[4]

[1] F. P. Ramsey, Truth and Probability, *The Foundations of Mathematics,* Kegan Paul, Trench, Trubner & Co. (London, 1931).

[2] J. Von Neumann and O. Morgenstern, *Theory of Games and Economic Behaviour* (2nd ed.), Princeton University Press (1947).

[3] B. De Finetti, La Prevision : ses Lois Logiques, ses Sources Objectives, *Annales de l'Institut Henri Poincaré* (1937).

[4] L. J. Savage, *The Foundation of Statistics, op. cit.*

(3.3.2) In the crude form in which it has been described above the operation is subject to the following objections. (i) The individual may decide to gamble or not to gamble not because he likes much or little the pay-off from the prize, or because he regards the outcome as likely or unlikely to come off, but because he likes or does not like the danger of a loss. The subjective pay-offs and the weights which the gambling operation defines are then numerical measures of the individual's preferences not only for the respective combinations of pay-offs and weights but also for the risks he has to assume. (ii) No provision is made in the operation for the separation of the subjective pay-offs from the weights in the prospect of the gamble. The fact that the individual chooses the gamble means that he prefers the particular combination of the subjective pay-off and of the weight attached to it to the pay-off from the sure prospect of not paying the stake. But it does not tell us anything about those pay-offs and weights taken separately. And (iii) the individual's indifference cannot be observed as an act of choice between any alternatives. Either, therefore, the operation must fall back again on introspection, or some other operation must be performed to determine whether the individual is or is not indifferent.

Nothing can be done about objection (i). If the individual likes or fears danger of a loss for its own sake, the numerical measures of subjective pay-offs and of weights cannot be ascertained by means of a gambling operation. The matter will be considered again in (6.3) and (6.4). Objection (iii) will be considered in (3.4). In the remaining paragraphs of the present section we will deal with objection (ii).

(3.3.3) As the first step consider n tosses with a coin. They may result in any of 2^n sequences of heads and tails. Suppose that these sequences do not differ one from another in anything except in the way in which the heads and the tails are arranged in them. The individual does not feel any pleasure or any distress when one of them comes off, nor is he interested in the result. He has only some views as to how likely they are to come off. And these determine the subjective weight which he attaches to the outcomes of them.

If the coin is true (in the sense that everything that can be said about it applies equally to the outcomes of heads and of tails) equal weights can be attached to the outcomes of all the

89

sequences on logical grounds. All of them are equally confirmed by the evidence. This does not mean, however, that if the subjective factors are taken into account, the outcomes must also be regarded by the individual as equally likely. The individual may have a hunch that one rather than some other sequence will come off and he may, therefore, attach to the outcome of it a greater weight than to those of the others.

To obtain a set of outcomes with equal subjective weights the individual may be asked to divide the whole set of 2^n sequences into groups so that he does not attach a greater weight to the outcome of a sequence from one group coming off than he does to that of a sequence from some other group coming off. If, for instance, the sequences are divided into two equal groups, and the individual turns out to be prejudiced in favour of one of them, some sequences must be removed from it and transferred to the other group so as to make both groups 'equal' to him in the sense that he does not think that the sequence which actually comes off is more likely to come from one of these groups than from the other. The same applies to a greater number of groups into which we may wish to divide the set of the sequences. They must be so balanced one with another as to make the individual feel that the sequence which actually comes off is as likely to be in one of them as in another. The respective outcomes are then subjectively equally likely cases.

(3.3.4) The segregation of the sequences could be made by the individual himself by introspection. If, however, this is not acceptable on methodological grounds, the individual may be offered a prize for guessing correctly the group to which the sequence which comes off will actually belong. If he decides on one group rather than on some other, the subjective weight which he attaches to the outcome that the sequence will be in the former is greater than that which he attaches to the outcome that it will be in the latter. The former group is then too large and some sequences must be removed from it and transferred to the other. If, however, the stage is reached at which the individual is indifferent which group to choose, the groups are subjectively 'equal' to him.

This operation is not likely to be ever performed. It shows, however, a way in which in principle at least it is possible to derive from the individual's choices a number of subjectively equally likely cases. If then the weight of unity is given to the outcome that the sequence which actually comes off is one of those in the whole set, and if the set of 2^n sequences is divided into say 100 subjectively 'equal' groups, the numerical weight of the outcome that a sequence from one particular group comes off is $1/100$; and the weight of the outcome that it will come from one or other of two specified groups is $2/100$. As the weights ascertained in this way are ratios of the numbers of groups with particular characteristics, the rules of probability calculus are applicable to them.

A scale constructed in this way may then be used to measure subjective weights of outcomes in expectations on other subjects. If, for instance, it turns out that the individual is indifferent whether a prize will be paid to him if the outcome of rain today comes off, or if the sequence of heads and tails which comes off in n tosses happens to be one of those in 50 out of 100 'equal' groups into which all the 2^n sequences have been divided, the weight of the outcome of rain is $0 \cdot 5$. The weights of all outcomes may thus be formalized in this way. They are ratios of numbers of equally likely cases and are, therefore, amenable to all the manipulations of probability calculus. Furthermore, if they appear in prospects derived from the same evidence, the logical relations between them are the same as those between objective probability weights. We may call them, therefore, *subjective probability weights*.

(3.3.5) The following objection may be raised against this procedure. The expectation of one of a number of sequences coming off in n tosses with a coin differs from that of rain today not only in the outcomes considered in the prospect but also in the evidence. It is, therefore, by no means certain that if a subjective probability weight is attached by means of a gambling operation to the outcomes of rain and to that of no rain, the two would add up to unity. A gambling operation on outcomes which appear in expectations on different subjects may easily lead to this result. The formalization of weights as subjective probability measures must then be either abandoned altogether, or the measures arrived at originally must be adjusted upwards (or downwards) so as to make them conform to the rule that the weight of a tautology is equal to unity.[1]

[1] The point is discussed more fully in W. Fellner, Distortion of Subjective

(3.3.6) If the weights of outcomes are formalized as probability measures, the formalization of the subjective pay-offs does not present any further difficulties. [1] Suppose that as in (3.2.5) the measures of zero and of unity are attached arbitrarily to the subjective pay-offs from some outcomes A and B; and let there be an outcome C the subjective pay-off from which is greater than that from A and less than that from B. The individual may then be asked to choose between C and a lottery ticket which offers him either A or B, the respective weights being $1 - p$ and p. The mean value of the measures of the subjective pay-offs from the outcomes A and B with the proper weights attached to them may then be accepted as the measure of the subjective pay-off from the lottery ticket. And if the conditions of the lottery (and in consequence the weights p and $1 - p$) are so adjusted that the individual is indifferent whether he gets the lottery ticket or C, the measure of the subjective pay-off from the latter is $0 \cdot (1 - p) + 1 \cdot p = p$.

The same would apply to any other outcome. If the subjective pay-off from it happens to be greater than that from B, the individual may be asked to choose between B and a lottery ticket which gives him a chance of either that outcome or A; and *vice versa* if the subjective pay-off from that outcome happens to be less than that from A. Whatever the subjective pay-offs may thus be, they can always be formalized by means of the gambling operation as numerical measures of the degree to which the respective outcomes are desirable.

(3.4) The Operation of Indifference

(3.4.1) The above elaborations dispose of the difficulty mentioned in the second objection in (3.3.2). Subject to the reservations made in (3.3.5) both the subjective pay-offs and the weights of the outcomes may be formalized by means of the gambling

---

Probabilities as Reaction to Uncertainty, *Quarterly Journal of Economics*, **LXXV**, November (1961), pp. 670–89.

[1] The operation has been introduced into economics by von Neumann and Morgenstern (*Theory of Games and Economic Behaviour, op. cit.*), and popularized by many others. See for instance M. Friedman and L. J. Savage, The Utility Analysis of Choices Involving Risk, *Journal of Political Economy*, **LVI**, August (1948); J. Marschak, Rational Behaviour, Uncertain Prospects and Measurable Utility, *Econometrica*, **18**, April (1950); and P. A. Samuelson, Probability, Utility and the Independence Axiom, *Econometrica*, **20**, October (1952).

operation, one separately from the other. We must now turn to the third objection. The theory must provide for a meaningful definition of the individual's indifference. The difficulties to which this may lead have been discussed in economics in connection with indifference curves. [1] The point is that indifference too is a subjective term. It too, therefore, must either be ascertained by introspection or an operation must be devised to derive it from the individual's behaviour.

(3.4.2) If an individual is confronted with two alternatives and prefers one to the other, it is reasonable to assume that he will choose that which he prefers. Preference may thus be revealed in the act of choice. Indifference cannot reveal itself in any act at all. It might perhaps do so in the hesitation to act. Hesitation, however, would also be difficult to ascertain by observation. For how long one has to hesitate to be called indifferent? And if one's mind is ultimately made up, hesitation may well go together with preference. A possible way to get rid of this difficulty is to confront the individual with a series of similar situations, to make a record of his choices, and to call him indifferent if his choices distribute themselves more or less evenly between the alternatives which are offered to him. [2]

(3.4.3) A possible solution is also to offer the individual a premium if he refrains from choosing himself one of the alternatives – one of the groups, for instance, into which the set of sequences of heads and tails has been divided – and agrees that the choice is made by somebody else to whom a premium is offered if he chooses the group from which the sequence has not come out. If the individual whose indifference we want to test regards the groups into which the whole set of the sequences has been divided as not 'equal', such delegation of the choice must mean to him that the chances of getting the prize become smaller. For the other person may choose the group to which the winning sequence is in the individual's opinion less likely to belong. The prize, however, is greater because a premium is added to it. If

[1] See for instance J. M. D. Little, *A Critique of Welfare Economics*, 2nd ed., Clarendon Press (Oxford, 1957), p. 23.

[2] This statistical approach to indifference (and to preference as well) gave rise to a probabilistic theory of consumer behaviour. See for instance, R. E. Quandt, A Probabilistic Theory of Consumer Behaviour, *The Quarterly Journal of Economics*, **LXX,** November (1956), pp. 507–36. These developments, however, are outside the scope of the present study and will not be discussed here.

thus he accepts the offer, the increase in the prize more than compensates, in his opinion, the reduction of the chance of getting it.

It may be further argued that the more 'equal' are the groups to choose from, the smaller increase in the prize would do the trick. If, therefore, it would be possible to divide all the sequences so that an infinitesimal premium would induce the individual to accept the group chosen by the other person, the individual could be described as indifferent what choice is actually made. The smaller is the premium which gives this result, the more precisely is the individual's indifference identified.

The same operation may be used to determine the individual's indifference with respect to other choices. If, for instance, he is confronted with the choice between a car and a certain amount of money and accepts the offer of a very small premium for abiding by the choice which somebody else makes for him, he may be regarded as indifferent whether he gets the car or the money.

(3.4.4) The operation described in this section is not more likely to be ever performed than the gambling operation described before. But it may be accepted as a definition of indifference in the latter. And then the gambling operation may serve as a definition of the subjective pay-offs and of weights.

(3.5) Potential Surprise

(3.5.1) The degree of potential surprise is an interpretation of a subjective weight of an outcome. It has been put forward by Shackle.[1] The theory in which it appears will be discussed in the third part of this book. In the present section a few words will only be said about the formal representation of the prospect to which it gives rise.

(3.5.2) The interpretation of the weights of outcomes as degrees of potential surprise has been introduced by Shackle to allow for the fact that if we think that an outcome is probable or that it is likely to come off, we do not experience any sensation. We do not experience probability or belief as we do fear, sorrow, or joy. We cannot, therefore, ascertain by introspection how probable the outcome seems to us or how much we believe

[1] G. L. S. Shackle, *Expectations in Economics*, 2nd ed., Cambridge University Press (1952).

that it will come off. All we can do is to ascertain it indirectly, through the experience of surprise which we would feel if an outcome which we thought not probable, or in the coming off of which we did not believe has in fact come off. If, for instance, we did not believe that rain would come today but rain has come, we are surprised that it has come. The less we believed in it the more surprised we are. The degree of surprise may thus be taken as a measure of the subjective weight of the outcome. And as surprise is a sensation which we experience as we do fear, sorrow, or joy, the measure can be ascertained by introspection.

The weight of the outcome is a *potential* surprise because we do not experience any surprise when we contemplate the outcome. We may experience it only if the outcome comes off. At the time of the expectation we may only imagine how surprised we would be if at the time of the subject the outcome comes off. At the time of the expectation the surprise is thus potential only.

(3.5.3) A prospect in which weights of outcomes are interpreted as degrees of potential surprise may be called a *potential surprise function*. Outcomes are one variable in it, and the corresponding degrees of potential surprise the other. In Shackle's analysis the outcomes are represented by their monetary pay-offs. The function summarizes, therefore, the relation between the monetary pay-offs from the possible outcomes and the degrees of potential surprise attached to them.

(3.5.4) Among the outcomes which appear in the prospect there must be always at least one, and usually more than one, to which a zero degree of potential surprise is attached. The fact that the individual would be surprised if a particular pay-off came off means that he has some other figure in mind which would not surprise him. If a greater than zero degree of potential surprise were attached to all possible pay-offs, the individual would be surprised whatever happens.

The outcomes to which zero degree of potential surprise is attached form the so-called *inner range* of the prospect. The degrees of potential surprise attached to the outcomes outside that range are greater than zero, usually greater the greater (or the smaller) are the monetary pay-offs from them. In a typical prospect, the inner range is somewhere in the region of small gains and losses, and the degrees of potential surprise increase monotonically with the increase of gains or of losses until they

95

reach a maximum when the gains or losses become so large tha' they are regarded as virtually impossible.

If the individual is very optimistic in his expectations, th(inner range may not contain any outcomes of losses; if he is very pessimistic, the inner range may not contain any outcomes of gains. It is also possible that the inner range consists of two or more parts separated one from another by outcomes with posi- tive degrees of potential surprises. The pay-offs from a particula· strategy may, for instance, depend on whether there will or will not be a revolution in a particular country. Either, therefore, very large gains are expected if there is no revolution or very large losses if there is one. The outcomes of medium gains or medium losses would be surprising.

(3.5.5) The weights defined in terms of the gambling operation cannot be interpreted as degrees of potential surprise. For they are related to belief in a positive sense: the greater the weight the greater the degree of belief that the particular outcome will come off. Potential surprise, on the other hand, is negatively related to belief: the greater the potential surprise the greater the degree of disbelief. But if these relations consistently obtain, the degree of potential surprise is also negatively related to the probability weight and may, therefore, be derived from it by means of a suitable transformation. It may, for instance, be defined as the difference between the highest probability weight and that of the outcome in question.[1] This is not how Shackle defines them. But the definition is not inconsistent with his theory. It does not imply more than that the more we would be surprised if a particular outcome came off, the less prepared we are to gamble on it.[2]

(3.6) Consistency of Surprise

(3.6.1) In (2.5) certain relations have been established between

[1] W. Edwards – Note on Potential Surprise and Nonadditive Subjective Probability, Mary Jean Bowman (ed.) *Expectations, Uncertainty, and Business Behaviour, op. cit.*, Mary Jean Bowman (ed.), p. 45 – suggested the formula: potential surprise is equal to one minus probability.

[2] The validity of this implication was questioned by Shackle and by Carter (see C. F. Carter, A Revised Theory of Expectations, *Economic Journal*, LXIII, December (1953), pp. 811–20) on the ground that the individual might regard one outcome as more probable than some other and yet not be surprised at all at the occurrence of either of them.

probability weights in expectations on different subjects if the expectations are held in virtue of the same evidence and are consistent one with another. The relations apply to objective as well as to subjective probability weights. In the present section we will consider the question whether any relations of this kind can also be established between degrees of potential surprise.

(3.6.2) Let us take again the example of a businessman's expectations of profits and of the results of the General Election on which these profits depend. Suppose, however, that the weights of the respective outcomes are degrees of potential surprise. Let these weights be as in Table 3.6.2.

Consider first the weights in the second and the third column. They represent the degrees of surprise which the individual would experience if he knew that the election will be won by the Conservative or by the Labour Party respectively, and if his profits happened to be as in the first column of the table. They are weights which appear in the individual's expectation of what his expectation of profits will be when the result of the election becomes known. The actual numbers have been derived from the probability weights in Table 2.5.3 by means of the formula suggested in (3.5.5). The degree of potential surprise is the

Table 3.6.2

Profits	Conservative Party won	Labour Party won	Result unknown and the weights			
			0 and 0		$2\frac{1}{2}$ and 0	
(1)	(2)	(3)	(4a)	(4b)	(5a)	(5b)
-2	3	1	1	1	1	1
-1	2	0	0	0	0	0
0	0	2	0	0	2	$\frac{1}{2}$
1	2	3	2	$1\frac{1}{2}$	$2\frac{1}{2}$	$1\frac{7}{8}$
2	3	4	3	$2\frac{1}{2}$	3	$2\frac{7}{8}$

difference between the highest probability weight and the weight of the outcome in question, multiplied by 10 for the sake of convenience. Thus the weight at the top of the second column is the difference between 0·4 in the third row and 0·1 in the first row of the second column in Table 2.5.3, multiplied by 10.

97

As in the case of probability weights we will consider two sets of weights of the outcomes in the prospect of the election results. One is zero degree of potential surprise for both parties. It corresponds to equal probabilities in (2.5). The other is 0 degree of potential surprise for Labour and $2\frac{1}{2}$ for the Conservative Party, and corresponds to the probability weights 0·625 and 0·375.

(3.6.3) The question now arises what weights of the outcomes of different levels of profits are consistent with the weights in the conditional expectations of profits and of the election results as given in the table. The problem is the same as in (2.5.5). It refers only not to probability weights, but to degrees of potential surprise.

Take first the case of 0 and 0 degrees of potential surprise in the prospect of the election results. It is possible to argue that if the individual would not be surprised at the Conservative Party winning the election, and if he would not be surprised at his profits being then equal to zero, he could not be surprised at his profits being equal to zero. The fact that he would be surprised if his profits happened to be zero when the other party has won the election does not matter. It is the alternative with the lowest degree of potential surprise that determines the weight of the outcome. For it would not make sense to say that the individual would be surprised if his profits happened to be zero, but that he would not be surprised if the Conservative Party won the election and his profits happened to be zero. The same applies to the outcomes of profits of -1 and of the Labour Party winning the election. In the example in Table 3.6.2 zero degree of potential surprise is, therefore, attached to the outcomes of profits of both 0 and -1.

Similar considerations apply to the outcomes of other levels of profits. The degree of surprise which the individual would experience if his profits happened to be -2 cannot be greater than the degree of surprise which he would experience if they happened to be -2 and either the Conservative or the Labour Party has won the election. Again, therefore, the least surprising alternative determines the weight of the outcome. In the case of the outcome of profits of -2 the weight in column (4a) is 1, that of the Labour alternative; and in the case of the outcome of profits of 1 and 2 the weights are 2 and 3 respectively, those of the Conservative alternative.

(3.6.4) This is *the first consistency rule* suggested by Shackle. If a particular outcome appears in several possible states of the world, the weight of the outcome is the lowest degree of potential surprise that is attached to it in any of them. The situation is more complicated if the degrees of potential surprise attached to the respective states of the world are not all zero. In Table 3.6.2 the last two columns refer to the case in which the degree of potential surprise attached to the outcome of the Conservative Party winning the election is $2\frac{1}{2}$. We cannot then argue that the individual would not be surprised if his profits happened to be zero, because although he would not be surprised if they were zero with the Conservative Party in power, he would be surprised if the latter happened to be the case; and although he would not be surprised if the Labour Party happened to be in power, he would be surprised if his profits happened to be zero then.

The rule which has been suggested by Shackle to deal with this case – his *second consistency rule* – is that if an individual would be surprised if both (i) a particular event has taken place, and (ii) some other event has taken place *when* the first has taken place, the degree of surprise which he would experience if both events have taken place must be equal to either that of (i) or to that of (ii) according to which of them is greater. Thus if in our example, the degree to which the individual would be surprised at the Conservative Party winning the election is $2\frac{1}{2}$; and the degree to which he would be surprised if his profits were 1 *when* the Conservative Party has won the election is 2; the degree of surprise which he would experience if both the Conservative Party has won the election and his profits happened to be 1 is $2\frac{1}{2}$. In the case of zero profits it would also be $2\frac{1}{2}$. But in the case of profits of 2 it would be 3 because now the individual would be more surprised at his profits being as high as that *when* the Conservative Party has won the election, than he would be at the fact that the Conservative Party has actually won.

The degrees of potential surprise which are attached to the outcomes of different levels of profits when the results of the election are still unknown can then be derived from those corresponding to the two alternative results of the General Election by means of the first rule. The weight in that state of the world is relevant in which it is the lowest. Thus for profits of -2 and -1 the state of the world with the Labour Party in power is relevant, and the weights in column (5a) of the table are the same as in (3) and in (4a). For zero profits the degree of potential surprise in the state of the world with the Conservative Party in power (adjusted for the fact that this particular result would itself be surprising) is 2½. This is greater than the weight 2 which would apply if the Labour Party were to have won the election. The latter, therefore, is the weight of the outcome. For profits of 1 the adjusted degree of potential surprise in the Conservative state of the world is relevant. For profits of 2 no adjustment is required, and the weight is 3, the same as in columns (2) and (4a). [1]

(3.6.5) It has been already pointed out that the degrees of potential surprise in the second and the third columns of Table 3.6.2 have been derived from the second and the third columns in Table 2.5.3 by means of the formula that the degree of potential surprise is the difference between the highest probability weight and that of the outcome in question. The same formula may now be applied to the probability weights in the fourth and the fifth column in Table 2.5.3. The result is shown in columns (4b) and (5b) in Table 3.6.2. The degrees of potential surprise in these columns are thus consistent with those in columns (2) and (3) according to the rules of probability calculus. Those in columns (4a) and (5a) are consistent with them according to the rules suggested by Shackle.

In the case of 0 and 0 weights of the two election results some of the numerical values of the degrees of potential surprise in column (4a) differ from those in (4b), but the ranking of the outcomes is the same. In columns (5a) and (5b) not only the numerical values differ but so does the ranking which they describe. For in column (5a) a greater degree of potential surprise is attached to the outcome of 0 profits than to that of −2, and in column (5b) the ranking is the other way round. This is no doubt true in a general sense. The consistency rules suggested by Shackle yield different results than the logical rules of probability calculus.

(3.6.6) The following example may help to see why this is so. Suppose that we intend to make a toss with a die which is loaded in favour of the ace. If we know about the die being loaded, we

---

[1] Compare G. L. S. Shackle, *Decision, Order and Time in Human Affairs*, *op. cit.*, Chapter XXIV.

will attach a zero degree of potential surprise to the outcome that the ace will come off and some positive degree of potential surprise to the outcomes of other results. Suppose then that we gain a premium if the ace comes off, and suffer a loss if this is not the case. What degrees of potential surprise should we attach to the outcome of the gain and to that of the loss? According to Shackle's first rule zero degree of potential surprise should be attached to the outcome of the gain and a positive one to that of the loss, *quite irrespective of how much the die is loaded in favour of the ace.* It may be argued, however, that if the die is only very slightly loaded this may not be the case. For the fact that we gain if one particular result occurs and lose if any one of five possible results occurs might then outweigh the fact that the die is loaded in favour of the former result.

To see what the second rule implies, suppose that the die is loaded not in favour but against the ace. Zero degree of potential surprise would then be attached to the five outcomes of the results other than the ace, and a positive degree to that of the ace. Suppose also that the die will be tossed not once but n times. The result of these n tosses may thus be any sequence of the six faces of the die. The amount of gain which we may receive depends then on how many aces appear in the sequence which actually comes off. As there are many sequences in which the number of aces is close to $\frac{1}{6}$ of the total number of tosses and only a few in which it is either very large or very small, the probability weights of the outcomes of gains corresponding to the former are higher than those of the outcomes of either very large gains or very large losses. For if the die is only very slightly loaded, the fact that many sequences would yield a particular gain may be more important for the probability weight of that gain than the fact that the die is loaded. According to Shackle's second rule we should, however, attach zero degree of potential surprise to the outcome of maximum loss, that which corresponds to the sequence in which no aces appear, and a positive degree of potential surprises to all the other outcomes of losses and gains, the same as that which we attach to the outcome of one ace in one toss. In other words we should then be no more surprised if n aces come off in n throws than we would be if their number happened to be smaller. This is not a very plausible conclusion. The result of all aces in n throws is likely to be much more surprising than that of a smaller number of them, quite irrespective of the load.

(3.6.7) The above considerations throw some doubts on the validity of Shackle's rules.[1] It must, however, be pointed out that validity means here plausibility only. A rule that the degree of potential surprise attached to one outcome is equal to the highest or to the lowest from those which are attached to some other outcomes is only a suggested description of what happens in our minds. They cannot, therefore, be rejected as illogical or as not true. All we can do about them is to ask ourselves what degree of potential surprise we would find if we performed a marking or a Jevonsian operation on ourselves with respect to the outcomes to which the rules apply. This is, in fact, what the argument in the preceding paragraphs amounts to. And if we discover that what we find does not conform to the rules, we may reject the latter as a wrong description of what actually takes place in our mind. But we cannot say on the ground of our experience that they are also a wrong description of what takes place in other people's minds.

(3.7) The Criterion of Disappointment

(3.7.1) It has been explained in (1.5.5) that as time goes by new facts become known, and the evidence in expectations with the time of the subject still far ahead may change. If the new evidence consists in answers to questions which could not have been answered before, expectations are clarified. If it consists in different answers to the same questions, expectations are revised. It has also been pointed out in (1.6.6) that if the result of an expectation depends on conditions which can be only guessed, the fact that expectations on the same subject, but with earlier times of it, have been confirmed by the actual results may be accepted as an indication that the guesses have been correct, and that the expectation is clarified only. If, however, the expectations with the earlier times of the subject are contradicted by the actual results, the guesses must have been wrong and the expectation with a later time of the subject is revised.

---

[1] See, however, the limitations discussed in the introduction to Chapter 7 and in paragraph (7.5.7). Shackle's theory of expectations is supposed to apply to those cases only in which calculation of odds is quite impossible.

In (2.6) some logical rules have been established for the adjust-ment of the prospect if the weights are formalized as probability weights. No distinction, however, could have then been made between clarification and revision, because no rules of logic could tell us whether the result of one out of several outcomes confirms or does not confirm the expectation. Now with the subjective factors allowed for, the analysis of clarification and of revision of expectations may be carried a little further. For if clarification implies confirmation of an earlier expectation by the actual result, the criterion of it may be that the individual is satisfied with the prospect at which he then arrived. And if revision implies no confirmation, the criterion of it may be that the individual is disappointed. The problem is then what results mean satisfaction and what mean disappointment.

The answer is simple if the prospect is a sure prospect. If, for instance, a businessman thought that the Conservative Party would win the election and then the Conservative Party has really won, his expectation has been confirmed by the result, and he is satisfied with the prospect at which he arrived in it. If the Labour Party won, he would be disappointed. In the examples in Tables 2.5.3 and 3.6.2 he would then substitute the weights in column (3) for those in (2). In general, however, prospects are not sure prospects. Several outcomes appear in them. The question is thus whether it is possible to formulate a criterion which would enable us to say that the individual is confirmed or disappointed in his expectations if one rather than some other outcome comes off.

(3.7.2) Consider first the case in which the weights of outcomes are formalized as degrees of potential surprise. The argument may run then as follows. A positive degree of surprise means that a result occurred which the individual did not quite expect. He did not regard it as impossible, but none the less he thought that something else would rather take place. He is, therefore, not only surprised but also disappointed. Only if the actual result happened to be an outcome to which a zero degree of potential surprise was attached, one of those in the inner range, only then could the individual regard his expectation as con-firmed by it. In this case, therefore, the criterion of whether a particular change in the expectation with a later time of the subject is a clarification or a revision of it is whether a zero or a

103

greater than zero degree of potential surprise was attached to the outcome which has come off at an earlier time.

(3.7.3) If this is accepted, some conclusions may be formulated with respect to the clarification of weights. It may be argued that if the weights are formalized as degrees of potential surprise and related one to another in accordance with Shackle's consistency rules, clarification of the respective expectation cannot result in a decrease of any of them. For the degree of potential surprise attached to an outcome at the time of the expectation is then either equal to or lower than that which would be attached to it if any of the outcomes in the inner range of the expectation with the earlier time of the subject came off. In our example in Table 3.6.2 the degrees of potential surprise in column (4a) are either those in column (2) or those in column (3) according to which of them is lower; and those in column (5a) are either equal or lower than those in (3). If, therefore, at the time of the election the prospect summarized in column (4a) is replaced by either that in (2) or in (3); or if the prospect summarized in column (5a) is replaced by that in (3); the degrees of potential surprise attached to some outcomes of profits may remain unchanged; those attached to some others may increase; but none may be reduced.

Nothing can be said about how the prospect will change if the expectation is revised. If in the example in Table 3.6.2 the Conservative Party wins the election and the weights in column (5a) are replaced by those in (2), the weights of the outcomes of profits of −2 and of −1 increase, the weight of 2 remains unchanged, and those of 0 and of 1 decrease.

(3.7.4) The analysis is much less straightforward if the weights of outcomes are formalized as probability measures. The logical rules of the adjustment of probability weights are then those of (2.6). But the criteria of satisfaction and disappointment are more difficult to formulate. The problem was considered by Hart in connection with his analysis of the role which anticipations play in the behaviour of firms.[1] He was interested in how the knowledge of prices which successively come off at earlier times may affect the expectations of prices which will come off at

[1] A. G. Hart, Anticipations, Uncertainty, and Dynamic Planning, *Journal of Business of the University of Chicago*, **13**, 4, (Chicago, 1940).

ater times. His analysis, however, may also be applied to our example of the expectations of profits.

According to Hart three conditions must be satisfied for an expectation to be confirmed by the actual result. (i) The actual result must be equal to the mean value of the outcomes. If, for instance, the weights in the prospect of profits are as in column (4) in Table 2.5.3, the businessman's expectations are confirmed if the actual profits turn out to be equal to -0.45. (ii) The knowledge of a particular result at an earlier time must not lead to a change in the mean value of the outcomes at a later time. The result of the General Election or the actual profits at t_k must thus be such that when they become known, the mean value of the outcomes of profits at t_s remains the same as it was before. And (iii) the result at an earlier time must be such that when the knowledge of it is added to the evidence in the expectation with a later time of the subject, the outcomes in the latter become more concentrated around their mean value. In other words the result of the election or the actual profits at t_k must be such that not only the mean value of profits at t_s remains the same as it was before, but the outcomes of some extreme values of profits drop out also, and the weights of those which are close to the mean value increase.

(3.7.5) An obvious restriction of these conditions is that they apply to those expectations only in which outcomes are measurable. The first condition, for instance, does not apply to expectations of the election results. For there is no mean value in that case. The result must be either one party or another. The second and the third condition allows for the outcomes not to be measurable in the expectation with the earlier time of the subject. In the example of the businessman's expectations of profits and of the election results, the latter must be simply such that the outcomes of profits in the former concentrate more closely around the same mean value. The outcomes must, however, be measurable in the expectation with the later time of the subject.

Furthermore, if the first condition is to be ever satisfied the outcomes must not only be measurable but they must also describe a characteristic which is continuous over the relevant range. Any amount of profits may, for instance, be an outcome in the prospect of profits. But if the subject of the expectation is the number of leaves on a stem of a clover, the actual result

105

can never be equal to the mean value of the outcomes. It must be either three or four.

(3.7.6) Hart's conditions are quite arbitrary. In very general terms they agree with the observations which in many cases we might be inclined to make on common-sense grounds. For if we do not know what our profits are going to be, the prospect in our expectation is likely to take the form of several outcomes with probability weights arranged more or less symmetrically around their mean value. Then if everything goes as we thought it should, the prospect is likely to become more and more definite in the sense that the outcomes cluster more and more closely around the same mean value, and finally the latter becomes the result. If the events in the time in-between are not as we thought that they would be, our expectation of profits is likely to change so that the outcomes cluster now around a different mean value or they are more dispersed.

The actual formulation of Hart's conditions is, however, arbitrary because in general the mean value is not the most probable outcome, and no significance can, therefore, be attached to the fact that the outcome which has come off happens to be equal to it. The probability distribution need not be symmetrical. Greater probability weights may also be attached to the outcomes at the extremes than to those in the middle of the range. And if an outcome with a lower probability weight happens to come off, the individual can hardly be described as satisfied with the result. Furthermore, the only precise meaning that can be given to the notion of the dispersion of outcomes is that of a statistical measure. And this too is arbitrary.

PART TWO

SURE-PROSPECT EQUIVALENTS

IT HAS been explained in the first part of this book that to be complete the prospect in an expectation must contain more than one outcome. Our knowledge of the future is always imperfect. Even if a prospect is derived from the evidence in accordance with some well established law, it cannot be accepted as a sure prospect. There is always the possibility that the result may be different. In principle, there may always be a mistake in the astronomers' view of the universe, and the sun may not rise tomorrow. The weight of this outcome is very small, but it is not zero.

This applies even more to expectations in economics, in which prospects are not derived from the evidence in accordance with any laws. None the less large parts of economic theory have been written as if they were sure prospects. Outputs of firms and quantities demanded by consumers are supposed to be determined by given prices, the volume of investment by given rates of return, and so on. Why this is so, and what is the sense of it? What hypotheses are implied in this procedure?

These are the questions with which we will be concerned in the next three chapters of this book. The sure prospects are called there sure-prospect equivalents because the individuals are supposed to behave *as if* the prospects at which they arrive were sure prospects. The actual hypothesis may take many forms. The sure-prospect equivalent may be a theoretical term, derived from the evidence by means of an arbitrary formula. In an expectation of a future price, for instance, the prospect is often the price ruling at the time of the expectation. It may also be derived from a multi-outcome prospect, the mean value of the possible outcomes of prices for instance. We will speak in such cases of multi-outcome prospects being reduced to a sure-prospect form by formula. The sure-prospect equivalent may be determined by the individual's subjective attitudes and dispositions. It may be, for instance, the mean value of the possible outcomes of prices less some premium for risk. The sure-prospect equivalent must then be chosen by the individual. We will speak, therefore, of the reduction by choice in that case. The sure-prospect equivalent may be also the mean value of utility pay-offs.

This is how the subject matter of this part of the book is divided between the three chapters which deal with it. Chapter 4 deals with sure-prospect equivalents arrived at by formula. Chapter 5 with the reduction by choice, and Chapter 6 with the hypothesis of moral expectation in which the sure-prospect equivalents are the mean values of utility pay-offs. In the cases discussed there sure-prospect equivalents differ one from another. In each case much attention, therefore, must be paid to the actual context of the hypothesis. In particular one has to distinguish clearly expectations of pay-offs to which behaviour is adjusted from intermediate expectations through which the former are arrived at. For if, for instance, expectations of profits are arrived at through intermediate expectations of prices, outputs, and costs, adjustment to sure-prospect equivalents of the former does not necessarily mean that behaviour is determined by sure-prospect equivalents of the latter.

4

The Hypothesis of a Formula

IF THE sure-prospect equivalent is derived from the evidence by a formula, the latter is not a hypothesis but a definition. The hypothesis of the theory is that the individual behaves *as if* he were adjusting his position to a theoretical term defined in this way. The whole procedure is usually an attempt to get rid of expectations altogether. The evidence is supposed to be given in an objective sense and the individual's behaviour is derived from it by means of a theory which does not say anything about what happens in his mind.

Not much will be said about this case in the present book. The subject is not within its scope. The sense of the hypothesis is explained in the first two sections of this chapter. The other sections deal with the hypothesis that a formula can be applied to reduce to the form of a sure-prospect equivalent a multi-outcome prospect. The latter may be formalized in terms of any of the operations described before. For the purpose of the problem in hand it will be accepted as given. The question will be only asked whether a whole set of possible outcomes and their weights can be reduced by means of a formula to the form of a sure prospect, so that the hypothesis that the individual behaves *as if* he were confronted with the latter provides a satisfactory explanation of how he actually behaves when he is confronted with the former.

(4.1) Sure Prospects by Definition

(4.1.1) Taken at its face value, the hypothesis that a prospect is a sure prospect means that the individual thinks, or behaves as if he thought, that he knows the future. One outcome only appears in his mind as a description of what is going to happen.

In terms of probability weights, the situation could be described as one in which the individual would never be prepared to gamble that the outcome does not come off, whatever the odds. In terms of subjective weights it would mean that the individual would never consider the possibility of any other outcome coming off, or of being surprised to less than a maximum degree if it did.

In neither of these two forms could the hypothesis be true. In business and in our everyday life we are usually confronted with situations in which we would accept a gamble against every possible outcome at favourable odds. And we are often surprised to less than a maximum degree. If, therefore, the formal representation of expectations is in terms of subjective probabilities or of subjective weights determined by introspection, the prospect in it cannot as a rule be a sure prospect.

(4.1.2) None the less, as has been already pointed out in the introduction to this part of the book, many chapters of economic theory have been written as if prospects in expectations were sure prospects. They have been often identified with the results which occur at the time of the expectations. Thus in elementary supply and demand theory the argument is that if demand increases, the price also increases, and the firms expand their outputs to earn as much profits as these higher prices permit. It is understood that as outputs cannot be increased instantaneously, they are not being adjusted to current prices but to the prices which the firms expect to be ruling when the increased outputs become available. The hypothesis implied in this argument is that the prospects in the expectations of prices are sure prospects of the same prices as those which are ruling on the market at the time of the expectation.

If the adjustments in output proceed very quickly and by very small steps, the results of the prices cannot differ much from their prospects. The time of the subject is then so close to the time of the expectation that neither supply nor demand can change much during the time in-between; the equilibrium price cannot, therefore, change much either; and if the sure prospect of the price is identified with the actual price at the time of the expectation, it cannot be also much different from the price which will be ruling at the time of the subject. If, however, the adjustment in output requires time, considerable changes in upply and demand may occur during the time in-between, and he result of the price may differ much from the sure prospect)f it. This is, for instance, the situation in the cobweb case. The ,ure prospect of the price is then equal to the actual price at the ime of the expectation; but during the time in-between so large adjustments in the output are made that the actual result of the)rice is much different from it.

(4.1.3) Similar considerations apply to models in which adjust-ments are made to expectations on other subjects. For instance, n Cournot's model of oligopoly the firms are supposed to fix their outputs so as to maximize their profits subject to the condition that the outputs of the other firms remain unchanged. The theory implies the hypothesis that the prospects in the expectations of the other firms' outputs are sure prospects of outputs which are observed at the time of the expectation.

The acceleration principle is often interpreted as an explanation of how capital stock adjusts itself to changes in demand for the product. It implies the hypothesis that if demand for the product increases, it is expected to remain at that higher level. Otherwise there would be no point in adjusting the capital stock to it. And if the relation which determines the numerical value of the accelerator is the capital output ratio, the prospects of output must be sure prospects if the accelerator is to have a definite value.

Many other examples could be given from other parts of economic theory. Whenever in fact the argument is that the firm, or whoever else is the relevant agent, adjusts itself to the environ-ment so as to achieve a certain objective at some time in the future, a hypothesis is usually implied in it that the adjustments are to sure prospects of some of the conditions which can be observed at the time of the expectation. There is hardly any chapter in economic theory to which these remarks would not apply.

(4.1.4) How can this be reconciled with the observation that in fact prospects in expectations are multi-outcome prospects? Two explanations are possible. One is that although in many cases prospects in expectations are not sure prospects, the cases in which they are *approximately* of this form are so important that the theory which postulates that they are sure prospects is useful; it permits us to say how in the particular circumstances

113

we would behave. The other explanation is that expectations in economic theory are not expectations proper but only theoretical terms introduced into the theory to establish a link between the evidence and the individual's behaviour. We will consider these two explanations in more detail in the next section.

(4.2) Two Alternative Interpretations

(4.2.1) Let us consider first the first explanation. A theory is refuted if observations of actual events contradict any of its hypotheses. In principle one observation contrary to any of the hypotheses is sufficient to refute the whole theory. In the practice of science the rules are much less strict. There is always the possibility of an error of observation. Instead of the theory being refuted, the observation may, therefore, be rejected as faulty. Furthermore, a theory which is refuted in principle may still be retained as useful, if nothing better can be put in its place. The theory of gravitation, for instance, although refuted by some observations of the whole universe, is useful as an explanation of what takes place in the neighbourhood of large agglomerations of matter in any small part of it.

The same may apply to the hypothesis that expectations are sure prospects. If the individual were offered a lottery ticket at sufficiently attractive terms, he would be prepared to bet against any of the possible outcomes. If asked what mark he would give to his subjective belief in the coming off of those outcomes, he would admit that he would attach some degree of belief to more than one of them. None the less, his actual behaviour may turn out to be not much different from that which the respective theory predicts. Although, therefore, the theory is in principle refuted (that is to say, although the businessman's possible betting on other outcomes and his own appraisal of the weights attached to them contradict the hypothesis that his expectations are sure prospects), it may none the less be useful because it permits us to predict the individual's behaviour. The theory of supply and demand, for instance, permits us to predict the fact that an increase in demand leads to an increase in the quantity supplied.

(4.2.2) The second interpretation is that sure prospects are not what we determine by introspection or by gambling operation,

114

but that they are theoretical terms only, a formal link between the individual's behaviour and the conditions in which it takes place. The theory may, for instance, contain the following statements : (i) expectations are sure prospects of the same events as those which can be observed at the time of the expectation; sure prospects of the same prices, for instance, of the same outputs or of whatever else is relevant ; and, (ii) the individuals behave *as if* they were adjusting their positions to these sure prospects.

The formal representation of the expectation is in this case the sure prospect of the same event as that which actually occurred at the time of the expectation. The expectation is defined in terms of the operation of ascertaining by observation what this event actually is. Statement (i) cannot then be refuted either by a gambling operation or by introspection. It is not a hypothesis but a definition. Statement (ii) can be refuted. If the behaviour of the individual turns out to be different from that which the respective theory predicts, (ii) is refuted. The refutation, however, is then not of the sure-prospect formalization of expectations, but of the whole theory.

If statement (i) cannot be refuted, then one may well ask why have it at all. The introduction of expectations as a theoretical term does not make the theory either particularly simple or elegant. Why, therefore, not to reformulate it so as to omit expectations altogether ? The hypothesis may be simply that the individuals adjust their positions not to their expectations of future events, but to the actual events, to those which occur at the time at which they make the adjustments. In this form, however, the hypothesis begs the question of what may be the motive of these adjustments. There is no purpose in adjusting ourselves to conditions which by the time at which the adjustment is completed belong already to the past. The hypothesis is thus not very plausible. But from the behaviouristic point of view, the question of the motive is irrelevant. What is important, is only whether the behaviour which the theory predicts is that which actually takes place.

(4.2.3) As far as the explanation of the actual behaviour is concerned, both theories come to one and the same thing. Both predict the same behaviour if the conditions in which it takes place are the same. How good these predictions are it is difficult to say. There seems to be a fairly general consensus of opinion

115

that the theory of supply and demand is quite satisfactory in this respect. In general, however, nothing definite can be said about how close is the correspondence between what economic theory predicts and what actually takes place. Not much formal research has been done in this field, and the subjective hunches and intuitive appraisals which we may have and profess, can hardly be taken as an evidence.

(4.2.4) The fact that the predictions derived from both forms of the theory are the same means that the form of the theory has no effect on its usefulness. The same results can be obtained by postulating that expectations are *approximately* sure prospects of the same events as have been actually observed as by disposing of expectations altogether and relating the behaviour directly to those events. If thus, the predictions which the theory enables us to make correspond to the facts in one case, the same must be true in the other.

There is a difference in the interpretation of the connection between the behaviour and the conditions which are supposed to determine it. If expectations are interposed between the behaviour and the conditions in which the behaviour takes place, the theory is teleological. The individual behaves in that way because he wants to achieve a certain objective; to earn, for instance, the greatest possible profits. If expectations are omitted, the theory is causal. The individual behaves in that way because the conditions in which his behaviour takes place call forth this particular reaction on his part.

Formally both interpretations are correct. It is, however, the teleological interpretation that we have usually in mind. The propositions that firms expand their outputs along their marginal cost curves or that they expand their capital equipment in proportion to how their outputs expand, command belief not because we see firms actually behaving in this way but because we think that in this way they achieve better the objective of earning the greatest possible profits. We ourselves would behave so if we were in their place. Although, therefore, the expectations which could be ascertained by gambling operation or by introspection are not of a sure-prospect form, the hypothesis that they are sure prospects does not make the theory less acceptable. On the contrary, it makes it even more so because it is both simple and gives the theory a teleological form. The fact that we can under-

116

stand the firms' behaviour (in the sense that we think that we ourselves would behave in that way) means more to us than a realistic interpretation of the prospect.

(4.2.5) The acceptability of a teleological theory is not independent of the degree to which the respective hypothesis corresponds to the facts as we can ascertain them. For the teleological interpretation of the theory to be accepted, expectations must at least approximate to sure prospects. In economics we do not know what these expectations are. We do not perform any gambling operations on businessmen, nor do we ask them to ascertain their expectations by introspection. The question, therefore, whether the actual expectations do or do not approximate to the form specified in the theory, cannot be answered in any other way than by an intuitive appraisal of one's own experience.

This is not a very reliable evidence. Some evidence, however, would have to be there if the approximations were to be accepted. For it is not generally true that people expect the present to continue whatever this present may be. In this general form, the hypothesis would cover not only the prospects that the price will be the same in the future as it is at present or that the outputs of competitors will be the same; it would cover also the prospects of prices or outputs changing in the future as they do at present. What obtains at present is not only a particular level of prices or outputs but also a particular rate of change in them. And it is impossible for both the level and the rate of change to remain the same.[1]

One might invoke here the principle of Gestalt psychology, and argue that our expectations approximate sure prospects of either the same level or of the same change in it according to how we perceive the present. If, for instance, the particular variable changes quickly, it is the change that makes a greater impact on our mind, and we may predict the change. If the variable changes slowly, we may perceive the level and predict no change. In this general form the hypothesis is by no means implausible. As a

[1] Sure-prospect expectations may also be derived by means of a formula from other characteristics of the present; from the deviations of the current prices from the sure prospects of prices, for instance, which were expected or from what is regarded as their normal level. As an example of what economic models can be built along these lines see M. Nerlove, Adaptive Expectations and Cobweb Phenomena, *Quarterly Journal of Economics,* **LXXIII,** May (1958).

part of a scientific theory it is, however, inadequate. For it does not say when we perceive the level and when the change. As has been explained in (3.1.4) Gestalt psychology may help us to understand why different prospects can be arrived at in virtue of the same evidence. But it does not tell us in virtue of what evidence what prospects are arrived at. If, therefore, a particular theory contains the hypothesis that expectations are sure prospects of the same prices as those which are ruling at the time of the expectation, there must be some ground for making the hypothesis refer to the absolute level of prices and not to the rate of change.

(4.3) The Formula of the Mean Value

(4.3.1) In the first two sections of this chapter, expectations were sure prospects derived directly from the evidence; the outcomes of the same prices, for instance, or of the same changes in prices as are observed at the time of the expectation. The theory was that businessmen adjusted their positions to these sure prospects so as to achieve some objective, the greatest possible profits for instance. In the present section we will consider the hypothesis that prospects are originally multi-outcome ones, but that they are then reduced to a sure-prospect form, the sure prospect being the mean value of the possible outcomes. The theory is that businessmen adjust their positions to these mean values *as if* these values were the only outcomes in the prospects at which they originally arrive.

It has been already pointed out in (3.7.5) that in many cases the mean value cannot be an outcome at all because the variable in terms of which it would have to be described is not continuous over the relevant range; or because the outcomes are not measurable. In an expectation of the number of leaves on a stem of a clover, the outcome cannot be 3½ but only either three or four ; and in the case of a General Election, the mean value of the possible results does not mean anything. The hypothesis discussed in this section can thus apply to a limited range of subjects only. The range, however, is so important that the hypothesis deserves careful consideration. [1]

[1] As an early example of the application of the mean-value hypothesis to a definite problem in economics see F. Y. Edgeworth, The Mathematical Theory of Banking, *Journal of the Royal Statistical Society*, LI (1888), pp. 113–27.

(4.3.2) The reason why the businessmen use in their calculations the mean values of possible outcomes as if they were sure prospects is often the tendency to what Knight called *consolidation*. A number of events at different points of time and place is treated as a repetitive event and strategy is adjusted not to expectations of individual instances but to those of the over-all result of the repetitive event. In insurance, for instance, and in gambling the prospect of a certain frequency distribution of results in a long repetitive event approximates a sure prospect. Insurance companies and professional gamblers adjust then their positions not to their expectations of individual results but to the sure prospects of the distribution of results in the repetitive event.

It has been, however, explained in (2.4.4) that if weights of outcomes are formalized as probability weights, the weights of the outcomes in the prospect of individual events tend to be equal to the frequency distribution of results in the repetitive event. The adjustment to a sure prospect of the latter implies, therefore, the adjustment to the mean value of the possible outcomes in the former. If, for instance, the repetitive event is a series of tosses with a 'true' coin, the sure prospect of the frequency distribution of heads and tails is one-half and one-half, and a professional gambler would be prepared to pay for either of these two results twice the stake (less some premium for his profits and costs). By consolidation, he would transform the single events of individual tosses into a repetitive event of a whole series of them, and would adjust his position to a sure prospect of the latter.

It may be argued that it is never certain whether a particular event is unique or an instance in a repetitive event. If, therefore, no other rules of behaviour are available, the adjustment to the mean values is always preferable to no adjustment at all. Consolidation is then potential only. But in this case too the adjustment is to a repetitive event. The adjustment to the mean value of possible outcomes in a single event is only implied in it.

(4.3.3) Formally there is no difference between the hypothesis that an individual adjusts his behaviour to the mean value of possible outcomes and that he adjusts it to a sure prospect of a frequency distribution in a repetitive event. Both represent the same relation between outcomes, probability weights and the individual's behaviour. But there is a difference in the ground on which they are supposed to be accepted. In the case of an individual adjusting his behaviour to the mean value of possible outcomes in individual events by implication, we accept the hypothesis because we believe that he adjusts his behaviour to a sure prospect of a frequency distribution in a repetitive event An adjustment to a sure prospect is always rational. For if we are sure that something is going to happen, we must also be sure that we will achieve our objective better if we adjust ourselves to what is going to happen. Thus if expectations of frequency distributions are sure prospects, our adjustment to them is also rational; and so is the adjustment to the mean values of possible outcomes in expectations of individual events which is implied in it. The ground for the acceptance of the implication is our belief that the individuals to whom our theory applies are rational.

If, however, the proposition that the individual adjusts his positions to the mean value of possible outcomes is a hypothesis in its own right, the ground for its acceptance must be different. For the adjustment of one's position to the outcome of the mean value is then no more rational than the adjustment to some other outcome. If the hypothesis is to be accepted, the whole theory of which it is a part must be accepted as a satisfactory explanation of our actual behaviour.

(4.3.4) The hypothesis of the mean value cannot be accepted as a description of what actually takes place. We very rarely go through the ritual of attaching numerical probability weights to all the outcomes which are considered, of calculating the mean values, and of adjusting ourselves to the latter as if they were sure prospects. There are cases in business in which this is done. But the purpose of the theory is then not so much to explain behaviour as to determine it.

(4.3.5) It may be argued that the reduction of a multi-outcome prospect to a sure-prospect mean-value form is made by intuition. The businessman weighs up the possible outcomes and arrives at a sure prospect which approximates the mean value to a significant extent, without being aware of what he is actually doing. Or, he may be dealing so often with repetitive events that he may be conditioned to behave according to the hypothesis of the mean value also in those cases in which the events are not repetitive.[1]

Two possibilities must then be considered. The weight in the original prospect may be a subjective or an objective probability weight. If the first is the case, the hypothesis cannot be tested directly by observation. For to find whether the approximation is or is not significant, we would have to calculate the mean values ourselves and compare them with the sure prospects to which the businessman adjusts himself. We would have, therefore, to ascertain first the outcomes which the businessman considers, the weights which he attaches to them, and the sure prospect to which he adjusts his position. The outcomes would have to be made explicit and the weights ascertained by means of a gambling or of a marking operation. The test would not be, therefore, one of how the businessman actually weighs up the outcomes, and at what reduction of the multi-outcome prospect he actually arrives, but how he would reduce it if all the elements in his calculation were made explicit. If the hypothesis is that the businessman weighs up the outcomes by intuition without being aware of what he is actually doing, the very fact that the outcomes were made explicit and the weights ascertained would change the conditions so that the hypothesis would no longer apply.

The hypothesis may be tested directly if the weights of the outcomes in the original prospect are objective probability weights. The relevant operations are then those of Chapter 2. If, for instance, the physical properties of a coin are such that it can be accepted as 'true', or if it has been observed that in a large number of tosses with that coin heads have been coming out as many times as tails, the objective probability weights of one-half may be attached to the outcomes of heads and of tails in the prospect of the next toss. They can be derived from the observation of the physical properties of the coin or from the frequency distribution of results which have occurred in the past. The mean value of outcomes can then be calculated by an observer and the result compared with the sure prospect to which the businessman adjusts his position.

[1] This point was made by G. Gould in, Odds, Possibility and Plausibility in Shackle's Theory of Decision : A Discussion, *Economic Journal*, LXVII, December (1957), p. 663.

(4.3.6) The theories which contain the hypothesis of the mean value, explain usually general features of our behaviour which are independent of the actual numerical measures of the weights and of the mean value of the outcomes. The question of the calculation of the latter does not then arise. Nor does that of any direct test of how well the hypothesis approximates the facts. The hypothesis can then be subjected only to an indirect test, whether the whole theory to which it belongs is useful.

An example of such an indirect test is the so called St Petersburg game. The hypothesis of the mean value leads then to quite wrong predictions of our behaviour. In fact, the hypothesis is contradicted by the fact that people gamble at stakes and insure themselves at premiums which cover profits and costs of the other side. We will postpone, however, the discussion of the problem of gambling and insurance till the end of this part of the book. In the present chapter we will proceed on the assumption that the negative results of these tests do not prejudice the usefulness of the hypothesis as an explanation of other forms of behaviour.

(4.4) Arbitrary Procedures

(4.4.1) In the preceding sections of this chapter we were interested mainly in how sure-prospect equivalents could be arrived at. They were sure prospects of the same events as those which actually took place at the time of the expectation or mean values of possible outcomes. The businessman was supposed to adjust his position to them so as to achieve best his objectives. Little, however, has been said so far about what these adjustments may be.

In the present section we will consider some of the difficulties to which the hypothesis of the mean value may lead if the nature of these adjustments is taken into account. The objective which a businessman is usually supposed to achieve is that of the greatest possible profits. This will, therefore, be also the assumption of the argument given below. The theory will be that businessmen adjust their positions to the mean values of whatever may be the relevant outcomes so as to maximize their profits.

(4.4.2) The very fact that a businessman adjusts something so as to maximize his profits means that some factors on which the level of profits depends are under his control. What he adjusts may be the price, the quantities of outputs or the quantities of inputs, according to what are the conditions in which he acts. The factors which he adjusts describe then his strategies.

Other factors are those which describe the possible states of the world, independent of what the businessman decides to do. These too may be prices and the quantities of outputs and inputs. For instance, the businessman may have to sell his product at the price ruling on the market; he may have to use a capital equipment which will be available; or he may have to dispose of a certain quantity of his product, a crop, or a catch of fish. His expectations of the price, of the capital equipment, or of the quantity of the product are then data to which he is supposed to adjust himself.

Between these two extremes there are also expectations of events which depend partly on the state of the world and partly on the businessman's strategy. The quantity of the product which he expects to sell may, for instance, depend on the conditions of demand and on the price which he decides to fix for it. What he expects is then the outcome from his strategy of charging a particular price.

(4.4.3) Bearing all this in mind, consider a simple textbook case in which a businessman adjusts his output and price to the conditions of demand and of costs so as to maximize his profits. Suppose that the demand and cost conditions are formalized as demand and cost curves. What expectations may then be relevant to the businessman's behaviour ?

Two cases are usually considered. The businessman may either fix a price and let the output be determined by the conditions of demand; or he may fix the output and let the price be determined by demand. In the first case the price is the description of his strategy ; and the output is the subject of his expectation of an outcome from it. In the second case the output is the description of the strategy, and the price is the expected outcome. On the side of costs, the prices of inputs may be descriptions of either states of the world or of outcomes from the businessman's strategy, according to whether they are independent of or are affected by his own demand for those inputs. The costs are outcomes because they are determined by both the prices and by the quantities of inputs which the businessman may decide to use.

123

(4.4.4) Consider now a general hypothesis that the business-man expects the present to continue. In what form can it be a part of a theory explaining his behaviour? On the side of demand it cannot refer either to the price or to the volume of output because both depend on the businessman's strategy. If it is admitted that he can make adjustments in them, he cannot be supposed to expect that they will remain as they are. Nor can the costs be expected to remain unchanged if the output can change. The hypothesis must thus apply not to prices, outputs or costs, but to some more fundamental factors on which these prices, outputs, or costs depend.

What these factors may be is the subject of the theory of demand and of the theory of costs. They may be tastes, prices of other products, incomes, capital equipment of the firms using the product, prices of the factors of production, technical co-efficients, capital equipment of the firms supplying the product, etc. It is difficult to give a complete list of all of them. The most common procedure is to subsume them in the condition that all factors which determine the demand curve and the cost curve are supposed to remain constant. In terms of expectations, the condition is equivalent to a hypothesis that the conditional expectations of outputs at particular prices, of prices of partic-ular outputs, or of costs of particular outputs, are as indicated on the given and constant demand and cost curves. At the back of one's mind is then a hypothesis that the businessman might have found by experience what these curves are and that he expects the factors which determine them to remain unchanged.

(4.4.5) The procedure does not lead to any difficulties if the expectations are sure prospects. To each strategy of a price corresponds then one expected volume of output, and *vice versa* to each strategy of output corresponds one expected price. The functions summarizing these relations are single valued both ways. The same outputs correspond to the same prices when the prospects of outputs are derived from the strategies of prices and when the prospects of prices are derived from the strategies of outputs.

The situation is different if the hypothesis is that businessmen adjust their positions to the mean values of outcomes. The functions are then not single valued. Those which determine the mean values of outputs from the particular strategies of prices are different from those which determine the mean values of prices from the particular strategies of outputs.

(4.4.6) The following example may help to make the point clear. Take again the case in which the General Election is supposed to be held before the time at which the businessman intends to maximize his profits. Two possible states of the world appear then in the prospect of the result of the election: the Conservative Party may win the election, and the Labour Party may win. Suppose that to either of them corresponds a different schedule of demand. If the Conservative Party wins, the schedule will be :

$$Q_c = 100 - 10.P_c$$

If the Labour Party wins, it will be :

$$Q_l = \frac{120}{P_l}$$

Q and P are the quantity demanded and the price. The businessman's expectations are summarized in Table 4.4.6. The possible strategies of price are 2, 3, 4, and 5; and the conditional outcomes from them, corresponding to the two possible states

Table 4.4.6

Price strategy	Q_c	Q_l	Q	P_c	P_l	Price expected
(1)	(2)	(3)	(4)	(5)	(6)	(7)
2	80	60	70	3	1·7	2·4
3	70	40	55	4·5	2·2	3·3
4	60	30	45	5·5	2·7	4·1
5	50	24	37	6·3	3·2	4·8

of the world, are the outputs in columns (2) and (3). The businessman expects, for instance, that if the Conservative Party wins the election, he would be able to sell 80 units of his product at the price of 2, 70 units at the price of 3, and so on for all other prices and election results.

Suppose further that the two states of the world are equally probable to him. The probability weights attached to the outcomes of the Conservative Party and of the Labour Party winning the election is 0·5 in either case. The mean values of possible outputs to which the businessman is supposed to adjust his position are then as in column (4). Combined with the prices in the first column they give a demand schedule with respect to which the businessman is supposed to maximize his profits. Drawn on a graph, it looks like QQ in FIG. 4.4.6.

This is, however, not the only demand schedule which the data of the example permit us to derive. We may also start with the outputs in the fourth column and determine the prices at which they could be sold. The outputs are then strategies and the prices the possible outcomes. Using the same formulae we arrive then at conditional outcomes of prices as in columns (5) and (6). If, for instance, the output were fixed at 55, it could be sold at the price of 3 if the Conservative Party won the election, and at

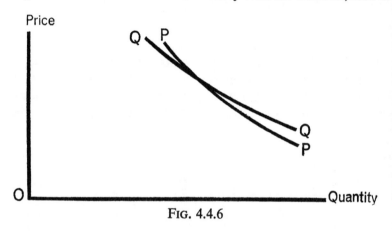

FIG. 4.4.6

1·7 if the Labour Party won. And so on for all other outputs in column (4). The mean values of the possible outcomes of prices are then as in the last column of the table, different from those in the first column. And the respective demand curve is as PP in FIG. 4.4.6, different from QQ.

(4.4.7) The same argument could be repeated with respect to costs. The proposition it helps to establish is that it is not enough to say that a businessman adjusts his position to the mean values of the possible outcomes of outputs or prices. In this general form the hypothesis is incomplete. For according to whether he asks himself what outputs he could sell at different prices, or at what prices he could sell different outputs, he arrives at different maximum profit positions. The determination of sure-prospect equivalents cannot be separated in this case from the hypothesis about the actual process of adjustment. For if the latter is that the businessman fixes his price and lets the output be determined by demand, QQ in FIG. 4.4.6 is relevant; and if the hypothesis is that he fixes his output and lets the price be determined by demand, PP is relevant.

(4.5) The Possibility of a Permanent Disequilibrium

(4.5.1) The points which have been made so far may be summarized as follows. The hypothesis that businessmen adjust their positions to sure prospects is subject to the criticism that if the prospects are arrived at by means of a formula, the formula is always arbitrary. If the sure prospect is of the same event as that which takes place at the time of the expectation, the arbitrariness consists in there being no ground for selecting one rather than another event as the one which is supposed to remain the same. The businessman may expect the level as well as the change in the price to be the same. If the sure prospects are mean values of possible outcomes, the arbitrariness is in the way in which the relation between strategies and possible outcomes is arrived at. According to whether the businessman adjusts his positions to the mean values of prices as possible outcomes from different strategies of outputs, or to the mean values of outputs as possible outcomes from different strategies of prices, he arrives at different maximum-profits positions.

(4.5.2) This criticism is valid if the purpose of the theory is to explain behaviour in any particular case. Why did a particular businessman decide to produce a particular output, or why did he fix a particular price for it? To answer such questions one needs a theory which permits to predict what output in the given conditions the businessman would produce and what prices he would fix. A theory which allows for an arbitrary selection of variables and procedures on which those outputs and prices depend does not satisfy these requirements. It cannot explain what the outputs and the prices actually are.

But the theory may also be interpreted in a more general sense. The questions for it to answer may be not about the actual prices or outputs which a particular businessman would choose, but

127

about some very general characteristics of his behaviour, inde
pendent of what in the particular circumstances this behaviou
might be. This is probably what many a theoretician has at th
back of his mind when he admits lack of realism in his theorie
but none the less insists on them being useful.

(4.5.3) The following point was made by Weintraub.[1] Suppos
that a businessman adjusts his position to a definite deman
curve for his product so as to maximize his profits. The curv
summarizes conditional prospects of outputs and prices. We ar
not interested in what the businessman's behaviour actually is
The exact form of the curve is, therefore, irrelevant; and so i
the fact that it may depend on an arbitrary selection of determining events and procedures. What is important is that a curve
of a sort exists in the businessman's mind and that he derives
from it his sure prospects of outputs at particular prices or of
prices of particular outputs. The curve need not describe the
actual conditions on the market at the time of the subject.
Maximization of profits with respect to it does not, therefore,
necessarily imply that profits are also maximized in an objective
sense, so that they could not be greater if in the conditions of the
market as they actually are some other output or some other
price were chosen. Is it possible that, if this is the case, the
businessman may not become aware of this?

The answer is that he may not become aware of this because
not all mistakes made in conditional prospects can be revealed
by subsequent results. The point is that the sure prospect of that
output only can be confronted with facts, which corresponds to
the actual price. Other points on the demand curve cannot be
revealed by subsequent results. The businessman, however,
maximizes his profits with respect to the whole curve. If, therefore, he has made a mistake in the outputs which he thought
that he could sell if he fixed a different price, but has not made
any mistake in the output which he thought that he would sell
at the actual price, he may not be maximizing profits with
respect to the market conditions as they actually are, and he may
not be aware of this.

---

[1] S. Weintraub, *Price Theory*, Pitman Publishing Corporation (New York,
1949), pp. 354–60. Sure prospect equivalents in Weintraub's analysis are not
determined by a formula. The point discussed here is, however, quite general and
may be included anywhere in this part of the book.

Suppose, for instance, that *EE* in FIG. 4.5.3 represents the demand curve from which the businessman derives his conditional sure prospects of outputs corresponding to different prices, and let his maximum profit position be at *M*. If then the actual relation between output and price happens to be as shown by *AA*, the businessman is not maximizing profits with respect to the latter if he does so with respect to the former. And he is not aware of this because the sure prospect of the actual output is confirmed by the result.

(4.5.4) The conclusion is that if businessmen adjust their positions to sure prospects, the positions to which these adjustments lead may not be those which they would choose if they

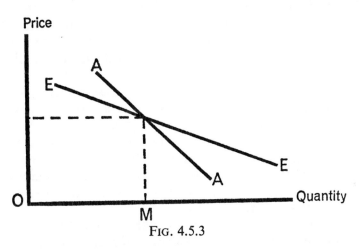

FIG. 4.5.3

knew the future. The actual positions may be quite accidental, determined by businessmen's mistakes which have not been revealed. This must not be regarded as a very serious criticism of the conventional theory. For the argument in the latter is usually that before equilibrium is established businessmen try other strategies as well. They have, therefore, a pretty good idea of what the respective relations actually are. If any mistakes persist, they are not likely to affect much the result.

On common-sense grounds it is difficult to find fault with this defence of the conventional theory. We all learn by experience, and our appraisal of the possible consequences of what we do is usually not so far off the mark as to make our behaviour erratic. But commonsense is not a theory. What we need in this case is a

129

theory of business behaviour in which the tendency towards equilibrium would follow as a necessary result. A general hypothesis that businessmen adjust their positions to sure prospects of costs or demand does not satisfy this condition. It allows for a permanent disequilibrium in relation to the actual conditions of the market. The theory of which it is a part may thus be interpreted so as to explain not only equilibrium but also disequilibrium behaviour. And as in fact we do not know whether the former or the latter is actually the case, we do not know for sure what the theory actually explains.

(4.5.5) It follows that no general propositions can be derived from Weintraub's point. The importance of the argument lies rather in its bringing to light the inadequacy of a teleological theory in which businessmen adjust their positions to what they expect. The conclusion that outputs and prices approximate their equilibrium values as determined by the actual conditions of the market is not necessarily valid.

This negative conclusion is general in the sense that it applies to any formalization of expectations. Irrespective of what arbitrary procedures we might use to define the prospects, the conclusion would always follow. This may be a sufficient ground for regarding ourselves relieved from the task of defining them at all. For if it is shown that all hypotheses of a certain kind lead to a negative result, it would be a waste of time to attempt to formulate any particular one.

(4.5.6) A different kind of disequilibrium may arise as a result of lack of symmetry between positive and negative deviations of the actual quantity demanded from the mean value of its possible outcomes. It has been pointed out by Mills[1] that if the product produced cannot be stored, and output and price are fixed in advance so as to maximize the mean value of possible outcomes of profits, demand greater than output cannot be satisfied at the chosen price, and total revenue is determined not by demand but by the chosen output. It follows that the mean value of the expected total revenue is then smaller than the mean value of the quantity demanded multiplied by the chosen price. Even, therefore, if the firm acts in accordance with the mean value hypothesis, the output and the price which it chooses is different

[1] E. S. Mills, Uncertainty and Price Theory, *Quarterly Journal of Economics*, **LXXIII,** February (1959), pp. 116–30.

from those which it would choose if the sure prospect of the quantity sold were the mean value of the quantity demanded.

(4.6) Flexibility of Plant

(4.6.1) The hypothesis of the present section is that the sure prospects to which the individuals adjust their positions are the mean values of the outcomes which appear in the original prospects. The argument, however, is general in the sense that the conclusions to which it leads do not depend on what these original prospects actually are. As in the case of Weintraub's point the theory is about some general feature of business behaviour. Again, therefore, we need not specify the operation in terms of which the original prospect is to be ascertained. The only conditions which it must satisfy is that the weights of outcomes in it are probability weights.

(4.6.2) The general feature of the business behaviour which the hypothesis helps to explain is that businessmen often choose techniques which do not minimize costs of any particular output. The textbook theory of the firm says that the cost curve of a firm shows the lowest possible costs at which the particular outputs could be produced. These lowest possible costs may be higher in the short run than in the long run, but they are always the lowest possible in the conditions to which the curve applies. The argument is that if the same output could be produced at still lower costs, by means of a different combination of factors, the firm would use this different combination and the costs would in fact be lower.

We will argue in this section that this need not be true if the firm adjusts its position so as to maximize not its profits from a sure prospect of a definite output, but the mean value of profits from a number of possible outcomes of outputs. For what is minimized then is not the cost of any particular output but the mean value of costs from those possible outcomes of output. The expectations to which the firm adjusts itself are those of profits, and it is to these that the hypothesis of a sure-prospect equivalent applies. What the conclusion amounts to is thus, that adjustment to a sure-prospect equivalent of profits may not be consistent in this case with the firm adjusting itself to a sure-prospect equivalent of output.

131

The argument was formulated for the first time by Hart.[1] A very elaborate model was used by him to explain all its steps. No attempt is made here to reproduce the model in all its details. We will concentrate on those of its aspects only which are relevant to the point with which this section is directly concerned.

(4.6.3) Consider again two possible states of the world, following two different results of the General Election. To either of them corresponds a different demand schedule for the firm's product. The schedules have no empirical content. They exist solely in the businessman's mind as generalizations from which he derives conditional prospects of outputs and prices. The result of the General Election is the only factor on which the form of the demand schedule is supposed to depend. Thus to each result corresponds only one schedule.

To simplify the argument suppose also that the result of the General Election has no effect on costs. The expectations of costs are sure prospects of conditional outcomes from combinations of two types of strategies: (i) outputs and (ii) methods of production. Outputs can be decided upon after the General Election. But the method of production must be chosen right now because the installation of the necessary capital equipment needs time. Let there be three methods to choose from. According to the hypothesis of the mean value of possible outcomes, the businessman will choose that method to which corresponds the greatest mean value of profits.

Suppose that the probability weights of the outcomes of the Conservative Party and of the Labour Party winning the election are 0·5 in either case. The mean value of profits from a particular method of production is thus the arithmetical mean of the profits which the businessman could earn in either of the two states of the world.

(4.6.4) Let the two demand schedules be as in Table 4.6.4a. The businessman believes that he could sell the outputs shown in the first column at the prices in the second column if the Conservative Party wins the election and at the prices in the third

[1] A. G. Hart, Anticipations, Uncertainty and Dynamic Planning, *op. cit.* and, Risk, Uncertainty and the Unprofitability of Compounding Probabilities, in O. Lange, F. McIntyre and T. O. Yntema (eds.), *Studies in Mathematical Economics and Econometrics*, In Memory of Henry Schultz, University of Chicago (1942), pp. 110–18.

column if the Labour Party wins. The total revenue schedules are then as in the last two columns. The curves which fit these

Table 4.6.4a

Output	Price		Total Revenue	
	C	L	C	L
1	75	56	75	56
2	64	55	128	110
3	52	53	156	159
4	39	45	156	180
5	25	30	125	150

schedules are shown in FIG. 4.6.4, *CC* being the total revenue curve in the Conservative state of the world and *LL* in that of Labour.

The cost schedules corresponding to the three methods of production are as in Table 4.6.4b. Method I requires very little of capital equipment. Marginal costs are constant and high, and fixed costs are negligible. The opposite is true of Method II. Fixed costs are very high, and the marginal costs negligible.

Table 4.6.4b

Output	Total costs corresponding to Method		
	I	II	III
1	55	147	60
2	105	149	111
3	155	152	158
4	205	156	163
5	255	161	170

Method I is thus more suitable for small outputs and Method II for large outputs. Method III is more flexible. It permits to produce small outputs at lower costs than those of Method II, and large outputs at lower costs than those of Method I. But the costs of small outputs would be still lower if Method I were chosen, and the costs of large outputs would be lower if Method II were chosen. Method III is flexible, but inefficient. It leads to higher costs of any output than either Method I or Method II does.

The total cost curves which fit these data are shown in FIG. 4.6.4. The curve corresponding to Method I is a straight line starting very close to the origin of the diagram; the fixed costs are low. The curve corresponding to Method II starts much higher up, it is less steep, and it is not quite straight; the fixed costs are high, and the marginal costs are low and increasing. And the curve corresponding to Method III shows marginal costs falling.

(4.6.5) There are six combinations of the production methods and of the possible states of the world. Thus the prospect of

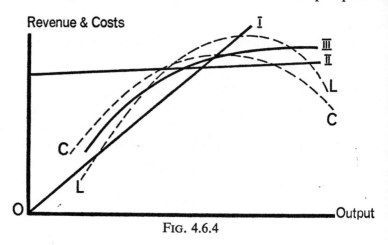

FIG. 4.6.4

profits consists of six conditional outcomes, each of them corresponding to a different state of the world and to a different method of production. These six outcomes are shown in Table 4.6.5. The highest possible profits which the firm could earn in each of the six combinations of the states of the world and of the production methods are printed in heavy type. If the businessman knew for certain that the Conservative Party would win the election, he would choose the first method of production. For he would then fix his output at 2 units and earn profits of 23. If he chose Method II or Method III, he could not earn more than 4 or 17 respectively. If he knew that the Labour Party would win the election, he would choose Method II and profits of 24. Method III would not be chosen in either case.

134

If the businessman does not know the results of the election, he is supposed to choose his method of production so as to maximize the mean value of the possible outcomes of profits. If he chooses Method I, he may earn 23 if the Conservative Party wins the election; but he must also be prepared for the possibility of earning not more than 5 if the Labour Party wins. And as the probability of either of these two alternative states of the world is 0·5, the mean value of maximum profits is 14. Similarly, if he chooses Method II, he may earn either 24 if the Labour Party wins or only 4 if the Conservative Party wins, and the mean value of maximum profits is 14 as well. If, however, he chooses Method III, he deprives himself of the chance of earning profits as high as 23 or 24; but at the same time he makes himself secure against the possibility of earning as little as 4 or 5.

Table 4.6.5

Outputs	Profits corresponding to the combination					
	I C	I L	II C	II L	III C	III L
1	20	1	−72	−91	15	−4
2	23	5	−21	−39	17	−1
3	1	4	4	−7	−2	1
4	−49	−25	0	24	−7	17
5	−130	−105	−36	−11	−45	−20

He can then earn 17 irrespective of which party wins the election. The mean value of maximum profits is thus also 17, greater than that from either of the other two methods.

(4.6.6) As in the case discussed in the previous section the conclusion is negative. If the businessman adjusts his method of production to the mean value of possible outcomes of profits, he may not choose the method which minimizes the costs of the output he ultimately decides to produce. This is not due to any mistake in his estimate of demand. It is rather because in the conditions in which he has to reach the decision no reliable estimate can be made. And the conclusion is valid whatever are the actual values of the outcomes of profits and of the probability weights attached to them in the original prospect. Again, therefore, we may feel relieved of the task of specifying the operation by means of which these weights would have to be ascertained.

Is, however, the hypothesis of the mean value really necessary to obtain this result? The argument could be put in a still more general form. Whenever a businessman takes into account the possibility of several outcomes, flexible methods may be preferred to inflexible ones, even if they lead to higher costs of any particular output. How the possible outcomes are taken into account is not particularly important. They may be weighted by their probability weights as in the hypothesis of the mean value of profits, averaged with equal weights, extreme prospects only may be averaged, or they may be combined in some other way and the same result might follow. Hart did not give any other justification for the formula of the mean value than that it is a special case of the reduction of a multi-outcome prospect to a sure-prospect form. The argument is a demonstration of the fact that if the future is uncertain an inefficient but flexible method of production may be preferred to an ultimately less expensive but also less flexible one.

Interpreted in this way it is, however, not a theory. It does not enable us to say that the businessmen choose inefficient methods. It is possible to construct an example in which an efficient method is chosen. As in the case of permanent disequilibrium the purpose of the argument is only to show that the textbook theory may go wrong if several outcomes appear in the prospect of profits. But it does not give us any indication of how it could be improved.

(4.7) The Value of Information

(4.7.1) The model described in the previous section may also be used to explain why in some cases firms are prepared to pay for information about what the future is likely to be. The respective theory has been developed as a part of decision theory.[1] It may, however, be also turned into a descriptive theory explaining the fact that information about the future is worth being paid for.

[1] For a more rigorous treatment and references, see F. Modigliani and K. J. Cohen, *The Role of Anticipations and Plants in Economic Behaviour and their Use in Economic Analysis and Forecasting, op. cit.,* pp. 69–78.

In the literature the value of information is usually expressed
n utility pay-offs. Formally the respective theory belongs, there-
ore, to Chapter 6. The condition, however, that the pay-offs
re in utility is by no means essential. The argument holds also
or monetary pay-offs. To make the exposition easier we will
eglect, therefore, the distinction between utility and monetary
ay-offs and consider the theory as an application of the
ypothesis of the mean value of the latter.

(4.7.2) Suppose that in the example used in the previous section
he General Election takes place too late for any adjustments in
utputs to be made in the light of the results. The position of the
emand curve and the level of profits depend on these results;
the data given in Tables 4.6.4 (a and b) and 4.6.5 are valid. The
difference is only that now both the method of production and
the volume of output must be decided upon before the election
akes place.

Suppose, however, that it is possible to obtain some information about what these results will be by means of a public
opinion poll. This costs money. But if the firm decides to pay
the price, it may know the results of the election before the
election actually takes place, and it may adjust its output accordingly. We will neglect the possibility of the information it obtains
being unreliable or incorrect.

The problem which the firm has then to solve is whether to
pay the price and adjust the method of production and the output to the conditions of demand as they actually will be, or not
to pay the price and act on the ground of the data which are
given in Table 4.6.4 (a and b) and 4.6.5. The answer must, of
course, depend on the price the firm would have to pay. Let us,
however, concentrate first on the demand side of the problem.
What is the highest price that the firm would be prepared to pay?

(4.7.3) Suppose first that the firm does not pay any price and
acts on the ground of the data in the tables. According to the
hypothesis of the mean value it adjusts the method of production
and the volume of output so as to maximize the mean value of
possible profits. As the probability weights of the outcomes of
either of the two parties winning the election are $\frac{1}{2}$ and $\frac{1}{2}$, the
mean value of profits corresponding to the first method of
production and to output of 1, for instance, is $10\frac{1}{2}$; that corresponding to the second method and to output of 4 is 12; and

137

Table 4.7.3

Output	Method I	Method II	Method III
1	$10\frac{1}{2}$	$-81\frac{1}{2}$	$5\frac{1}{2}$
2	14	-30	8
3	$2\frac{1}{2}$	-3	$\frac{1}{2}$
4	-37	12	5
5	$-117\frac{1}{2}$	$-22\frac{1}{2}$	$-32\frac{1}{2}$

so on for all other strategies. The respective figures are shown in Table 4.7.3. The highest is 14, that which corresponds to the first method and 2 units of output. This is, therefore, the strategy which the firm will choose.

The method of production is different from that which the firm was supposed to choose in the previous section. The reason is that the output must now be decided upon before the result of the election becomes known. To maximize the mean value of profits the firm must adopt that method which minimizes the costs of that particular output. The possibility of choosing an inefficient but more flexible method does not arise.

(4.7.4) Suppose now that the firm decides to pay the price of the public opinion poll and obtains an advance information about what the result of the election will be. The profits which it can then earn are shown in Table 4.6.5. If the Conservative Party is going to win the election, the best strategy is to choose the first method of production and 2 units of output. Profits would then be 23. If the Labour Party is going to win, the best choice is the second method and the output of 4 units. This would give 24 units of profits.

But when the firm decides to pay the price of the public opinion poll, it does not know yet which of these two situations will actually arise. All that it knows is that both of them are equally probable. For it attaches equal probability weights to the outcomes of either of them coming off. Either of these two figures is thus an outcome in the expectation of profits which it holds at that time.

The mean value of profits is then $23\frac{1}{2}$, more than the firm could obtain if it did not know the result of the election. For in this latter case the respective mean value would be 14. The difference

138

between these two figures is the maximum price that the firm would be prepared to pay for the information about what the result of the election will be. If the actual price of the public opinion poll happens to be greater than $9\frac{1}{2}$, the businessman would give up the idea and choose the first method of production and the output of 2. If the actual price happens to be less than $9\frac{1}{2}$, he would pay it and adjust the method and the output to the information he then obtains.

(4.7.5) The following special case[1] yields a very neat result. Suppose that profits of the firm depend on the strategy of its

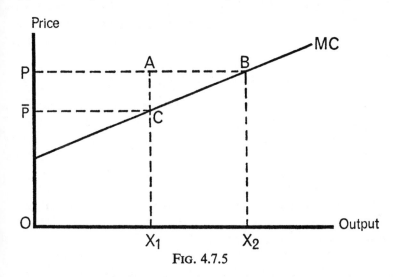

FIG. 4.7.5

output and on the price of its product. The firm determines the former but has no influence on the latter. Suppose also that the marginal cost curve is linear as in FIG. 4.7.5. If then the firm had no information at all of what the price was going to be, it would fix its output so as to make marginal costs equal to the mean value of the possible outcomes of the price (at X_1 in FIG. 4.7.5). For the mean value of profits would then be at a maximum. If, however, the firm knew that the price would be P, for instance, it would fix its output at X_2. It would then earn extra profits represented by the triangle ABC, equal to $(P - \bar{P})^2/2S$, if S is the slope of the marginal cost curve.

[1] Taken from R. R. Nelson, Uncertainty, Prediction and Competitive Equilibrium, *Quarterly Journal of Economics*, **LXXV**, February (1961), pp. 42–5.

139

As in the case discussed in (4.7.4) the firm does not know whether the information about the future price of its product, will be that of P or of some other outcome. The extra profits which the firm expects to earn as a result of buying the information are thus not $(P - \bar{P})^2/2S$ but a prospect of possible outcomes of those profits for all possible P's, each outcome qualified by a probability weight. The maximum price which the firm would be prepared to pay for the information is thus the mean value of those possible outcomes of extra profits $E(P - \bar{P})^2/2S$. If, for instance, P depended solely on the result of the General Election, and the probability weights attached to the outcomes of the Conservative and of the Labour Party winning the election were $\frac{1}{2}$ and $\frac{1}{2}$, the value of the information about the election results would be

$$(1/25) \left[\tfrac{1}{2}(P_1 - \bar{P})^2 + \tfrac{1}{2}(P_c - \bar{P})^2\right]$$

The expression $E(P - \bar{P})^2$ is simply the variance of outcomes in the prospect of the price. In this particular case the value of the information is thus proportional to that variance. It is independent of the mean. For it is only if the price may deviate from the mean, that the information about what it actually is going to be becomes valuable. The value of information is also greater the less steep is the marginal cost curve. For the possibility of increasing profits by adjusting output to what the price may happen to be is then also greater.[1]

(4.7.6) These very simple examples do not do justice to the scope and the elegance of the analysis which has been done in this field. They give us, however, an idea of what is the sense of it. People are prepared to pay a price for information about what the future is likely to be, because they are then able to choose a more suitable strategy. The hypothesis of the mean value permits us to calculate the value of this information to them. In principle it enables us, therefore, to predict whether they will or will not pay a particular price.

[1] For the development of the ideas expressed in this paragraph see the already quoted article by R. R. Nelson in the *Quarterly Journal of Economics*.

5

Reduction by Choice

THE hypotheses considered in the previous chapter had one feature in common. In all of them, the individual was supposed to adjust his position to something that he knew for certain. In the case of a sure prospect by definition the parameter to which he was adjusting himself was a definite outcome, one outcome only, with a full weight attached to it. In the hypothesis of the mean value the parameter was that mean value. In either case, the fact that the future was not known did not play any part in the adjustments. The individual might not know what would be the actual outcome from his strategy, and he might consider several outcomes in his original prospect; but he was supposed to adjust his position to a prospect arrived at by means of a formula as if it were a sure prospect.

The hypothesis to be considered in the present chapter is of a different kind. No prospects are supposed to be sure prospects. By means of whatever formula the outcomes may be aggregated, the result need not be a sure prospect. Multi-outcome prospects can be reduced to their sure-prospect equivalents by choice only. Nobody but the individual himself can tell us (or reveal by his behaviour) what they are.

(5.1) Lucrativity and Risk

(5.1.1) In his analysis of the valuation of assets Marschak[1] introduced the terms 'lucrativity' and 'risk' to describe two basic properties of assets on which their value depends. Lucrativity is the property of a gain being expected from the asset. Risk is the property of its being not known what this gain will be. The

[1] J. Marschak, Money and the Theory of Assets, *Econometrica*, **6**, October (1938), pp. 311–25. See also H. Makower and J. Marschak, Assets, Prices and Monetary Theory, *Economica*, **5**, August (1938), pp. 261–88.

problem of the valuation of assets is then (i) to find measures of these properties, one for risk and one for lucrativity, and (ii) to reduce these measures to a common denominator.

Similar considerations apply to strategies and expectations. The attractiveness of a strategy depends on the level of pay-offs that can be expected from it and on how far it is possible to say which pay-offs will come off. In a sense it depends thus on the lucrativity and the risk of the strategy. Lucrativity describes the level of pay-offs from it, and risk describes the fact that one rather than some other pay-off may come off. If the two could be reduced to a common denominator, the level of pay-offs could be adjusted for the amount of risk, and the result could be treated as an index of the attractiveness of the strategy. Buying an asset is in fact only a special case of a strategy.

(5.1.2) The common-sense idea behind this argument is that lucrativity is that characteristic of the prospect which makes the individual look forward to the outcome. It is an inducement for him to adopt the strategy which gives rise to it. Risk, on the other hand, is a negative characteristic of the prospect. It discourages the individual from adopting the respective strategy.

A formal representation of lucrativity and risk must take these facts into account. The formula by means of which it is derived from the original prospect must be such that the theory does not lead to predictions which are obviously wrong. A formal representation of lucrativity may, for instance, be a measure expressed in the same units as the pay-offs in the original prospect, not greater than the pay-off from the most attractive outcome and not less than that from the least attractive one. If the pay-off is the price which a businessman expects to receive for his product, the formal representation of lucrativity may be a sum of money which is not greater than the highest price and not smaller than the lowest price in the original prospect. If the pay-offs from all outcomes are the same, lucrativity is equal to them. And if the prospect is a sure prospect, lucrativity is the pay-off from that sure prospect. A formal representation of risk may be a number which increases from zero when the pay-offs from all outcomes are equal, to a greater and greater number as the differences between them increase. Risk of a sure prospect is then zero, and it becomes infinitely large if there is no limit to positive and negative pay-offs.

142

(5.1.3) This is, however, only a first approximation, arrived at by eliminating the alternatives which most obviously would lead to wrong predictions. For if the measure of the level of pay-offs were greater than the pay-off from the most attractive outcome, it could be positive when all the pay-offs in the original prospect are negative. The individual might then be looking forward to the outcome from a strategy which gives rise only to negative pay-offs. If risk were greater than zero in a sure prospect, the individual might be discouraged by a sure prospect of a positive pay-off.

The limits imposed by such considerations are very wide. Lucrativity might, for instance, be formalized as the mean value of pay-offs from all outcomes in the prospect, as the mode of those pay-offs, as the greatest or the least pay-off, the average of the two, and so on. The measure of risk might be the variance, the standard deviation of pay-offs, the difference between their extreme values (in absolute terms or in relation to the mean), and so on. All these formulae satisfy the requirement that if lucrativity is a positive characteristic, and risk a negative characteristic of the prospect, the predictions to which the theory leads are not obviously wrong.

But each of these formulae may lead to a different prediction of the individual's behaviour. Suppose, for instance, that in two prospects the pay-offs from the extreme outcomes are the same and those between the extremes are different. If lucrativity is then formalized as the average of the extreme values of pay-offs and risk as the difference between them, the respective measures are the same in both cases, and the strategies which give rise to them are equally attractive. If, however, lucrativity is formalized as the mean value of pay-offs, its measures in these two prospects are different, and one strategy is more attractive than the other.

(5.1.4) The ultimate choice of the formula must depend on which explains better the actual behaviour. The more, however, the range of the alternatives is reduced by the elimination of those which on closer inspection turn out to be wrong, the less apparent become the relative merits of those which remain. The worst alternatives can be eliminated on common-sense grounds. The best would require a very subtle test.

No tests of this kind have ever been made. We must, therefore,

143

be satisfied with a rather vague formalization of lucrativity and of risk. The formulae in terms of which they are defined are only representative members of a class which satisfies certain minimum requirements. No significance must be attached to their precise form.

(5.2) Indifference as the Criterion of Equivalence

(5.2.1) The essential difference between the hypotheses discussed in the present and in the previous chapter, is that in the previous chapter the sure-prospect equivalent was derived by means of a formula from the original prospect, whereas in the present chapter the measures of lucrativity and of risk only can be so derived from it. A second operation is needed to reduce these measures to a sure-prospect equivalent. In whatever way we might average, aggregate, or simplify the outcomes in the original prospect, the uncertainty inherent in the multiplicity of outcomes would always remain. To get rid of it we have to establish an equivalence between the reduced and the original prospect on the ground of data which do not appear in either of them.

(5.2.2) The crucial question is in what sense the two are to be equivalent one to the other. The criterion is usually described as that of indifference. A sure-prospect equivalent is simply that sure prospect which is as attractive to the individual as the original one. The individual is indifferent whether he is confronted with one or with the other. A strategy which gives rise to one of them is as good to him as that which gives rise to the other.

If the original prospect is reduced, by means of a formula, to a pair of measures of lucrativity and of risk, the indifference curve technique may be used to represent diagrammatically the reduction of the respective measures to a sure-prospect equivalent. As lucrativity is a positive element and risk a negative element in the prospect, several combinations of them may be equally attractive to the individual. They may be plotted on a diagram, with lucrativity measured along the horizontal axis and risk along the vertical axis. The result is an indifference curve as in FIG. 5.2.2. Each point on it represents all those prospects in which lucrativity and risk are as indicated along

he two axes. A different point represents a prospect with
different lucrativity and different risk, but the latter are so
balanced one with the other that the individual finds the strategy
which gives rise to it equally attractive.

An indifference curve of this kind is sloping upwards because
f lucrativity of one prospect is higher than that of another, its
risk must be greater if the strategy which gives rise to the
former is to be equally attractive as that which gives rise to the

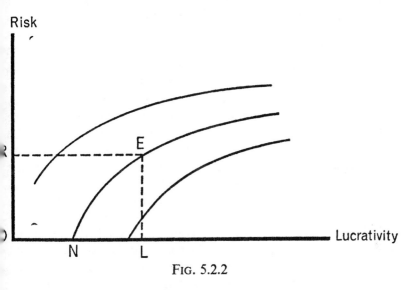

FIG. 5.2.2

latter. As points corresponding to the same risk, but to a greater
lucrativity, are on higher indifference curves, and points corresponding to the same lucrativity and a greater risk are on lower
curves, the curves are arranged in an ascending order as we
move from left to right. Whether they are bending upwards or
rightwards depends on the 'tastes' of the individual, and on the
formulae which have been used to derive the measures of
lucrativity and of risk from the original prospect. [1]

(5.2.3) The reduction of a pair of measures of lucrativity and
of risk to a sure-prospect equivalent corresponds then to a movement along the respective indifference curve down to the point
at which it intercepts the horizontal axis. In FIG. 5.2.2 *OL* is

[1] Compare J. Marschak, Rational Behaviour, Uncertain Prospects, and
Measurable Utility, *op. cit.*, pp. 118–20.

145

lucrativity of the original prospect, OR is risk, and ON is the sure-prospect equivalent. The difference between the level of lucrativity and the sure-prospect equivalent is the premium for risk.

The exact position of the point E depends on the content of the individual's original prospect and on the formulae by means of which the measures of lucrativity and of risk are derived from it. The form of the indifference curve depends on the latter and on the individual's 'tastes'. The value of the sure-prospect equivalent is independent of the formulae by means of which the measures of lucrativity and of risk are derived. It depends solely on the individual's 'tastes' and on the content of the original prospect. The premium for risk depends on both the 'tastes' and the measures of lucrativity and of risk.

The measures of lucrativity and of risk are theoretical terms. The relation of the individual's indifference cannot, therefore, be between any combinations of them. It must be between the views of the future described by the prospects from which they are derived. And these are independent of any of the formulae used. Only if lucrativity and risk were observable data which determine the individual's assessment of the views of the future described by the respective prospects, only then the relation of indifference could be between some combinations of them. Then, however, the question of the choice of the formulae would not arise. Lucrativity and risk would not be measures arrived at by means of a formulae, but facts ascertainable by inspection.

(5.2.4) The technique of indifference curves permits us to represent on a diagram the reduction of a multi-outcome prospect to a sure-prospect equivalent. The reduction, however, which we represent cannot be a basis for a theory of the individual's behaviour. The reason is that the meaning which we give in this case to the notion of indifference makes the theory circular. For the word indifference has been used here to describe equality of attractiveness of strategies which give rise to the respective prospects. In more precise terms, the sure-prospect equivalent is a sure prospect which satisfies the condition that if the individual were adjusting his position to it, his behaviour would be the same as that which results from the adjustment to the original prospect. This, however, means that to be able to reduce a multi-outcome prospect to a sure-prospect equivalent we must know the individual's behaviour. Such reduction cannot, therefore, be a part of a theory which is meant to predict that behaviour. For to predict the behaviour we would have to reduce the original prospect to a sure-prospect equivalent; and to do the reduction we would have to know the behaviour.

The analogy with the theory of consumer behaviour should not blind us to the fact that the problems considered are fundamentally different. In the theory of consumer behaviour, we do not endeavour to explain what quantities of goods a consumer will buy in the given conditions of prices and income. These quantities are determined by the consumer's tastes. In the case of an individual adjusting his position to a multi-outcome prospect the choice of a strategy is just what the theory is meant to explain.

(5.2.5) There is also the following point. The pay-offs which are relevant to businessmen's behaviour are their profits, sales or whatever else the context of the theory prescribes. The expectations of these pay-offs are usually secondary expectations arrived at through the expectations of prices. The reduction of prospects in them must, however, proceed in the opposite direction. The prospect of pay-offs must be reduced first and the prospect of prices next. The latter reduction is determined by the choice made in the former. The sure-prospect equivalents of prices cannot, therefore, be regarded as data for the choice of the strategy. For they are determined by that choice. [1]

(5.3) Elasticity of Expectations and Stability

(5.3.1) Reduction of a multi-outcome prospect to a sure-prospect equivalent may also be a part of a more general theory. The argument is then as follows. It is true that we cannot determine the equivalent if we do not know the behaviour. The former cannot, therefore, be a term in a theory which is meant to explain the latter. But if the hypothesis is understood in a general sense, as that the reduction of a multi-outcome prospect to a sure-prospect equivalent requires an adjustment of the level of lucrativity by a premium for risk which depends on the individual's tastes, it may be used in a theory explaining not the

[1] Some formal elaborations of this point are given in P. B. Simpson, Risk Allowances for Price Expectations, *Econometrica*, **18**, 3, July (1950), pp. 253–9.

actual behaviour in any particular case but some general aspects of it, independent of what the premium for risk actually is.

Two examples of a theory of this kind have been discussed in Chapter 4. In one of them it was shown that if a businessman adjusts his position not to the actual conditions on the market but to sure prospects of these conditions, he may remain in permanent disequilibrium with them (in the sense that if these conditions were fully revealed to him he would choose a different position). In the other example, the conclusion was that if a businessman adjusts his position to the mean value of profits, he may choose an inefficient method of production. In either case the results were negative. Something that might have been thought to be known turned out to be not known. Prices and outputs of firms might have been thought to be known as those which are determined by the objectives of the firms and the actual conditions of the market. If expectations are taken into account, this may no longer be true. It may not be possible to predict those prices and outputs on the ground of the market conditions only. Methods of production used by firms might have been thought to be known as those which minimize costs of the actual outputs. If, however, the firms' adjustments are to the mean values of the possible outcomes of profits, the methods may be different. They may be inefficient with respect to all possible outputs.

The remaining sections of this chapter follow a similar line. The theories discussed in them are of this general, qualitative kind. The difference is only that the sure prospect equivalent to which the individuals are supposed to adjust themselves are determined not by a formula but by the individuals' 'tastes'.

(5.3.2) The present section deals with Hicks'[1] and Lange's[2] analysis of stability of equilibrium. No attempt is made in it to reproduce the analysis in detail, or to compare the two versions one with the other. The stress is again on the general significance of the argument and on the part which expectations play in it.

Whether equilibrium is or is not stable depends on how expectations change as a result of a possible displacement of it. An important question is thus how to formulate the relation between

[1] J. R. Hicks, *Value and Capital* (2nd ed.), Clarendon Press (Oxford, 1946).
[2] O. Lange, *Price Flexibility and Unemployment*, Cowles, Commission for Research in Economics, Monograph, No 8, Principia Press (1944).

the change of expectations and the displacement of equilibrium so as to make it identifiable and amenable to formal manipulation.

(5.3.3) The concept of *elasticity of expectations* is supposed to serve this purpose. It is a measure of responsiveness of prospects to changes in results, and has been defined as the ratio of the proportional change in the former to that of the latter. If, for instance, expectations are sure prospects of prices, the elasticity of expectations is the ratio of the proportional change in the expected future price to the proportional change in the price which has been observed in the past. If the elasticity of expectations is equal to unity, a 10% increase in the actual price leads to a 10% increase in the expected price. Thus, if formerly the price was expected to remain unchanged and then it increased by 10%, it is now expected to remain unchanged at the new, higher level. If the elasticity of expectations is zero, no adjustment in the expected price takes place; the prospect is that the price will return to its former level. If the elasticity of expectations is greater than unity, an increase in the actual price gives rise to a prospect that it will increase still further.

In principle, the concept of the elasticity of expectations applies to one time of the subject only. To simplify the analysis it has, however, been assumed by Hicks that prospects of what is going to happen at different points of time are always adjusted all of them in the same proportion. If thus there is an increase in the current price of a good by 10% and the elasticity of expectations is unity, the prices which the individual expects to rule at several points of time in the future are supposed to be increased all of them by 10%. In a theory, assumptions of this kind are hypotheses which may turn out to be true as well as not true. It is, therefore, only if the theory is so general that its predictions are independent of what the expectations actually are, that the assumption made by Hicks could be accepted as an expository device.

The concept of the elasticity of expectations does not apply to multi-outcome prospects. We could speak of a percentage change of a multi-outcome prospect if the values of all outcomes were changing all of them in the same proportion and if the weights attached to them were constant. Otherwise, the notion of a percentage change in the prospect does not apply. It is for this reason, therefore, that both Hicks and Lange insisted on the reduction of multi-outcome prospects to their sure-prospect equivalents. For only if the prospects are in the sure-prospect form, can changes in them be expressed numerically and the concept of the elasticity of expectations be applied to them.

(5.3.4) The general line of the argument is as follows. There is a certain degree of substitutability between inputs of firms at different points of time, or between goods demanded by consumers. A firm, for instance, may use less durable capital equipment or over-work the existing one, and increase in this way its current output at the cost of its future output. A consumer may postpone some purchases or make them sooner at the cost of buying less in the future. Formally the inputs to be made and the goods to be purchased at different points of time may be treated as different inputs and different goods, and their substitutability as covered by the general hypothesis that inputs are substitutes one for another in production and consumer goods are substitutes in consumption. The general theorem that the quantity demanded increases as the price falls may thus be applied to inputs and goods which are described not only in terms of their physical characteristics but also in terms of the point of time at which they appear.

It may then be argued that the production and consumption plans in which inputs and goods to be obtained in the future appear are determined by the expected prices of those inputs or goods. Whether, therefore, current inputs and current purchases of consumer goods are substituted for future inputs and future purchases, or the other way round, depends on how the expected prices of those inputs and goods change in relation to their current prices. And this is where the concept of the elasticity of expectations has to be brought in. For it can then be shown that if the elasticity of expectations of prices is greater than unity, prices expected to be ruling in the future change more than the current prices do, and there is a tendency to substitute future for current inputs and future for current goods if current prices fall, and current for future inputs and goods if current prices rise. In either case the quantities currently demanded tend to change in the same direction as prices, and the tendency is not towards but away from equilibrium. If, on the other hand, the elasticity of expectations is less than unity, the expected prices change less than the current prices do, the substitution is the other way round, and the tendency is towards equilibrium.

Similar considerations apply to supply. If the elasticity of expectations is greater than unity, current supply tends to fall if current prices increase, and the latter tend to increase still further. If the elasticity of expectations is less than unity, an increase in the current prices leads to an increase in the current supply, and the current prices tend to fall back to their former level.

(5.3.5) If the argument is applied to the system as a whole, the conclusion depends also on monetary effects of changes in prices. It must also be borne in mind that stability of equilibrium depends not only on the direction in which supply and demand change in response to changes in prices but also on the extent and on the position in time at which they change. No verbal argument about stability can be conclusive. Let us, however, neglect these difficulties. Suppose that if further refinements were introduced into the analysis, the difficulties would be removed. In what sense then could this analysis enhance our understanding of what actually takes place?

It has been already pointed out before that the reduction of expectations by choice cannot be a part of a theory of business behaviour. For in order to perform the reduction we must first know the behaviour. The argument that the economic system is stable if expectations are inelastic cannot, therefore, be accepted as a theory explaining stability in terms of the elasticities of expectations. To be able to say that expectations are inelastic we would have to reduce them to their sure-prospect equivalents; and to reduce them to this form we would have to know whether the businessmen behave so as to render the system stable. Even, therefore, if we could discover what prospects arise in what circumstances, we would not be able to say whether the system is or is not stable because we would not be able to reduce these prospects to a sure-prospect form if we did not already know the conclusion.

The value of the argument consists rather in its bringing to light one of the causes of our ignorance. We cannot say whether the system is stable or not, because this depends on how expectations change in response to a disturbance in the system; and we do not know in fact either how expectations change or what changes in them render the system stable or unstable. The concept of the elasticity of expectations does not seem, therefore to serve any other purpose here than to make it clear in a very elegant way that both conclusions are possible.[1] The only useful conclusion which can be derived from this analysis is that stability of the economic system depends not only on how the prospects change but also on how the businessman's attitudes towards them change. For if the sure-prospect equivalent cannot be derived from a multi-outcome prospect by means of a formula but depends on the individual's 'tastes', the elasticity of expectations must also depend on the individual's 'tastes'.[2]

(5.4) Short-term and Long-term Expectations

(5.4.1) The formal representation of expectations in Keynes's General Theory is the same as that in Hicks's and Lange's stability analysis. The original prospect is supposed to consist of several outcomes with probability weights attached to them. These are subsequently reduced, by means of an arbitrary formula, to the measures of lucrativity and of risk. And then a premium for risk is deducted from the measure of lucrativity and a sure-prospect equivalent arrived at to which the individual is supposed to adjust his position. The equivalence is by choice, defined quite explicitly in terms of equal behaviour. The sure-prospect equivalent to which the individual adjusts his position is that sure prospect which would call forth the same behaviour on his part as does the original multi-outcome prospect. If left at that, Keynes's theory of business behaviour would thus be as circular as that of Lange and Hicks.

Keynes, however, did not leave it at that. With respect to some cases, he formulated hypotheses about the formation of expectations which enabled him to perform the reduction of the whole original prospect by means of a formula. With respect to

[1] For a more constructive line of criticism see J. H. Power, Price Expectations, Money Illusion and the Real Balance Effect, *Journal of Political Economy*, LXVII, April (1959), pp. 131–43. Compare also Milton Friedman's review article, Lange on Price Flexibility and Employment: A Methodological Criticism, *American Economic Review*, XXXVI, September (1946), pp. 613–31.

[2] No attempt is made in this book to review the literature on stability of equilibrium for its own sake. Some hypotheses about expectations are always implied in it. Very little, however, can be said about them in general terms.

others, he refrained from going much further than providing only an interpretation of what actually takes place.

(5.4.2) Different hypotheses were formulated by Keynes with respect to what he called 'short-term' and 'long-term' expectations. The distinction is quite fundamental. It cuts across the whole field of business behaviour in such a way that two distinct theories can be formulated for either of them.

Short-term expectations are expectations of proceeds and costs to be received and paid by firms when the process of production on which they embark now will be completed. The process of production is understood as the actual turning out of products, using the productive resources which are now at the firms' disposal. The firms have at their disposal a certain capital equipment and organizational set-up, and in the light of their expectations of proceeds and of costs they decide how to use them. They choose, in other words, one particular strategy of outputs and inputs out of a number of alternatives according to the conditional expectations of the proceeds from them and of costs.

Long-term expectations are expectations of proceeds from, and costs of, an additional capital equipment. The subject of expectations is then not the proceeds and costs of a strategy of output from a given capital equipment but the proceeds and costs of an optimum strategy of output from an increase in the capital equipment. The distinction runs along the same lines as the Marshallian distinction between the short run and the long run in the theory of the firm: the criterion is whether the capital equipment and the set-up of the firm is constant or may be changed. It only serves a different purpose. In the case of the Marshallian analysis the purpose is to isolate the effect of changes in capital equipment on output and prices. In the Keynesian theory of expectations, the purpose is to separate the theory of production behaviour from that of investment behaviour.

(5.4.3) The theory of production behaviour is very simple. The interval between the time of the expectation and the time of the subject, that is to say the interval between the time at which the decision about the strategy of output is made and the time at which the inputs are bought and the outputs sold, is very short. There is, therefore, little uncertainty as to what the actual

153

result will be. For the proceeds and the costs cannot then change much in relation to what they would be at the time of the expectation if the same strategy was chosen. In other words, great weights are attached in the prospects of proceeds and costs to outcomes which do not differ much from what these proceeds and costs would be at present. The strategies chosen must not then differ much either. It seems, therefore, that no great mistake can be made if short-term expectations are treated as if they were sure prospects of the proceeds and costs which the firms receive and incur, at the time of the expectation. Short-term expectations and the actual experience of proceeds and costs overlap so closely one with the other that one may be substituted for the other without much effect on the adjustments which they would call forth.

This is how Keynes used the concept of expectations in his theory of production behaviour. The actual expectations are not sure prospects of the events which take place at the time of the expectation. But in this particular case they may be formalized so, because if they were sure prospects of those events, the behaviour of firms would not be much different from what it actually is. In principle, the assertion that it would not be much different requires a test. In view, however, of the obvious technical difficulties this is not likely to be attempted. A common-sense argument that the actual prospects cannot differ much in this case from the sure prospect is, therefore, offered as a substitute for it.

(5.4.4) Long-term expectations refer to proceeds and costs which will be received and incurred at more distant points of time. The prospects in them must, therefore, be less definite than those in short-term expectations. It may be even misleading to speak of them as expectations of proceeds and costs. Keynes spoke of expectations of returns without laying down any rules about how these could be derived from the prospects of proceeds and costs.

If these long-term expectations of returns were formalized as multi-outcome prospects, their form might differ quite radically from that of a sure prospect. It is, therefore, impossible to substitute for them sure prospects of the same returns as those which obtain at the time of the expectation, on the ground of their close overlap as in the case of short-term expectations.

154

The idea of such substitution must be either completely rejected or some other ground must be found for it.

Keynes introduced at this point, the hypothesis of a *convention*. In their estimates of future returns from particular investments, businessmen are supposed to follow a convention that the market knows what these returns are likely to be. Some dealers may be more optimistic, others less so, but on the whole, if no drastic changes in the conditions take place, the market valuations of the particular forms of investment give a correct estimate of their future profitability. As long, therefore, as this convention holds the businessmen's expectations of returns cannot be much different from a sure prospect that the returns will be as the market valuations indicate. Thus if the latter is accepted as a formal representation of these expectations, the theory cannot go much wrong in what it says about actual events. Only when the convention breaks down, the returns become uncertain, and the hypothesis that the businessmen behave as if their expectations were sure prospects no longer applies.

(5.4.5) Thus as far as both the production behaviour and the conventional investment behaviour are concerned, the hypotheses accepted by Keynes make the concept of expectations redundant. Formally they permit us to derive predictions of behaviour from observable data. No expectations need to be taken into account. The businessmen are supposed to behave as if they were adjusting their positions not to their expectations but to these observable data. It is only to justify this hypothesis that an appeal is made to a possible correspondence between the data and the expectations which in those conditions might arise. Without this link the argument might seem incomplete. For why should a businessman adjust his position to the data which can be observed at present if he is interested in the pay-offs from a strategy which he adopts for the future? But from the formal point of view the link is outside the theory. What it actually amounts to is that if expectations were taken into account and the theory thus made acceptable on intuitive grounds, a formal representation of these expectations could not be much different from the data which in the present form of the theory are taken into account.

(5.4.6) In investment behaviour without convention the link is no longer there. On the contrary, it may be argued that the

155

more the outcomes differ one from another and from the data currently observed, the less likely is a businessman to behave as if the latter were the prospect. A hypothesis of this kind would no longer be acceptable. One is rather inclined to believe that the more dispersed are the outcomes, the more important is the negative element of risk, and the smaller is the sure-prospect equivalent to which the businessman adjusts his position. A breakdown of the convention may, therefore, be identified with a sudden collapse of the parameter to which the businessman adjusts himself. This is in fact all that Keynes needed for his theory and all that he said. The sure-prospect equivalent of long-term expectations of returns is the marginal efficiency of capital, and its sudden collapse the breakdown of the trade cycle. In what conditions the convention may be expected to break down, the theory does not say. The latter cannot, therefore, be tested by confronting what actually takes place with what the theory predicts. It does not predict anything in fact. It only makes a collapse of a sure-prospect equivalent understandable in terms of 'how we would feel' or 'what we would do in that case'.[1]

(5.5) Pure Profits

(5.5.1) Uncertainty is a crucial factor in Knight's theory of profits.[2] Expectations are more implied in it than explicitly taken into account. The implication, however, is so obvious and the theory so important, that it is impossible not to give it a place in a book which deals with the element of expectations in economic theory.

The place is in this chapter because the argument is in terms of sure-prospect equivalents by choice. This is again by implication only, because the question of the formal representation of expectations has not been discussed by Knight at all. But this is the only representation which is consistent with what he said. The people whose behaviour is the subject matter of his theory, not only behave as if they were adjusting their positions to sure-prospect equivalents, but they also determine those sure

---

[1] See also A. G. Hart, Keynes' Analysis of Expectations and Uncertainty, in S. E. Harris (ed.), *The New Economics*, Alfred A. Knopf (New York, 1948).
[2] F. R. Knight, *Risk, Uncertainty and Profits, op. cit.*

prospects in accordance with how they feel about the situations with which they are confronted.

(5.5.2) The basic hypothesis of Knight's theory is that uncertainty in business cannot be abolished. It can be reduced by grouping together situations in which the same strategy can be adopted, and by adjusting that strategy not to expectations of what will be the result in each individual case but to expectations of frequency distributions of results in all of them. This may take the form of what Knight called *consolidation*, of people pooling together their pay-offs from the strategies they adopt, as in the case of insurance; or it may take the form of *specialization*, of people restricting their activities each to a narrow range of situations which can be met with a strategy adjusted to the frequency distribution of results, as in the case of a businessman allowing in his calculation for a certain proportion of his output to be faulty. There are, however, limits to either of these procedures. The majority of the situations with which the businessmen become confronted cannot be met with a common strategy, and the possibility of adjusting the latter to an expectation of the frequency distribution of results does not arise. By consolidation and specialization uncertainty can be reduced; but it cannot be abolished altogether.

It follows that if expectations of businessmen were formalized as multi-outcome prospects, the outcomes in them would differ much one from another. The expectations of pay-offs in these cases could not, therefore, be approximated by sure prospects as in the case of Keynes's short-term expectations. They would have to be reduced to sure-prospect equivalents, and the result of the reduction would depend not only on the content of the original prospect but also on the individual's 'tastes'. For some individuals the sure-prospect equivalents might turn out to be very high, for others very low. If, therefore, the individuals can choose between being entrepreneurs with expectations of outcomes which differ much one from another, and having contractual incomes the expectations of which approximate more closely sure prospects, then even if the expectations were the same for everybody, some individuals would choose the former and others the latter.

This is Knight's explanation of why some people accept contractual incomes and others assume the rôle of entrepreneurs

157

with residual income.[1] To accept a contractual income means to choose a strategy to which correspond expectations of that contractual income as a sure prospect. In principle some uncertainty is always there, but there is little doubt that even if the expectations were formalized as multi-outcome prospects, they would approximate very closely sure prospects of the contractual income. To become an entrepreneur, on the other hand, means to choose a strategy to which correspond multi-outcome prospects of pay-offs. Thus the fact that the former are chosen means that for this particular individual the sure-prospect equivalent of the entrepreneurial income is below the sure prospect of the contractual income. The opposite must be true if the entrepreneurial income is chosen.

(5.5.3) Pure profits are defined as the entrepreneur's residual income. If somebody accepts the role of an entrepreneur, the sure-prospect equivalent of his expectation of profits is greater than the sure prospect of a possible contractual income. But the sure-prospect equivalent is not the actual result of income. The fact, therefore, that the former is higher than the contractual income does not necessarily mean that the latter is also higher. If it is higher, the difference represents a profit; but it may also be lower, and then the difference represents a loss. In either case, income is residual because it is arrived at by deducting the contractual incomes of all those who contribute to the enterprise, from the actual receipts from it.

Pure profits are not a reward for uncertainty-bearing because they are neither offered nor necessarily received. The fact that profits are uncertain means that not profits as such but only a chance of profits is offered. Profits may not be received because, in the case of the majority of entrepreneurs, the sure-prospect equivalents of their expectations of receipts may turn out to be higher than the actual results of receipts. And the obligations which they accept towards those who choose contractual incomes may then be also higher than the receipts. This is in fact what Knight thought to be generally the case.[2]

(5.5.4) In what sense may the notion of expectations in

---

[1] Similar explanation was given by Irving Fisher, *The Nature of Capital and Income*, The Macmillan Company (New York, 1927), p. 289.

[2] Compare, however, the treatment of this point by Pigou in his *Economics of Welfare* (4th ed.), Macmillan & Co. (London, 1932), Appendix I.

Knight's theory help us to understand what actually takes place? The first part of the argument, that the pay-offs from business strategies are always uncertain, is a substitute for a test of the hypothesis that the original multi-outcome prospects can be reduced to their sure-prospect equivalents by choice only. If there were no uncertainty we would know the future events, either single or repetitive ones, as we know those which have already taken place, and we would adjust ourselves to what we know for sure. There could then be no profits. Different individuals might choose different lines of activity because they might like them better than others. But they would know the rewards from them and no discrepancy could arise between what they actually receive and what they might have thought in the past that they would receive.

It does not follow, however, that if we accept these conclusions, expectations are an indispensable element in the second part of the theory. It is possible to restate the latter so as to turn it into a causal theory of profits, without any expectations at all. Instead of the hypothesis that people's behaviour is the result of them adjusting themselves to their expectations of the future so as to achieve a certain objective, the prospects in those expectations being determined by what people have experienced in the past and by their inner attitudes and dispositions, we could have a hypothesis that people's behaviour is determined directly by their experiences and attitudes. Some of them assume the rôle of entrepreneurs, others seek contractual incomes, according to what these experiences and attitudes actually are. The actual pattern of behaviour could then be explained in terms of the differences in people's responses to what they have experienced in the past, determined by their inner dispositions and attitudes.

(5.5.5) By giving the theory of profits this causal form we could get rid of the problem of how to formalize expectations. The prediction that residual incomes would arise, could then be derived from the hypothesis that there would be always people who respond to the conditions in which they happen to act by assuming the rôle of entrepreneurs. No questions would have to be asked about what they think or what they expect.

In spite of this advantage, a teleological explanation seems, however, to be preferred. The reason is that in the causal theory we would explain the existence of profits by means of a

159

hypothesis about our behaviour, which itself would have to b explained. And in the teleological theory we have that explana tion. People behave that way because they adjust their position to their expectations so as to achieve a certain objective. The explanation is not in terms of any generally accepted law o which the present case would be an instance. But we accept the hypothesis because we think that we ourselves would behave so

(5.6) Risk Taking and Taxes on Income

(5.6.1) The hypothesis of the reduction of prospects by choice and the technique of indifference curves for lucrativity and risk have been used by Domar and Musgrave[1] to analyse the effec of taxes on the amount of risk which businessmen are prepared to accept. As economic progress depends to a large extent or the activities of the entrepreneurs, any discouragement from risk taking is usually regarded as a bad thing. The problem therefore, is important from the policy point of view and come: up in every discussion of relative merits of various types of taxes.[2] From the theoretical point of view, the analysis repre- sents an attempt to find out what predictions about the entre- preneurs' reactions to taxes on their incomes can be derived from the hypothesis of the reduction of prospects by choice.

(5.6.2) The analysis is as follows. Suppose that a businessman has a certain amount of resources and that he can choose between a number of ways in which to invest them. These different ways are his strategies. They need not be restricted to one form of investment in each case. A strategy may be a distribution of resources between several forms of investment.

To each strategy corresponds a certain prospect of profits. In order to compare the prospects the businessman is supposed to reduce them first to a measure of lucrativity and of risk. Let the mean value of all possible pay-offs be the measure of lucrativity and the mean value of the negative pay-offs only the measure of risk. Thus if q_i's are possible outcomes of pay-offs arranged so that $q_i < q_i + 1$ for every i; if p_i's are probability weights

[1] E. D. Domar and R. A. Musgrave, Proportional Income Taxation and Risk Taking, *Quarterly Journal of Economics*, LXIII, May (1944), pp. 388–422.
[2] See, for instance, N. Kaldor, *An Expenditure Tax*, Allen & Unwin (London, 1956), Chapter III.

ittached to these outcomes, and if $q_k = 0$; the measure of ucrativity (to be called yield) is

$$y = \sum_{i=1}^{n} q_i . p_i$$

ınd the measure of risk (to be called risk) is

$$r = -\sum_{i=1}^{k} q_i . p_i$$

These two parameters determine the rank of the prospect to vhich they refer. Thus if in two different prospects the yield and :he risk happen to be the same, the individual is indifferent oetween the strategies which give rise to them.

(5.6.3) Every prospect may be represented by a point in FIG. 5.6.3. The yields are plotted along the horizontal axis and the :isks along the vertical axis. As yield is a positive element in the prospect and risk is a negative element, the prospects to the left and further up than some others may be discarded straightaway in favour of those others. The prospect ultimately chosen must thus be on the boundary of all those which are available. The boundary is the individual's opportunity curve. In FIG. 5.6.3 it is represented by OQ.

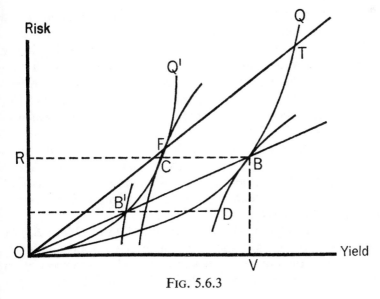

FIG. 5.6.3

161

It is sloping upwards and convex downwards because there is some limit to the mean value of pay-offs. Every successive increase in it can be obtained only at the cost of a greater and greater increase in risk.

The individual's tastes are represented by a system of indifference curves which too are sloping upwards. This follows from the assumption that lucrativity is a positive element in the prospect and risk is a negative element. As, however, the marginal rate of substitution of yield for risk is most likely to be increasing as more yield is combined with more risk, the indifference curves are convex upwards. Furthermore, the marginal rate of substitution of yield for risk is probably greater the greater is the yield even at the same level of risk. In other words, the indifference curve at D is less steep than that at B^1.

The indifference curves more to the right represent combinations of yield and risk which the individual ranks higher than those represented by indifference curves more to the left. Thus his optimum position is at B where the opportunity line OQ is tangential to one of the indifference curves. That strategy will be chosen which gives rise to the mean value of pay-offs equal to OV and to the mean value of negative pay-offs equal to OR.

(5.6.4) Suppose now that a tax is imposed on all incomes at a constant rate and that all losses can always be deducted from profits before the assessment of the tax. The result is that in the prospect of profits from various forms of investment all outcomes of pay-offs, positive as well as negative, become reduced by the rate of the tax. If, for instance, the rate of the tax is 50%, the prospect which was originally at B is now B^1 half-way between B and O. The same applies to all other points on the opportunity curve OQ. As a result of the tax the whole curve shifts towards the origin in such a way that if a straight line is drawn through O, the new opportunity curve OQ^1 bisects that segment of the line which is between the origin and the former opportunity curve OQ.

The slope of OQ^1 at B^1 is then equal to that of OQ at B. For if both the ordinates and the abscissae of every point along OQ are reduced at the same rate, they must bear the same proportion one to the other as they did before. The indifference curve passing through B and D is steeper at D than at B, and the indifference curve at B^1 is steeper than that at D. This means that the indifference curve at B^1 must also be steeper than that at B. At B it is as steep as the opportunity curve OQ. At B^1 the opportunity curve OQ^1 is as steep as OQ at B. At B^1 the indifference curve must, therefore, intersect the opportunity curve as on the diagram, and the individual's new optimum position must be at some point F above and to the right from B^1.

(5.6.5) It is impossible to say whether F is above or below the horizontal line through B. Its exact position depends on the form of the indifference curves. The tax may, therefore, induce the businessman to choose investments which give rise to a smaller as well as to a greater risk of losses after tax.

The actual yield and risk from investment is, however, that before the tax. By imposing a tax the government does not reduce the yield and the risk but participates only in the former and takes upon itself a part of the latter. The actual yield and the actual risk from the investment which gives rise to the investor's yield and risk after tax at F are thus those of the point T. And these are always greater than the yield and the risk at B. For if F is above B^1 along OQ^1, T must also be above B along OQ. Thus the conclusion is that if the form of the opportunity curve and of the indifference curves is as we think that it is most likely to be, a proportional income tax which allows for all losses to be deducted from profits before the assessment of the tax should induce the investors to choose projects which give greater mean values of profits before tax and greater risk of losses before tax.

(5.6.6) Consider now the case in which the tax is imposed on profits only. No losses can be deducted from profits before the assessment of the tax. The outcomes of positive pay-offs only are then reduced by the tax. The negative outcomes remain unaffected. The result is that the risk of an investment is not affected either, and the yield is reduced more than in proportion to the tax. For it follows from the definition of yield and of risk that the mean value of positive pay-offs is

$$\sum_{i=k}^{n} q_i \cdot p_i = y + r$$

This is now reduced by the rate of the tax. The yield, therefore, is

163

reduced by $(y + r).t$, and the rate of that reduction is $(1 + r/y).t > t$.

The fact that the risk to which the particular strategy of investment gives rise remains unaffected by the tax means that the opportunity curve OQ shifts horizontally over its whole length, each point by $(1 + r/y).t$ of its former distance from the vertical axis. If OQ^1 in FIG. 5.6.3 satisfied this requirement, CB would be equal to $(OV + OR)$ multiplied by the rate of the tax. The slope of the opportunity curve would then increase in proportion to the rate of its shift. The indifference curve passing through C would probably be also steeper than that at B. It is, therefore, possible that the businessman's new optimum position would be at C. As, however, we do not know how much the indifference curve at C is steeper than that at B, we cannot say whether the new optimum position would be exactly at C, above it, or below it.

In this case the result of the analysis is inconclusive. If the new optimum position happens to be at C, the actual yield and the actual risk remain the same as they were at B. If the new optimum position is above C, the result of the tax is that the businessmen tend to choose more risky projects. If the new position is below C, they tend to choose less risky projects.

(5.6.7) All actual tax systems fall somewhere between these two extremes. Some possibility of profits being offset by losses is always there. For even if the law does not allow for them being offset by losses suffered in other lines of business or in other accounting periods, there is always the possibility of them being offset by those which have been suffered in the same line of business and in the same accounting period. Thus with respect to any actual tax system some degree of inconclusiveness must always remain. The more scope is given in the tax laws to the offset of profits by losses, the more risky projects the investors will choose. Whether, however, the projects chosen by them will be more risky than those which they would choose without the tax depends on how much scope is given to the off-set.

This is about all that Domar and Musgrave's analysis permits us to say. It does not enable us to make any definite predictions of how investment in the real world is influenced by taxes. But it may help to make some guesses of how it could be influenced[1]

[1] On the ground of their analysis of the income and the substitution effects

164

and to settle some points of controversy which otherwise might remain unresolved.[1]

(5.7) Liquidity Preference

(5.7.1) Liquidity preference may be interpreted as preference for less risky forms of investment. For if an individual buys bonds, he exposes himself to the risk of having to sell them at lower prices if and when he needs his funds back in the form of money. He does not know either when he will need these funds back or at what price he will have to sell the bonds. The prospect of the return which he may obtain from his investment consists, therefore, of many outcomes, and the element of risk plays an important part in it. There is no risk of return if the funds are kept in the form of money. Thus the greater proportion of funds is kept in bonds and the smaller in money, the greater is the risk of pay-offs from them. To accept this risk the individual must obtain some compensation in the form of greater lucrativity of these pay-offs.

This does not explain, however, why money is held at all. For suppose that lucrativity and risk are formalized as in the previous section. Each combination of money and bonds may then be represented by a point in FIG. 5.6.3. The respective points need not be on the opportunity curve OQ. They may be above and to the left of it. Or if some of them happen to be on the curve, the individual's optimum point B may not be one of them. Although, therefore, Domar and Musgrave's analysis could yield the prediction that a proportional income tax with all losses allowed for would induce the individual to hold more bonds and less money *if money was held by him at all*, it could not yield the prediction that money would be held by him. Nor could it yield any prediction of how his money balances would respond to changes in the rate of interest.

of taxes Domar and Musgrave arrived, for instance, at the conclusion that the greater is the rate of the tax, the more likely are the businessmen to choose less risky projects than those which they would choose without the tax. (*op. cit.*, pp. 406-7).

[1] See for instance E. Cary Brown, Mr. Kaldor on Taxation and Risk Bearing, *Review of Economic Studies*, **XXV** (I), October (1957), pp. 49-52, and N. Kaldor, Risk Bearing and Income Taxation, *Review of Economic Studies*, **XXV** (3), June (1958), pp. 206-9.

(5.7.1) An explanation of liquidity preference in terms of risk and lucrativity has been given by Tobin.[1] His technique is again that of opportunity and indifference curves, and his measure of lucrativity is the same as that of Domar and Musgrave: the mean value of possible outcomes of pay-offs. The measure of risk, however, is different. It is not the mean value of negative pay-offs but the standard deviation of all of them.

As the pay-offs to which the analysis applies are those from holding bonds, they may be of two kinds only: (i) the interest r, and (ii) the capital gain g. If an individual invests a certain proportion of his funds in bonds and keeps the rest in money, the mean value of his total return is

$$\eta_R = a(r + \eta_G)$$

where η_G is the mean value of the capital gain per £ invested and a is the proportion of his funds which is invested in bonds. It may be further argued that current prices of bonds adjust themselves to the expected prices so that η_G is equal to zero,

$$\eta_R = a.r \tag{I}$$

The mean value of the return is then determined solely by the rate of interest and by the proportion in which the funds are divided between money and bonds.

The risk of that return is due to the risk of the capital gain. For the rate of interest is fixed and known. Thus the measure of risk is

$$\sigma_R = a.\sigma_G \tag{II}$$

where σ_G is the standard deviation of the capital gain. If a from this relation is substituted into (I), we obtain

$$\eta_R = \frac{r}{\sigma_G} \cdot \sigma_R \tag{III}$$

This last equation determines the opportunity curve for lucrativity and risk of various combinations of money and bonds.

(5.7.3) Relations (II) and (III) are represented diagrammatically in Fig. 5.7.3. The standard deviations σ_R and σ_G are

[1] J. Tobin, Liquidity Preference as Behaviour Towards Risk, *Review of Economic Studies*, **XXV** (2), February (1958), pp. 65–86. Compare also J. R. Hicks, Suggestion for Simplifying the Theory of Money, *Economica*, **II**, February (1935), pp. 1–19.

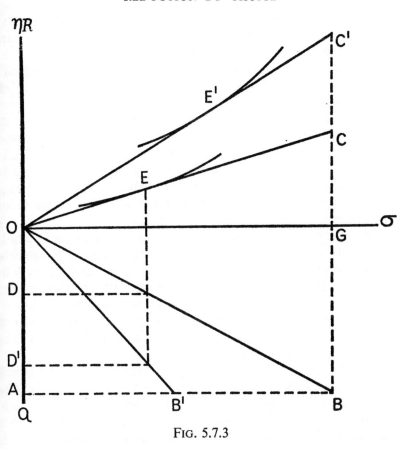

$$\text{Fig. 5.7.3}$$

measured along the horizontal axis, the mean values of return η_R along the vertical axis from O in the upward direction, and the proportion a along the vertical axis from O in the downward direction.

The upper part of the figure is used as a diagram of (III). Suppose that the prospect of the capital gain is such that the standard deviation σ_G is equal to OG and that the rate of interest r is equal to GC. Relation (III) is then represented by the line OC. The slope of that line is equal to r/σ_G, and if $\sigma_R = \sigma_G = OG$, the mean value of return is $\eta_R = r = GC$.

Relation (II) is represented in the lower part of the figure. If the individual invests all his funds in bonds, a is equal to unity, and $\sigma_R = \sigma_G$. This is the situation at the point B. If a smaller

167

proportion of funds is invested in bonds, the standard deviation of the return is as indicated by the line OB. The slope of that line is equal to the reciprocal of $\sigma_G = OG$.

(5.7.4) As in Domar and Musgrave's analysis the individual' optimum position is at the point E at which one of the indifference curves touches the opportunity curve OC. The indifference curves are now convex downwards because the axes of lucrativity and of risk have been reversed. Their form embodies, however the same features of the individual's scale of preferences as in FIG. 5.6.3. The opportunity curve is a straight line because in the present case the mean value of pay-offs is a weighted average of zero return from holding money and of a given mean value of return from the funds invested in bonds.

The proportion of funds which the individual invests in bond is equal to OD, and the proportion held in money is equal to DA. A corner solution is not impossible. The individual may be paying so little attention to the risk of pay-offs that his optimum position may be at C. As long, however, as the indifference curves are convex downwards, a sufficiently low rate of interest (that is to say a sufficiently flat opportunity line) would induce him to hold a part of his funds in money.

(5.7.5) This is Tobin's explanation of why not all money which is not needed for current transactions is invested in bonds. The explanation is independent of the hypothesis that the individual who holds that money expects the prices of bonds to fall. Relation (II) implies that the mean value of capital gains is zero. Tobin's explanation has, therefore, that advantage over the current textbook one, that it provides for a motive for holding money also in those situations in which the same expectations of the future prices of bonds are held all over the market and the current prices of bonds adjust themselves to these expectations so quickly that on the average no capital gains are expected.

No predictions, however, can be derived from it of how money balances would change in response to changes in the rate of interest. For suppose that the rate of interest is doubled. The result is that the slope of the opportunity line doubles as well; the new opportunity line is OC^1; and the new optimum position E^1. On the diagram E^1 is to the right of E. But this needs not necessarily be so. The point E^1 may also be to the left f E. And as the increase in the rate of interest has no effect on the position of the line OB, it may lead to a reduction as well as to an increase in the proportion of funds which are held in money.

(5.7.6) The effect of an income tax may be analysed as follows. Suppose that the initial position of the opportunity line is OC and that a proportional tax is then imposed on all incomes, including capital gains, with all losses allowed for in the assessment of the tax. The result is that from the point of view of the investor both r and σ_R are reduced in proportion to the tax. The opportunity line becomes shorter, but its slope does not change. Unless, therefore, the tax is so high that the line becomes shorter than OE, the individual's optimum position remains at E. The line OB becomes steeper. Thus the proportion of funds invested in bonds increases from OD to OD^1, and the proportion held in the form of money falls from AD to AD^1. This corresponds to Domar and Musgrave's conclusion that a proportional tax with all losses allowed for leads to more risky forms of investment.

Nothing definite can be said about the effect of the tax if capital gains are exempted from it. Only the rate of interest is then reduced by the tax. Standard deviation of pay-offs remains unchanged. Thus the opportunity line OC shifts now downwards in proportion to the tax and the line OB is not affected by it. The effect of the tax is identical with that of a fall in the rate of interest, and as in this latter case its direction is indetermined. It depends on whether the new optimum position happens to be to the right or to the left of the optimum position before the tax.

(5.7.7) In this brief outline of Tobin's analysis, little attention has been paid to an explicit formulation of the conditions which must be satisfied for it to be valid. Homogeneity of bonds, no change in the total amount of funds invested in bonds or kept in the form of money, no effect on bond prices of changes in the individual's demand for them, constant purchasing power of money, no connection between the prospects of capital gains and changes either in the rate of interest or in taxes, etc., are implied in the argument. For a more careful discussion of these conditions the reader is referred to Tobin's original article. [1]

[1] See also R. C. O. Matthews, Expenditure, Plans and the Uncertainty Motive for Holding Money, *Journal of Political Economy*, **LXXI**, June (1963), pp. 201–18.

As an attempt to derive predictions from the hypothesis of the reduction of prospects by choice, the analysis may be regarded as superior to that of Domar and Musgrave because predictions apply to facts which can be objectively observed. Whether people hold more or less money in relation to bonds can be ascertained by inspection. Domar and Musgrave's predictions apply to prospects of pay-offs. Those chosen in some circumstances are predicted to be more risky and more lucrative than those chosen in some other circumstances. Neither prospects, however, nor their lucrativity or risk can be ascertained by inspection. Domar and Musgrave's predictions could, therefore, be tested indirectly only, through the facts which they may be found to imply.

6

Theories of Moral Expectation

THEORIES of moral expectation differ from those discussed in the previous chapters in the nature of pay-offs to which the individuals adjust their positions; they are expressed not in money but in utilities. This raises the question of what these utilities are and how they are to be ascertained. The matter was already discussed at some length in the first part of this book. Very little, therefore, will be added here to what was said before.

The main topic of this chapter is the original formulation of the moral expectation theory and its subsequent development. As in all the other chapters, the stress is on what the theory is supposed to explain and on the sense in which it contributes to our knowledge of the world in which we live.

(6.1) St Petersburg Paradox

(6.1.1) The term 'moral expectation' was introduced by Daniel Bernoulli in the first half of the eighteenth century.[1] The purpose of Bernoulli's argument was to improve upon the hypothesis of the mean value of monetary pay-offs which was holding the field at that time but was unable to account for some features of our behaviour in the conditions of risk. The argument implied some notion of diminishing marginal utility of money.[2] The idea of diminishing marginal utility was thus introduced into the analysis of choice involving risk long before Jevons, Menger and Walras introduced it into the general theory of value. It turned out, however, that Bernoulli's moral-expectation theory was

[1] His paper, Exposition of a New Theory on the Measurement of Risk, was translated by Louise Sommer and published in *Econometrica*, 22, January (1954), pp. 23.
[2] The term covers marginal utility of income or of the individual's total wealth according to what the context requires.

inconsistent with other features of our behaviour just because of this hypothesis of diminishing marginal utility of money.

(6.1.2) The shortcomings of the theory of the mean value of monetary pay-offs were brought to a focus in the so-called St Petersburg paradox. Consider the following game. Suppose that a 'fair' coin is tossed and that if it falls heads, the player receives two pounds and the game is finished. If the coin falls tails, it is tossed again. If then it falls heads, the player receives 2^2 pounds; if it falls tails, it will be tossed for the third time. Heads at the third toss mean 2^3 pounds for the player; if tails come out, the coin will be tossed for the fourth time. And so on, if the game goes on till the n-th toss, either the player receives 2 pounds if heads come out or one more toss is made if tails come out.

The question is now how much the player might be prepared to pay for the privilege of playing that game. If the value of the game to him were determined by the mean value of the outcomes of the objective pay-offs, he should pay any price. For if the coin is 'fair', the probability of winning 2 pounds is $1/2$, the probability of winning 2^2 pounds is $1/2^2$, of 2^3 pounds is $1/2^3$, and so on. Each outcome of pay-off multiplied by its probability weight is equal to unity, and the mean value is infinitely large. Whatever price the individual might thus be asked to pay for being admitted to the game, it would be always lower than the sure-prospect equivalent to which he is supposed to adjust himself.

This is, however, not how people usually behave. It is quite obvious that nobody would be prepared to pay a very high price for being allowed to play St Petersburg game. The difficulty is not lack of money. For the maximum price which we would be willing to pay would certainly be far below what we could pay if we wanted to. There must be something wrong in the hypothesis itself.

(6.1.3) It was precisely to meet these objections that Bernoulli put the mean-value theory in terms not of monetary pay-offs, but of utilities which the individual derives from them. His argument is as follows. The utility of money income (its intrinsic value as Bernoulli called it) increases as that income increases. But it increases less than in proportion. Thus if heads do not come out at the first toss of St Petersburg game, and the minimum pay-off from it increases from 2 to 2^2 pounds, the utility of that pay-off increases less than that. The same applies to further tosses. The product of the utility pay-offs from them, and of the probability weights of the respective outcomes coming off, becomes less and less as the number of tosses increases. The mean value of those utility pay-offs need not, therefore, be infinitely large. If, for instance, the utility of a particular amount of money is equal to its logarithm, [1] the moral expectation of pay-offs from St Petersburg game is $\frac{1}{2} \log 2 + \frac{1}{4} \log 4 + \frac{1}{8} \log 8$ $\ldots = 2 \log 2$. The value of the game to the player is then not infinite.

The logarithmic measure of utility is quite arbitrary. It is important in this case only because it brings into relief the principle of diminishing marginal utility of income on which the whole argument depends. There are also other forms of the utility function which satisfy this condition. They too might lead to a finite value of St Petersburg game, though a different one. Unless, therefore, an operation is specified in the context of the theory in terms of which utility is defined and the utility function determined, the moral-expectation theory does not permit us to say whether the player will or will not be prepared to pay a particular price to take part in the game.

Bernoulli did not specify the method. It is doubtful if he was really interested in the actual value of the game. What he wanted to show was only that it need not be infinite. And this limited objective could have been achieved by means of any utility function which satisfies the condition that the mean value of utility pay-offs is finite. From his particular point of view the hypothesis that utility of income can be measured by the latter's logarithm was as good as any other which satisfies this condition.

(6.1.4) The matter received more consideration when the concept of utility was introduced into the general theory of value. The question of how it can be measured became then of crucial importance. For if value is determined by utility, a way must be found to describe what this utility actually is. Otherwise the statement must be meaningless. [2] In the early formulations of the subjective theory of value, utility was understood as a

[1] Bernoulli's hypothesis. Cramer thought that utility might vary as the square root of income. See Note VIII, in Marshall's *Principles*.

[2] Compare G. J. Stigler, The Development of The Utility Theory, *Journal of Political Economy*, **LVIII**, August (1950), pp. 307–27; and, October (1950), pp. 373–96.

measure of satisfaction to be ascertained by introspection. Either the marking or the Jevonsian operations would thus be relevant to it. Few writers, however, were aware at that time of the difficulties of a precise definition.

(6.1.5) Marshall tried to get rid of them by expressing utility in terms of money. His argument was that if an individual decided to buy a unit of a particular good, the utility which he derived from it could not be less than the utility of money which he payed for it. For infra-marginal units the former must be greater than the latter, and at the margin it must be equal to it. If, therefore, the unit of utility was so chosen that the utility of the marginal unit of money (that is to say the marginal utility of income) was equal to unity, the price which the individual was prepared to pay for the last unit of a good was a measure of the marginal utility of it.

The Marshallian measure hinges upon the assumption that marginal utility of income is constant. For if this were not the case, the unit itself in which utility is measured would vary from one instance of measurement to another. The measure might thus be applicable to marginal utilities of goods in conditions in which the individual's income is so adjusted that the marginal utility of it remains unchanged. But it cannot be applied to pay-offs from a game which lead to a change in the marginal utility of income. If, in this latter case, the marginal utility of income were constant, the moral expectation of a gain from St Petersburg game would be infinite, and the paradox of it would remain unresolved.

Marshall had in fact no measure of utility of income. He thought that it must be diminishing but like his predecessors did not provide for any operation in terms of which it could be defined. He did not object to Bernoulli's argument that the value of a game is determined by the moral expectation of the possible pay-offs from it. But he followed it up in a different direction. He argued that as the marginal utility of income is diminishing, the moral expectation of pay-offs from a gain must always be lower than the utility of their mean value. [1] To stake an amount equal to the latter would thus mean to pay more than what one receives in exchange is really worth. Hence the conclusion

[1] The proof of this proposition is given in Note IX in Marshall's *Principles* (8th ed.). See also (6.1.6) below.

that from the economic point of view fair gambling is irrational. And as the actual gambling is usually less than fair because the stakes must cover not only the prizes but also the other party's profits and costs, it is a folly to indulge in it. Bernoulli's explanation of St Petersburg paradox became thus in Marshall's hands a normative theory, more concerned with prescriptions for rational behaviour than with explanation of the actual behaviour.[1]

(6.1.6) We will use in this chapter the following diagram (invented by Friedman and Savage[2]) to elucidate the relation between the mean value and the moral expectation of pay-offs. Let us measure total wealth of an individual along the horizontal axis and the utility which he derives from it along the vertical axis, as in FIG. 6.1.6. The relation between the former and the latter may then be represented by a utility curve UU. The curve is convex upwards because the marginal utility of wealth is supposed to be diminishing.

Let the present wealth of the individual be OW. Suppose then

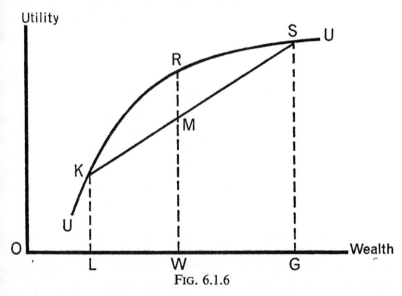

FIG. 6.1.6

[1] A possible explanation of the latter is then that people gamble because they like the game. For criticism of this hypothesis see H. Markowitz, The Utility of Wealth, *Journal of Political Economy*, LX, April (1952), pp. 157–8.

[2] M. Friedman and L. J. Savage, The Utility Analysis of Choices Involving Risk, *Journal of Political Economy, op. cit.*

that the following gamble is offered to him. If he pays a stake equal to LW, he may win LG. Thus if he accepts the gamble and loses, his wealth will be reduced from OW to OL; if he wins it will be increased from OW to OG. If the gamble is fair, the probability weights of these two outcomes must be inversely related to the amounts which may be lost or won. The weight of the outcome that the individual's wealth will be reduced to OL is thus WG/LG, and the weight of the outcome that his wealth will be increased to OG is LW/LG. As the utility pay-offs from these two outcomes are LK and GS respectively, the moral expectation of the individual's future wealth is $LK.(WG/LG) + GS.(LW/LG) = MW$. The utility which the individual derives from his present wealth is RW. Hence fair gambling is an economic loss.

Insurance on the other hand is an economic gain. For if we re-label the above diagram so that OG represents the individual's present wealth, LG the loss against the possibility of which the individual may insure himself, and WG the insurance premium which he would then have to pay, MW is the moral expectation of his future wealth if he does not take up the insurance, and WR is the utility of the sure prospect of his wealth when he takes up the insurance.

(6.2) Von Neumann and Morgenstern's Theory

(6.2.1) A moral-expectation theory is intuitively more acceptable than that of the mean value of monetary pay-offs because it seems more reasonable to suppose that people adjust their behaviour in risky situations to how much they desire the pay-offs from particular strategies than to what is the actual description of these pay-offs. The theory, however, is less satisfactory in certain other respects.

(6.2.2) In the first place, the hypothesis that the individual adjusts his position to the mean value of objective pay-offs may seem plausible on grounds explained in (4.3.5). In all those cases in which the individuals adjust themselves to sure prospects of pay-offs from repetitive events, they adjust themselves also by implication to the mean values of pay-offs from the single events out of which the repetitive events consist. For the probability weights in the latter are then equal to the frequency distribution ɔf results in the former, and the sure-prospect pay-off from the ʻepetitive event is a multiple of the mean value of pay-offs from he single event. If, therefore, an individual chooses a strategy ɔecause the sure-prospect pay-off from a repetitive event, which ʻs associated with it, is greater than that which is associated with ʒome other strategy, he would choose it also if he compared ɥot the sure-prospect pay-offs from the repetitive events but the mean values of pay-offs from the single events. Habits of thought might thus develop that whenever an individual is confronted with a risky situation, he always has at the back of his mind the mean value of possible pay-offs as a first approximation of what any particular strategy might be worth to him. And if the theory is not supposed to go much further than these first approximations, the hypothesis of the mean value of pay-offs may serve this purpose quite well.

It is, however, not so if the hypothesis is that the individual adjusts himself to the moral expectation of pay-offs. If the pay-offs are in some measure of utility which satisfies the condition that the marginal utility of income diminishes as the amount of income increases, the proposition that the sure-prospect pay-off from a repetitive event is a multiple of the mean value of pay-offs from single events is no longer valid. As the number of the latter increases, only the objective pay-off from the repetitive event increases in the same proportion. The pay-off in terms of utility increases less than that. The relation between the sure prospect of the utility pay-off from the repetitive event and the moral expectation of pay-offs from the single event to which the individual is about to adjust himself, depends then not only on the number of the latter in the former, but also on the form of the utility function. It is, therefore, not true in this case that if the individual adjusts himself to sure-prospect pay-offs from repetitive events, he chooses the same strategy as he would choose if he adjusted himself to the mean value of pay-offs from single events; and no habits of thought could develop which would identify the latter adjustment with the former.

(6.2.3) Bernoulli's theory of moral expectation is subject to the criticism that (as was explained in the previous section) it does not provide for any operation in terms of which utility could be defined and objectively ascertained. The individual is supposed to determine the utility of the possible pay-offs by

177

introspection as the degree of satisfaction which he would derive from having them. This makes the hypothesis more acceptable as a part of a teleological theory. But it makes the predictions to be derived from it dependent on introspection which has an inferior status as an operation in science.

(6.2.4) These criticisms do not apply to Von Neumann and Morgenstern's theory. It provides for an operation in terms of which utility can be defined without an appeal to introspection and it gives reasons for the hypothesis of moral expectation to be accepted as plausible which have nothing to do with sure-prospect pay-offs from repetitive events.

(6.2.5) Normative elements play an important part in it. It may, however, be also interpreted as a positive theory. Its general outline is then as follows. The individual is confronted with a number of outcomes, the weights of which are given as proba-bility weights. Nothing is said explicitly about the operations in terms of which these weights are defined. It is implied, how-ever, that the probability weights are objective, and that they may be formalized as classical probabilities, to be ascertained either by inspection of the physical characteristics of the mech-anism on the working of which the result depends, or by extra-polating the frequency distributions of results which have been observed in the past.

Utilities are defined in terms of a gambling operation. If the individual is indifferent between a sure prospect of A and a lottery ticket which gives him a p chance of B and a $(1 - p)$ chance of C, the utility of A is equal to the mean value of the utilities of B and C, i.e. $U(A) = p . U(B) + (1 - p) . U(C)$. Thus if arbitrary values are accepted as the utilities of the outcomes of B and C, the utilities of all the others may be derived from them by adjusting p so as to make the individual indifferent between those others and the respective lottery tickets. The operation was described in (3.3.6).

The essence of Von Neumann and Morgenstern's formal analysis is that if certain conditions are satisfied, the empirical utility measure is unique up to the arbitrary choice of the origin and of the unit of the scale, and it ranks consistently all the strategies according to which the individual prefers to which. If the weights in the prospects of pay-offs to which these strategies give rise are formalized as probability weights, the moral expectations of those pay-offs are indices of the ranks of those strategies on the individual's scale of preferences. Thus the theory not only provides for an operation in terms of which utility is defined, but it gives also reasons for the hypothesis to be accepted as a plausible explanation of the choices which are actually made.

(6.2.6) The conditions which must be satisfied for these conclusions to be valid are mostly idealizations of the actual state of affairs. They ensure that there is always a p which satisfies the equation $pU(A) + (1 - p)U(B) = U(C)$ for all possible values of A, B and C. The probability measure must thus exist, it must be continuous, and the individual must be able to discern clearly whether he is indifferent between the pay-offs which he expects from alternative strategies or prefers one to the other.

In addition, however, to the conditions idealizing the actual state of affairs it is necessary to accept a hypothesis of a restrictive character. If the utility measures are to be consistent and unique, the individual must be guided in his choices of strategies by the attractiveness of the pay-offs which they promise, and not by the pleasure or displeasure of exposing himself to risk. For otherwise it would be possible to find such p, A, B and C that the condition $pU(A) + (1 - p)U(B) = U(C)$ would be satisfield for A not greater and for B less than C, and the utility function would have to be a constant.

(6.2.7) Whether these conditions are approached in any actual case to a sufficient degree for the theory to explain the actual behaviour is a matter for an empirical test. Thus experiments have been devised in which predictions derived from the theory have been confronted with the actual choices made by the individuals who participated in them.[1] No conclusive results, however, have been obtained. On the whole the actual behaviour has been found not inconsistent with the theory. But the correspondence between the predictions and the facts has not been so clear as to throw much light on how choices are made in individual cases.

This may be ascribed to the fact that it has not been possible in any of the experiments to have all the conditions of Von

[1] For references and appraisal see R. D. Luce, Psychological Studies of Risky Decision Making, *Social Science Approaches to Business Behaviour*, J. B. Strother (ed.), Tavistock Publications (London, 1962).

Neumann and Morgenstern's theory satisfied. The difficulties are quite fundamental. For it is impossible to ensure by any means that the individual is not guided in his behaviour by the pleasure or displeasure which he derives from exposing himself to risk in the experiment. It is even impossible to find out *ex post* whether this has or has not been the case. Furthermore, owing to limitations of time it has not always been possible to make the individual so familiar with the rules of the experiment as to give him a clear idea of the actual probability weights of the possible pay-offs.[1]

This, however, does not change the fact that if the experiments are interpreted as a test of how well the theory fits the actual facts in the individual instances of behaviour, the results must be described as negative. The theory does not permit us to predict what an individual will do even in those cases in which all the necessary data can be derived from the conditions of his environment and of his tastes.

(6.3) A Linear Utility Measure

(6.3.1) The theorem that, if the conditions mentioned in (6.2.6) are satisfied, a linear utility measure can be derived from the ranking of prospects plays such an important part in the modern moral expectation theory that it deserves a section for itself. We do not intend to reproduce here either the axioms which formalize the conditions or the proof that a linear utility measure is implied in them. It may, however, be useful to have a geometrical demonstration of the proof to give the reader a better idea of the nature of the measure and of the limitations of the theory in which it appears.

The technique of the demonstration has been invented by Marschak.[2] It permits us to represent on a two-dimensional diagram prospects consisting of up to three possible outcomes. It could not be used to determine utility measures of more than

---

[1] If the individual's scale of preference satisfies certain, rather obvious, but more restrictive conditions than it is usually assumed, a cardinal utility measure can be derived from his choices between even-chance prospects only. See J. Debreu, Cardinal Utility for Even-chance Mixtures of Pairs of Sure Prospects, *Review of Economic Studies*, XXVI (3), June (1959), pp. 174–7.

[2] See J. Marschak, Rational Behaviour, Uncertain Prospects, and Measurable Utility, *op. cit.*

three outcomes at a time. The sense of the argument is, however, independent of the number of the latter. The conclusions arrived at in the course of the demonstration may, therefore, be generalized to cover any number of outcomes.

(6.3.2) The geometry is as follows. Consider three different outcomes: A_0, A_1 and A_2. Let the probability weight of A_1 be measured along the vertical axis and that of A_2 along the horizontal axis. Thus point A_1 (at the unit distance from the origin)

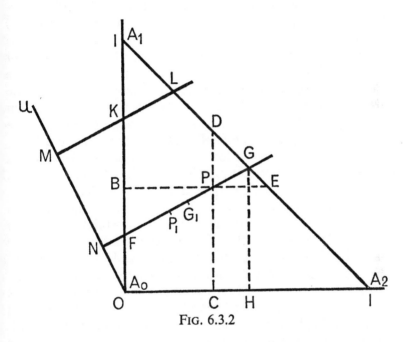

FIG. 6.3.2

represents the sure prospect of A_1, and point A_2 (also at the unit distance from the origin) represents the sure prospect of A_2. As A_0 is the only alternative to A_1 and A_2, the sure prospect of A_0 is represented by the origin. It is a prospect in which the probability weights of both A_1 and A_2 are equal to zero.

Every point within the triangle $A_0A_1A_2$ represents a prospect in which the outcomes A_1 and A_2 appear with the probability weights as indicated by its co-ordinates, and the outcome A_0 with that of unity less the sum of the other two. Thus point F represents a prospect in which outcome A_1 appears with the probability weight OF, and outcome A_0 with that of FA_1; and point P represents a prospect in which outcome A_1 appears with the weight CP, A_2 with BP, and A_0 with $PE = PD$. Alternatively, point P may also be interpreted as representing the prospect in which prospects F and G appear as possible outcomes with probability weights PG/FG and FP/FG respectively. For the weight of A_1 in P is equal to $OF.(PG/FG) + HG.(FP/FG) = CP$; the weight of A_2 is $OH.(FP/FG) = OC$; and that of A_0 is $A_1F(PG/FG) = PD$.

(6.3.3) The postulate which summarizes the conditions discussed at the end of the preceding section is that if the individual is indifferent between outcomes a and a^1, then he must also be indifferent between the prospects $p.a + (1-p).b$ and $p.a^1 + (1-p).b$ for every b and p. Thus if on our diagram the individual happens to be indifferent between P and G, then he must also be indifferent between P_1 (which is half-way between F and P) and G_1 (which is half-way between F and G). The postulate rules out the possibility of A_2 being preferred to A_1 and yet D being preferred to E; or of A_1 being preferred to A_0 and yet F being preferred to A_1. To quote Marschak's example, if A_1 means survival and A_0 means death, a man who loves danger and deliberately exposes himself to the danger of death does not behave in accordance with this postulate; nor does so a gambler who likes the thrill of being confronted with the possibility of a loss. Similarly, if both A_1 and A_2 are preferred to A_0, the latter must not be preferred to a prospect along A_1A_2.

(6.3.4) If this postulate is accepted, it can be easily shown that a locus of prospects with respect to which the individual is indifferent whether he is confronted with one of them or with another is a straight line. For suppose that the individual is indifferent between P and G. Then, as we have seen in (6.3.3), he must be also indifferent between P_1 and G_1. If, however, we vary the probability weights for P and G, we can show that he must also be indifferent between other points on FG. And if we start not from P and G but from some of those other points, we can show that he must be indifferent between still other points. The whole line in fact represents prospects with respect to which the individual is indifferent whether he is confronted with one of them or with some other.

Furthermore, if the individual is not to be indifferent between all prospects in the triangle, he must not be indifferent between those on FG and any of the prospects which are not on that line. For if he were indifferent between F, G and L, for instance, he would have to be also indifferent between all those on the line A_1A_2 plus all those on the line DC, on BE, A_1O, and so on, on any line in fact that can be drawn across the triangle. Hence, if FG is a locus of prospects with respect to which the individual is indifferent, and if there are also prospects in the triangle with respect to which he is not indifferent, all those with respect to which he is indifferent must be on FG.

Finally, it can be shown that the lines representing the indifference loci of prospects must be parallel one to another. For suppose that FG and KL are such loci. It follows then from the postulate that $A_1L/LG = A_1K/KF$. The lines are thus parallel.

(6.3.5) All this leads to the conclusion that the utilities of different prospects can be measured by the distance from an arbitrary origin of the indifference lines which pass through them. If, for instance, the origin is fixed at A_0, and OU is perpendicular to the indifference lines, the distance OM may be accepted as the measure of utility of the prospects represented by the points on KL, and ON as the utility measure of the prospects represented by the points on FG.

The measures are subject to an arbitrary origin because the distance of indifference lines may be taken from any point on the graph. If, for instance, we take it not from A_0, but from N, the utility measure of the prospects K or L would be MN, and that of A_0 would be $-ON$. The measures are also expressed in arbitrary units because a line cutting the indifference loci at some other angle could be used as well. The utility of A_1 could, for instance, be identified with OA_1, that of K with OK, and so on. Subject to an arbitrary choice of these two parameters the measures are, however, unique; they rank consistently all the prospects; and they are linear. The utilities of prospects are linear combinations of the utilities of the outcomes which appear in them, probabilities of those outcomes being the respective coefficients.

(6.4) Utility and Tastes

(6.4.1) The relation between the attitudes to risk and the utilities of sure prospects may be further elucidated by means of the following technique which was originally used by Krelle.[1] Let us plot along the horizontal axis in FIG. 6.4.1 outcomes of monetary gains or losses (to the right and to the left from C respectively) and along the vertical axis the probability weights attached to them, assuming always that the weight equal to one minus that indicated on the vertical axis is attached to the outcome of no gain and no loss. Thus point H, for instance, represents the prospect of either a gain of OG with probability OK or no gain and no loss with probability $KM = 1 - OK$.

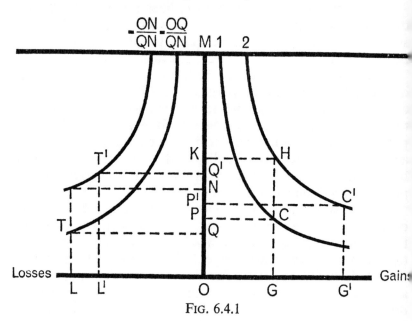

FIG. 6.4.1

The greater is the probability weight of the outcome of gain and the greater is that gain, the more desirable is the prospect. By reducing the probability weight and increasing the gain we may, therefore, find prospects (such as C^1, for instance) which are as desirable as H. The locus of these prospects forms an indifference curve which slopes downwards from left to right. Other indifference curves may be drawn from points representing more desirable or less desirable prospects. As all points along the vertical axis represent a sure prospect of no loss and no gain,

[1] W. Krelle, Preistheorie, Y. C. B. Mohr (Paul Siebeck, Tübingen) and Polygraphiseher Verlag A.G. (Zürich, 1961), pp. 89–107.

he vertical axis is also an indifference curve. And as greater osses mean less desirable prospects, the indifference curves to he left of the vertical axis slope downwards from right to left.

(6.4.2) Let us now attach indices to these indifference curves iccording to the following rules: (i) the index of the curve which coincides with the vertical axis is equal to zero; (ii) the nore desirable is the prospect, the greater is the index of the respective indifference curve; and (iii) if prospects consist each of several outcomes, the sum of the indices of the indifference curves of these outcomes is greater the more desirable is the prospect. This last condition implies that if two prospects are equally desirable, and the zero outcome in them is then replaced wholly or partly by some other outcome, the prospects with these other outcomes are also equally desirable.

(6.4.3) The conditions summarized in these rules impose the following restrictions on the form of the indifference map. The index of the curve passing through H is so much higher than the index of the curve passing through C as OK is greater than OP. For if OK is, for instance, twice as large as OP and both are probability weights, one outcome of OG with the probability weight OK is equivalent to two outcomes of OG with probability weights OP each. The sums of the respective indices are the same. To satisfy the condition of rule (iii) the index of the indifference curve passing through H must, therefore, be twice as high as the index of the curve passing through C. Thus if we know the form and the index of one indifference curve, we can derive from them those of the others by shifting the curve and adjusting the index upwards or downwards, both of them in the same proportion.

This applies to both the right-hand side and the left-hand side of the diagram. The indifference curves on one side cannot, however, be derived from those on the other side. To draw all of them we must be given at least one indifference curve on one side of the diagram and one on the other. This has nothing to do with the division of the map between gains and losses. For the same is true for the curves to the right and to the left of any point on the diagram. To draw the whole map we must be given at least one indifference curve to the right of C and at least one to the left of C.

The indices of the curves on the two sides of the diagram are

185

not independent one from another. For suppose that the individual is indifferent between two prospects. In one of them outcome OG appears with the weight OP and outcome $-OL$ with OQ (and the zero outcome with the weight $1 - OP - OQ$). In the other prospect outcome OG^1 appears with the weight OP^1 and outcome OL^1 with OQ^1 (and the zero outcome with $1 - OP^1 - OQ^1$). According to (iii) the difference between the indices of the curves passing through T and T^1 respectively must be equal to that between the indexes of the indifference curves passing through H and C (equal to one). The former, however, must also be so much greater than the latter as ON is greater than OQ. Hence both of them are completely determined. The index of the curve passing through T is $-OQ/QN$, and the index of the curve passing through T^1 is $-ON/QN$.

(6.4.4) The form of the indifference curves depends on the individual's tastes. If the probability weight of a gain is reduced, the individual who likes risk would need a smaller increase in the gain to remain on the same indifference curve than an individual who does not like risk. We may take the case in which the individual behaves in accordance with the hypothesis of the mean value of possible outcomes as a norm. A reduction in the probability weight of a gain is then compensated by an increase in the gain in the same proportion, and all the indifference curves are rectangular hyperbolae of unit elasticity. For if the mean value of the prospect H is to be equal to the mean value of C^1, the product $OG.OK$ must be equal to the product $OG^1.OP^1$. If the elasticities of the indifference curves are less (or greater) than unity, and a less (or more) than proportional increase in the gain is required to compensate a reduction in the probability weight which is attached to it, the individual may be described as one who likes (or dislikes) risks.

It may, however, be also argued that the indices of Krelle's indifference curves are utility measures. The only way to ascertain the form of the indifference map from which they are derived is by asking the individual to choose between different gambles. The indices of the curves passing through the successive points along a horizontal line drawn through M correspond then to sure prospects of the gain or losses indicated along the horizontal axis. They are, therefore, the utility measures of those gains or losses, arrived at by gambling operation.

It can be also shown that if Krelle's indices are interpreted as utility measures, the indifference map which satisfies the conditions listed in (6.4.2) satisfies also those of the moral expectation theory. For suppose that the pay-offs of gains and losses along the horizontal axis are utility pay-offs. The indices of the indifference curves passing through the successive points along the horizontal line drawn through M are then identical with those points' pay-offs (as in FIG. 6.4.4); and the condition that the index of the curve passing through 2 is so much greater than the index of the curve passing through C as OM (=1) is greater than OP is equivalent to the condition that *all* the

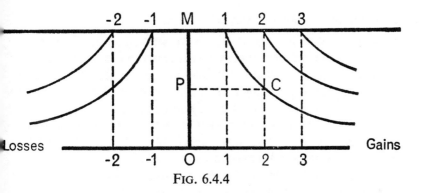

FIG. 6.4.4

indifference curves are rectangular hyperbolae.[1] The individual ranks the prospects according to the mean value of the utility pay-offs.

(6.4.5) The question now arises, which interpretation is correct? Do the terms arrived at by the gambling operation reflect the individual's valuations of sure prospects, or do they reflect his attitudes to risk?

The moral expectation theory does not give us any answer. The reason why people prefer a gamble to a sure prospect may be that they value greater pay-offs more than in proportion to their monetary worth or it may be that they like the gamble. Both interpretations are consistent with the condition that the measures of pay-offs are determined by the gambling operation. Whether these measures are called indices of indifference curves

[1] Krelle's assertion (*op. cit.*, p. 89) that his analysis is not affected by utilities being substituted for objective pay-offs is thus not correct.

or utility measures is quite irrelevant. No other significance must be attached to them than that they are numbers to be ascertained by that operation.

Following a well established usage we will call them utility measures. We must, however, bear in mind that their actual values depend on the individual's tastes, and that these cover also the individual's attitudes towards risk. Some forms of the love of danger are ruled out by the postulate discussed in (6.3.3) or by the conditions listed in (6.4.2). The utility measures reflect, however, the individual's attitudes to the gambles between which he is asked to choose. [1]

(6.5) *Friedman, Savage, and Markowitz*

(6.5.1) The conclusions at which we arrived in (6.2.7) apply to the moral-expectation theory as an explanation of instances of choices made by particular individuals in particular conditions. They may not apply if the theory is interpreted as an explanation not of any particular instance of behaviour but of some general feature of it. It may then turn out that although in particular instances the theory is not useful, it none the less predicts correctly something that is common to all of them.

This is how we must interpret Friedman and Savage's analysis of gambling and insurance. [2] The general feature of behaviour which it purports to explain is that the same people are often prepared both to gamble and to insure themselves. Marshall argued that if marginal utility of income diminishes as the amount of income increases, no rational person would accept a fair gamble. A fair insurance would be all right, because the utility of the sure prospect after the premium has been paid is less than the utility of the uncertain prospect which must be faced otherwise. In fact, however, people both gamble and insure themselves. Friedman and Savage's theory is an attempt to explain why this is so.

(6.5.2) The explanation hinges upon an empirical interpretation of the utility function. In Bernoulli's theory the subjective pay-offs are in terms of the 'intrinsic value' of what the individual

---

[1] Compare J. Marschak, Rational Behaviour, Uncertain Prospects, and Measurable Utility, *op. cit.*, pp. 137–9.

[2] M. Friedman and L. J. Savage, The Utility Analysis of Choices Involving Risk, *op. cit.*

may win. Marshall's utility is the degree of satisfaction which the individual would derive from the objective pay-offs. In either case the relevant term describes what the individual would experience or what would be his state of mind if the respective outcome came off. The operations in terms of which they are defined are anticipations of these experiences or states of mind to be ascertained by introspection. They may take the form of a marking operation or of a Jevonsian operation according to which of them is thought to be more suitable.

Friedman and Savage's argument is based on Von Neumann and Morgenstern's utility which is defined in terms of a gambling operation. It may serve as an index of the intrinsic value or of the degree of satisfaction because the individual is supposed to prefer the pay-offs to which a greater numerical value of utility is attached to those to which a smaller value is attached. But Von Neumann and Morgenstern's utility is not a cardinal measure of value or of satisfaction. The fact that the utility of a particular pay-off is twice as large as that of some other does not mean that the satisfaction from getting the former is twice as large as that from getting the latter. Utility in this case is only a theoretical term which has no other significance than that it is the result of a particular operation.

In Friedman and Savage's analysis we have to go even further than that. Utility of each pay-off is defined in it in terms of a gambling operation, but no significance is attached to its actual value. For in the actual fact it cannot be ascertained. What can be ascertained is only a certain description of the form of the utility function. It is, therefore, this description of the form of the utility function that we can accept as an essential element of the theory. The utilities themselves must not appear in it.

(6.5.3) The description of the form of the utility function is in terms of the utility curve being convex upwards or downwards. The fact that people often accept gambles which are not unfair to the other side implies that over the relevant range the utility curve is convex downwards. For if it were convex upwards, as in FIG. 6.1.6, the utility of the individual's present wealth would be greater than the moral expectation of pay-offs from the gamble, and no rational individual would accept the latter. If insurance is to be rational, the utility curve must be convex upwards. The individual would then find the moral expectation of pay-offs without insurance smaller than the utility of what he has got when he has paid the premium. Thus the implication of the fact that people both gamble and insure themselves is that the utility curve is convex upwards over the range which is relevant to insurance, and convex downwards over that which is relevant to gambling. How these two ranges combine into a single curve can be derived from the observation that the stakes in gambling and the premiums in insurance are usually small in relation to possible gains and losses.

The argument is as follows. The fact that stakes in gambling are usually small in relation to prizes which may be won, implies that the worst pay-off from the gamble that the individual needs to consider is only slightly smaller than the sure prospect of retaining what one has already got if one does not gamble. For the worst that the individual may expect from the gamble is that he pays the stake and does not win the prize. The worst pay-off must thus be represented by a point on his utility function which is only slightly to the left from that which represents his present position. The pay-offs from the other prospects must be represented by points more to the right. The part of the utility curve which is convex downwards must thus be to the right of the point which represents the individual's present position.

If the individual contemplates insurance, the arrangement is the other way round. If he insures himself, he is certain that he will keep what he has got now less the insurance premium. If he does not insure himself, the best that he can expect is that he will keep what he has got now and has not paid the premium. The worst is much less than that because if he is not insured he may suffer losses which are much greater than the insurance premium. Thus in this case the relevant range of the utility curve is to the left of the point representing the individual's present position. It is, therefore, to the left of that point that the curve must be convex upwards. [1]

[1] The utility curve need not be convex downwards in the range which is relevant to gambling, and it need not be convex upwards in the range which is relevant to insurance, if gains from bamgling and losses due to lack of insurance are cumulative. Large gains may put the individual in a better position to have further gains from his business or from his work, and large losses may make his position worse and lead to further losses. (See K. J. Arrow, Alternative Approaches to the Theory of Choice in Risk-Taking Situations, *op. cit.*) In our discussion of the moral expectation theory we will disregard this complication, but we will return to it in (9.5).

(6.5.4) The conclusion is thus that if an individual is willing both to insure himself against large losses and to gamble for large prizes on terms which are not unfair to the other side, his utility curve is convex upwards to the left and convex downwards to the right of that point on it which corresponds to his present position. This is what within the context of the moral-expectation theory can be derived about the form of the utility curve from observable facts. The actual level of utility at each point on the curve may not be ascertainable. But the form of the curve can be ascertained. Its description in terms of convexity upwards and downwards is as explained in the preceding paragraph.

(6.5.5) Friedman and Savage's original formulation of this conclusion was slightly different. The utility curve was described by them as turning from one form to the other at a point which might not correspond to the individual's present position. The inflexion point had its own independent existence. The hypothesis was rather the other way round. Most people were supposed to have their present position at that point and were, therefore, both gambling and insuring themselves. But there were also very poor people whose present positions were much to the left and very rich people whose present positions were much to the right of the inflexion point. They behaved differently. The observation that people both gamble and insure themselves was accepted as established for the middle income groups only. No evidence seemed to be available for those who were below or above the middle.

The formulation in which the inflexion point is determined by the individual's present position is that of Markowitz.[1] He thought that Friedman and Savage's original hypothesis might easily lead to predictions which are contrary to the facts. For it implies that a very poor individual, whose present position is very far to the left of the inflexion point, would never accept a fair gamble; and a very wealthy individual would never insure himself. Furthermore, an individual whose wealth is moderately above the inflexion point would always prefer a fair gamble to what he has actually got. None of these is true. The hypothesis that a poor individual's present position is to the left and that

[1] H. Markowitz, The Utility of Wealth, *Journal of Political Economy*, **LX**, April (1952), pp. 151–8.

of a rich individual is to the right of the point of inflexion doe
not seem, therefore, to be acceptable. All we can say is that i
an individual does not accept fair gambles for large prizes o
does not insure himself against large losses, his utility curv
must not be convex downwards over the range which is relevan
to the former and not convex upwards over the range which i
relevant to the latter. And if he both gambles and insures him
self, the inflexion point of his utility curve must correspond t
his present position. No connection, however, can be establishe
between these possibilities and the amount of wealth which th
individual has got.

To explain certain aspects of our behaviour in repetitive game
Markowitz distinguished also between present wealth (that whicl
the individual has actually got when he makes up his mind
whether to accept or reject the next gamble) and customar
wealth (that which he regards as truly his, net any windfal
gains or losses which may easily go or be made up as the game
proceeds). The argument about the position of the point of in
flexion applies then more to the latter than to the former. The
distinction, however, is not very relevant to our present discussion and may be neglected.

(6.6) Further Refinements

(6.6.1) Some further information about the form of the utility
curve can be derived from the fact that lotteries have usually
more than one price. Friedman and Savage have shown that to
offer several smaller prizes rather than a single big prize can be
a reasonable policy on the part of the lotteries only if the convexity downwards of the utility curve of those who buy the
tickets turns again into convexity upwards further to the right.
Markowitz derived the same conclusion from the fact that if all
prizes from a lottery are increased in the same proportion, there
is always a limit beyond which the price of the ticket has to be
increased less than in proportion. For otherwise the individual
would refuse to gamble.

(6.6.2) Friedman and Savage's argument is as follows. Suppose that n lottery tickets are going to be sold and that the total
amount offered in prizes is equal to a. Two strategies may be
considered. In one of them one prize only is offered, equal to a.

192

The probability of winning it is $1/n$. In the other strategy two prizes are offered, each equal to $a/2$. The probability of winning $a/2$ is then $2/n$. Suppose further that the prizes which the individuals have to pay for their tickets are p_1 in the first case and p_2 in the second. The possible monetary gains and losses of those who buy the tickets are then $(a - p_1)$ and $(-p_1)$ if the lottery chooses the first strategy, and $(a/2 - p_2)$ and $(-p_2)$ if it chooses the second. Let finally the present wealth of individual j, different probably for different individuals, be w_j. The moral expectations of pay-offs are then

$$\frac{1}{n} U\left[(w_j - p_1) + a\right] + \left(1 - \frac{1}{n}\right) U\left[(w_j - p_1)\right] =$$
$$\frac{1}{n} \left\{U\left[(w_j - p_1) + a\right] - U\left[(w_j - p_1)\right]\right\} + U\left[(w_j - p_1)\right]$$

for the first strategy, and

$$\frac{2}{n} U\left[(w_j - p_2) + \frac{a}{2}\right] + \left(1 - \frac{2}{n}\right) U\left[(w_j - p_2)\right] =$$
$$\frac{2}{n} \left\{U\left[(w_j - p_2) + \frac{a}{2}\right] - U\left[(w_j - p_2)\right]\right\} + U\left[(w_j - p_2)\right]$$

for the second strategy.

If now the objective of those who organize the lottery is to maximize their profits, both p_1 and p_2 must be set so that the marginal buyers of the tickets are indifferent whether they buy them or not; their moral expectations of pay-offs must be equal to the utility of their present wealth. Thus if profits were maximized in either of the above two cases, the moral expectations arrived at above must also be equal one to the other and

$$\frac{1}{n}\left\{U\left[(w_j - p_1) + a\right] - U\left[(w_j - p_1)\right]\right\} -$$
$$\frac{2}{n}\left\{U\left[(w_j - p_2) + \frac{a}{2}\right] - U\left[(w_j - p_2)\right]\right\} =$$
$$U\left[(w_j - p_2)\right] - U\left[(w_j - p_1)\right]$$

Otherwise either, not all the tickets would be sold, or the prices set for them would not be the highest possible that the buyers would be prepared to pay.

The second strategy would then lead to greater profits only if the marginal utility of income was diminishing. For p_2 greater

193

than p_1 implies that the right-hand side of the above equation is negative, and thus

$$2\left\{ U\left[(w_j - p_2) + \frac{a}{2}\right] - U\left[(w_j - p_2)\right]\right\} >$$
$$U\left[(w_j - p_1) + a\right] - U\left[(w_j - p_1)\right]$$

This could not be satisfied if the marginal utility of income were constant. For the increase in utility due to $a/2$ being added to $(w_j - p_2)$ would then be exactly one-half of the increase in it due to a being added to $(w_j - p_1)$ – quite irrespective of what are the utilities of $(w_j - p_1)$ and $(w_j - p_2)$ – and the above expression would be an equality. Nor could the inequality be satisfied if the marginal utility of income were increasing. For the increase in total utility due to $a/2$ being added would then be less than one-half of that due to a being added even if p_1 were equal to p_2; and it would be even more so if p_2 were greater than p_1. The left-hand side of the above expression would thus be less than the right-hand side. The condition can be satisfied for $p_2 > p_1$ only if the marginal utility is diminishing. Hence Friedman and Savage's conclusion that as most lotteries offer more than one prize, the prices which they can obtain for their tickets must be higher in that case than they would be if one very big prize only were offered, and thus the utility curve must be convex upwards over the relevant range.

(6.6.3) It has been already mentioned in (6.6.1) that Markowitz arrived at the same conclusion in a different way. He asked himself what would be the most likely response to offers of lottery tickets at higher and higher prices, giving the same chances of higher and higher prizes. Suppose, for instance, that we are prepared to buy a ticket which gives us a 1/100-th chance of winning £100 if the price of the ticket is £1. Would we be prepared to buy a similar ticket if the possible prize were £1000 and the price of the ticket £10? Or £10000 and £100 respectively? The answer is that even if we were prepared to pay £1 for a 1/100-th chance of winning £100, we would not be prepared to pay £n for a 1/100-th chance of winning £100n if n were sufficiently large. For rich people n may be very large. For poor ones it may be very small. But everybody has his limit beyond which he would not be prepared to go. For everybody, therefore, the utility curve must turn from convex downwards to convex upwards at some point to the right of his present position.

194

The observation that people who gamble at small prices for small gains are not prepared to do so if both prices and gains become very large, plays in Markowitz's argument the same part as does the observation that lotteries have usually more than one prize in the argument of Friedman and Savage's. It is an empirical generalization from which we derive certain characteristics of the form of the utility curve.

(6.6.4) Similar considerations apply to insurance. For it may be argued that although many people might be prepared to insure themselves against losses of £100 at a premium of £1, they would not do so if the losses were £100n and the premium £n. There is a certain limit for n beyond which they would not go. At some distance to the left from the individual's present position his utility curve must thus turn from convex upwards to convex downwards.

(6.6.5) The conclusion that the utility curve turns from convex upwards to convex downwards somewhere to the left of the individual's present position could also be derived from the fact that the insurance policies are often comprehensive, covering several risks at a single premium. The argument would then follow the same line as that of Friedman and Savage with respect to lotteries with several prizes. For it could be shown that only if the utility curve turns from convex upwards to convex downwards for large losses, insurance companies would be able to obtain higher premiums on comprehensive policies than on those covering single risks up to the same total amount. Comprehensive insurance policies, however, are not a general rule, at any rate less so than lotteries with more than one prize. It is doubtful, therefore, if the actual practice in this respect would justify any definite conclusions about the form of the utility curve. Friedman and Savage did not make this point at all. The convexity downwards at the extreme left of the utility curve was introduced by Markowitz on quite different grounds.

(6.7) Appraisal and Criticism

(6.7.1) The conclusion that over certain parts of the utility curve marginal utility of income is increasing may not be acceptable to those who regard utility as a measure of satisfaction. For to discover what this utility is they appeal usually to introspection, and then they find their experiences not quite in line with the marginal utility increasing over any range of the utility curve. It has been pointed out in (6.5.2) that a criticism along these lines would not be valid. Von Neumann and Morgenstern's utility is not a measure of satisfaction, and the tendency for marginal utility to increase cannot be disproved by introspection. Even, however, if utility were a measure of satisfaction, the conclusion that marginal utility is increasing over some ranges of the utility curve may not be as contrary to what we actually experience as might seem at first sight. For a movement along the utility curve means often not only an increase in the individual's income but also a change in his status, a jump from a lower to a higher socio-economic group. Increasing marginal utility over the segments of the curve which cover such jumps might thus be quite acceptable even as a description of the experience which can be gained by introspection. Small increases in income which do not lead to any changes in the individual's status may not give him as much satisfaction as to make him accept a fair gamble for them; and large increases, which help him to jump to a higher socio-economic group may give him so much more of it that he may be prepared to gamble for them even on conditions which are not quite fair to him. Over those ranges of income which do not exceed the limits of a particular socio-economic group the marginal utility of income may thus be diminishing; but over those which cover the jumps from one group to another it may be increasing, even if it is defined in terms of a Jevonsian or a marking operation.

(6.7.2) The argument applies both to Friedman and Savage's and to Markowitz's versions of the theory. The difference is only that in the latter case the range of the utility curve around its main inflexion point corresponds to the level of wealth of that socio-economic group to which the respective individual actually belongs, whereas in the case of Friedman and Savage the position of the inflexion point is independent of the income group. Markowitz's version is consistent with a subjective interpretation of utility at the other points as well. For it may be argued that as soon as the individual reaches a higher socio-economic group, the satisfaction he would derive from further and further increments of income would be less and less, and the utility curve would become again convex upwards. Similarly a loss which would bring him to a lower socio-economic group might mean to him a very large drop in the degree of satisfaction which he derives from his income, and losses which are greater than that might not make much more difference to him. Thus further to the left, the utility curve turns from convex upwards to convex downwards.

(6.7.3) One may, however, well ask what is the purpose of tracing all these waves of the utility curve. What does the theory explain? In Von Neumann and Morgenstern's rendering it might be supposed to explain the actual choices made in actual conditions. For if we could determine the utilities of all the possible pay-offs, we would be able to predict what choices the respective individual would make. And if these predictions turned out to conform to the facts, the theory might be accepted as an explanation of these facts.

If, however, we take the view that the operation specified in Von Neumann and Morgenstern's theory does not permit us to determine utility but only defines it, and that the most that the theory enables us to do is to derive from the observation of our behaviour certain general characteristics of the utility curve, no predictions of actual choices can be obtained from it and no actual choices explained. The question thus arises, what does the theory explain? Perhaps if some other aspects of our behaviour were taken into account, further waves in the utility curve could be added to those which are already there. But this would not change the fact that in tracing out these waves we move from the facts which we know to the utility curve and not the other way round, not from the waves on the utility curve to the prediction of facts of which we do not know.

(6.7.4) Friedman and Savage have shown that it is possible to move also in the opposite direction, from the waves on the utility curve to the prediction of facts other than those from which the waves have been derived. We have got a whole list of such predictions. Most of them are valid only if the form of the utility curve is independent of the individual's present position. They would not, therefore, be acceptable to Markowitz. But none the less it may be useful to consider some of them to have a clearer view of the whole theory.

Consider the following example. Suppose that the present wealth of the individual is small, and that his present position

197

is, therefore, at some point on that part of the utility curve to the left of the main point of inflexion which is convex upwards. An individual of this type would not gamble for moderate prizes. He would insure himself against moderate risks. He might gamble for large and improbable prizes. But on the whole he would prefer more secure investments to more risky ones. Thus the prediction which can be derived from the theory is that most people in lower income groups should receive their incomes from property in the form of interest and rents. This seems to be confirmed by facts.

Similar considerations apply to individuals in higher income groups, whose present positions are in the upper part of the utility curve convex upwards. They too prefer to play safe. Those, however, who are in the middle prefer more risky investments. They are then likely to move quickly up or down according to whether they win or lose. There should, therefore, be relatively few investors in this group and a relatively small supply of funds seeking this type of investment. Hence the prediction that the rate of return to moderately risky investments should be higher than that to very safe or very risky ones. And this too seems to be confirmed by facts.

(6.7.5) Neither of these predictions can be derived from Markowitz's version of the theory. For no distinction is made in it between different income groups. The form of the utility curve is supposed to be the same for everybody. It would be possible to argue that as in the lower and in the higher income groups wealth is usually held in more secure form than in the middle income groups, the form of the utility curves of the individuals who belong to the former must deviate in some consistent way from that in the latter. In lower income groups the curves must have their main inflexion points to the right of the respective individuals' present positions, and in higher income groups the inflexion points must be more to the left. This, however, would have nothing to do with the prediction of any new facts. Further refinements would only be added to the hypothesis about the form of the utility curve.

(6.7.6) The modern developments in the moral-expectation theory are a perfect example of the application of the Popperian methodology of science. First a hypothesis is formulated to accommodate certain known facts. Then predictions of other facts are derived from it. These are confronted with what actually takes place. And if the two do not agree, the hypothesis is modified so as to accommodate also those other facts. Von Neumann and Morgenstern's hypothesis was formulated to accommodate the facts that people are consistent in their ranking of the available alternatives, that they prefer a greater to a smaller income, that they prefer a more probable income to a less probable one, and so on. It was then supplemented by Friedman and Savage with some details about the form of the utility curve to accommodate the facts of gambling and of insurance. From these details predictions were derived that most people in the lower income groups should receive their incomes in the form of interest and rents, that the rate of return to moderately risky investments should be higher than that to very safe or very risky ones, and so on. Those predictions have been confirmed by facts. Other predictions, such for instance as that the individuals in the middle income groups should as a rule be prepared to pay premiums for symmetrical gambles have been contradicted by what actually takes place. Further refinements, therefore, have been added to the theory by Markowitz to make its predictions conform with these facts as well.

This is how science is progressing in all its fields. Hypotheses are formulated. They are then disproved by some facts, amended so as to accommodate these facts, disproved again, and again amended. As a result of this process theories develop which accommodate more and more facts and give us more and more insight into the actual working of the world in which we live. In the case of the moral-expectation theory we seem, therefore, to be on the right road. But this does not mean yet that we have gone very far on it. In its present form the theory can accommodate only some very general facts.

PART THREE

SELECTIVE REDUCTIONS

In ALL the theories discussed in Part Two the individuals were supposed to behave as if their expectations were sure prospects. The hypothesis was that the original prospects were either sure prospects, or that they could be reduced to their sure-prospect equivalents, and that the individuals behaved as if they were adjusting themselves to those equivalents. The method and the significance of the reduction differed from one case to another. The outcomes in the original prospect were aggregated by means of a formula; or the sure-prospect equivalents were arrived at (as we called it) by choice. The pay-offs were either in their original, monetary form; or they too had to be reduced first to subjective utility measures. All cases, however, had this in common that the expectations in them were reduced (i) to a sure-prospect form, and (ii) before the choice of the strategy. The pay-offs from the possible states of the world might have been determined by the strategy. But the reduction of those pay-offs was thought to be independent of it.

The hypotheses to be discussed in the next two chapters differ from this pattern in either one or the other of these two respects. Chapter 7 deals with Shackle's theory in which the equivalents to which the original prospects are reduced are not sure prospects. The reduced form contains not one but two outcomes. And Chapter 8 deals with the theory of games, in which the state of the world which is supposed to come off depends not only on the behaviour of the world but also on the individual's strategy. The reduction of the original prospect depends, therefore, on the latter.

Chapter 9 is a mixture of several things. It deals with hypotheses which do not fit very well into any of the categories which have been discussed before. But they have no common features which would justify putting them together as members of yet another class. None of them has ever played a very important part in economic theory. They will, therefore, be treated more summarily than those in the other parts of the book. They deserve, however, attention as interesting contributions to the field which the book is supposed to cover.

7

Shackle's Theory of Expectations

As HAS been already mentioned in the introduction to this part of the book, Shackle's theory of expectations presupposes a reduction of multi-outcome prospects to the form of not one but of two outcomes. They are not sure prospects because two different outcomes cannot be both of them sure. They are only of zero degree of potential surprise. The individual is supposed to be not at all surprised if one rather than the other comes off. The adjustment of the individual's position does not take then the form of choosing a strategy to which corresponds the greatest sure-prospect equivalent of pay-offs. It requires some weighing up of the two outcomes to which the original prospect has been reduced.

The theory has its place between those which were discussed in Chapters 4–6 and the theory of games which will be discussed in Chapter 8. For although it presupposes a reduction of multi-outcome prospects, it provides also for adjustments to more than one outcome at a time. In the theories discussed in the preceding chapters the second element was not there because the adjustments were to sure-prospect equivalents as if there were no other outcomes at all. In the theory of games the first element is absent because the choice of the strategy determines the sure-prospect equivalent.

An important limitation of Shackle's theory is that it applies to expectations in those cases only in which no objective probability weights can be attached to the respective outcomes. This rules out the possibility of either ratios of equally likely cases being derived from the characteristics of the mechanism on the working of which the result depends, or of any habits of thought to use frequency distributions of results in repetitive events as probability weights of outcomes in the prospects of single events.

Situations in which these conditions are not satisfied are outside the scope of the theory.

(7.1) Focus Gain and Focus Loss

(7.1.1) Shackle's formal representation of a multi-outcome prospect was discussed in (3.5) and (3.6). Its main feature is that the weights of the outcomes are measures of potential surprise to be ascertained by introspection. Potential surprise measures the degree to which the particular outcome is regarded as possible. If there is nothing in the evidence that could prevent the coming off of the outcome, the outcome is absolutely possible, and the degree of potential surprise attached to it is zero. The individual would not experience any sensation of surprise if the outcome happened to come off. If the evidence is such that the outcome is virtually impossible, a maximum degree of potential surprise is attached to it.

The actual numerical value of the maximum degree of potential surprise is arbitrary. As soon, however, as it is decided upon numerical measures may be attached to the degrees of potential surprise of other outcomes by means of a marking or of a Jevonsian operation. The individual must only be able to mark consistently the intensity, or to rank the differences in intensity, of potential surprise. If this condition is not satisfied, potential surprise can be ranked only. Shackle maintained that his argument was independent of whether potential surprise was ranked or measured. In fact this is not quite so. We will see in a while that in his theory potential surprise appears as a variable in a function which ranks combinations of prospects and weights. The form of the function which determines the latter ranking cannot then be independent of the form of the function which has been chosen as the index of the former.

(7.1.2) The subject of expectations in Shackle's theory is profits and losses. The prospects are the amounts of money which an individual may gain or lose. The weights of potential surprise attached to them may thus be treated as a function of profits and losses, and the prospect as a particular form of that function. To each strategy corresponds a different prospect of profits and losses, a different potential surprise function. The individual's decision which strategy to choose, depends on his evaluation of each of these functions from the point of view of the objective which he wants to achieve.

In general, the objective is to have the greatest possible profits. But at the time when the decision is taken neither profits nor losses are yet there. The choice is not between different levels of profits but between different potential surprise functions representing prospects of profits. Thus what the individual really obtains when he chooses a particular strategy is not profits but only his being in a position to contemplate a certain prospect of profits. The prospect is a particular view of the future. This view of the future is, therefore what determines his decision. The individual chooses that strategy which makes the future the most pleasurable for him to contemplate.

(7.1.3) The question now arises, how is this choice actually made? The relevant hypothesis is that in evaluating the prospects people concentrate their attention on two outcomes only, on one outcome of a gain and on one outcome of a loss. Which outcome they select depends on how strongly their imagination is stimulated by the particular combinations of profits or losses and degrees of potential surprise. When they contemplate a particular prospect, some of the combinations of profits or losses and degrees of potential surprise which appear in it, attract their attention more than others. The reason may be that the respective profits or losses are higher, or that the degrees of potential surprise are lower. Shackle's hypothesis is that the combination of profits and potential surprise which attracts the individual's attention more than any other in which profits appear, and the combination of losses and potential surprise which attracts his attention more than any other in which losses appear, are the only ones that are relevant to the evaluation of the respective prospect.

These two combinations of pay-offs and the corresponding degrees of potential surprise are called *primary focus gain* and *primary focus loss*. They are points on the potential surprise function, one in the region of the outcomes of gains and the other in the region of the outcomes of losses. Shackle has given a formal and very elaborate analysis of the selection of these points. First, all possible combinations of outcomes of profits and losses and of the degrees of potential surprise are ranked according to how strongly they stimulate the individual's imagination. And then the combinations which belong to a particular prospect are superimposed on all the possible ones, and the degree to which each combination in the former stimulates the individual's imagination is read off from the ranking of the latter. We will neglect the details of these technical parts of the theory. A summary diagram may be found at the end of this section. What is important is that the individual is supposed to focus his attention on two combinations of pay-offs and degrees of potential surprise only. The information that the combinations are those which attract most his attention does not add anything to what has already been said.

(7.1.4) Primary focus gain and primary focus loss are each a combination of a pay-off and of a weight. They are two-dimensional. But they can be reduced to a one-dimensional form if we find an outcome of a gain or of a loss with zero degree of potential surprise which attracts the individual's attention as much as the primary focus gain or the primary focus loss does. We have such zero-surprise outcomes, one on the side of gains and one on the side of losses. They are one-dimensional and have been called by Shackle the *standardized focus gain* and the *standardized focus loss*. As they attract the individual's attention as much as the primary focus gain and the primary focus loss do, the evaluation of the prospect from which they have been derived is not affected by them being substituted for the primary ones.

(7.1.5) Is it always necessary for a prospect of pay-offs to include the outcomes of both gains and losses? It is possible that in the individual's opinion a particular strategy cannot lead to a monetary loss or that it cannot lead to a monetary gain. Would not then maximum degrees of potential surprise be attached to all outcomes of losses in the first case and to all outcomes of gains in the second case? The difficulty, however, is more semantic than real. Gains and losses must here be understood in a relative sense. The criterion of them being regarded as gains or as losses is that the individual experiences pleasure or displeasure when contemplating the possibility of them coming off. If all the outcomes with less than maximum degree of potential surprise promise some monetary gain, this does not mean yet that the possibility of any of them coming off must be contemplated by the individual with pleasure. He looks at them as if he already were in possession of some gain. If, therefore, only a very small gain came off, he would not regard it as a gain at all. In the subjective sense it would be for him a loss.

(7.1.6) Without going into the details of Shackle's elaborate geometrical technique, it may be useful to illustrate his ideas by means of the following diagram. Let the monetary pay-offs be measured along the horizontal axis. Point N represents a neutral pay-off. The possibility of its coming off is looked upon by the individual neither with pleasure nor with displeasure. To the right of N are the outcomes of gains; to the left of it are outcomes of losses; greater the further away they are from N.

The vertical axis represents the degrees of potential surprise. Zero is at N, and the maximum at some arbitrary point M. The

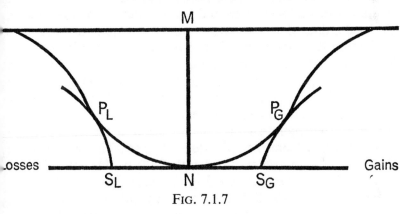

FIG. 7.1.7

prospect is represented by a curve of potential surprise which at first follows the horizontal axis to the left and to the right from N, and then moves upwards towards the maximum. The part of the curve which coincides with the horizontal axis is the inner range of the prospect. The greater are the gains or the losses the possibility of which the individual takes into account, the more surprised he would be if they came off. Hence the curve of potential surprise slopes upwards as we move to the right and to the left from the inner range.

Let the primary focus loss and the primary focus gain be represented by P_L and P_G respectively. They attract the individual's attention more than any other points on the respective sides of the curve. Standardized focus loss and standardized focus gain are S_L and S_G. They are on the horizontal axis because zero-degree of potential surprise is attached to them; and they are also on the two loci of the combinations of pay-offs and degrees of potential surprise which attract the individual's attention as much as the primary focus gain and focus loss do. We will call these two loci *standardization loci*. As the primary focus gain and focus loss attract the individual's attention more than any other outcome of gains and losses in the prospect, the standardization loci $S_L P_L$ and $S_G P_G$ are tangential to the potential surprise curve at P_L and P_G.

(7.2) Gambler Indifference Curves

(7.2.1) The reduction of multi-outcome prospects, each to a pair of standardized focus gains and focus losses, is the first step in the evaluation of the strategies which give rise to them. The evaluation is on the basis of these two outcomes only. As soon as they are selected, all others are supposed to be forgotten. A multi-outcome prospect is a datum for the selection of the focus gain and focus loss. In the ultimate evaluation of the strategy which gives rise to it, it plays no part at all.

(7.2.2) The second step is the derivation of the actual choice of the strategy from the individual's 'tastes'. The hypothesis is that there exists a system of rankings of all possible pairs of focus gains and focus losses, according to which the particular individual prefers to which. If the view of the future summarized in one of them is more attractive to the individual than that summarized in some other pair, the former is ranked higher than the latter.

If all the prospects are reduced to the form of standardized focus gains and standardized focus losses, their ranking may be represented by a system of indifference curves. Shackle called them *gambler indifference curves*. In FIG. 7.2.2 standardized focus gains are measured along the vertical axis and standardized focus losses along the horizontal axis. Thus each point on the diagram represents a pair of standardized focus gains and focus losses. The view of the future summarized in such a pair is more desirable to contemplate, the greater is the element of focus gain in it, and the smaller the element of focus loss. Thus a locus of points representing equally desirable pairs, those with respect to which the individual is indifferent whether he contemplates one or the other, must be a curve sloping upwards as we move to the right. For if a view of the future with a smaller focus gain is to be as desirable as a view with a greater focus gain, its focus loss must also be smaller.

At the origin the standardized focus gain and the standardized focus loss are both of them equal to the neutral prospect N. The individual does not pay then any attention to the possibility of either gaining or losing anything in relation to what he thinks he has already got. The points on the indifference curve which passes through the origin represent the views of the future which

Standardised
Focus Gain

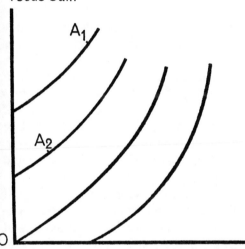

FIG. 7.2.2

the individual regards as equally desirable as that of no gain and no loss. The curves more to the right represent views which are less desirable than no gain and no loss; and those more to the left represent views which are more desirable than that. The more to the left is the curve, the more desirable are the pairs of focus gains and focus losses which correspond to it. The more to the right it is, the less desirable are those pairs.

(7.2.3) The exact form of the indifference curve depends on the individual's 'tastes'. If, for instance, the individual is very cautious, he needs a large increase in the focus gain to compensate even a small increase in the focus loss. His indifference

211

curves are thus very steep. A more reckless individual has more shallow curves. Each individual has probably a certain limit of a focus loss, which means a complete ruin to him and which he would never be willing to contemplate. Most probably, all the indifference curves bend, therefore, ultimately upwards and approach asymptotically a vertical line corresponding to that limit. The more the standardized focus loss approaches the limit, the greater must be the increase in the standardized focus gain to compensate it.

But it may also be argued that reckless individuals need not be repelled by a focus loss which means a complete ruin to them. A high value of the focus gain may still be sufficient to make the respective view of the future desirable. A further increase in the focus loss may then be quite irrelevant. For ruin is the worst that may actually happen. In this case the indifference curves might thus be getting less and less steep the further away from the origin we move along them.

It seems, therefore, that nothing conclusive can be said about the exact form of the gambler indifference curves. Any form in fact may be derived from our common-sense knowledge of human nature. The only restriction that quite definitely must be accepted is that the curves are sloping upwards. This, however, leaves plenty of room for special cases which the theory could cover but which it could not predict.

(7.2.4) The act of choice of a strategy consists in reading off the ranks of the pairs of standardized focus gains and focus losses to which various strategies give rise from the system of the individual's gambler indifference map and in selecting that strategy which gives rise to a pair with the highest rank. Thus if the standardized focus gain and the standardized focus loss from strategy A_1 are as indicated by point A_1, and those from strategy A_2 are as indicated by point A_2, the individual will choose strategy A_1. It is on a higher indifference curve and has, therefore, a higher rank.

(7.2.5) Does the concept of a gambler indifference map imply any hypotheses about our behaviour? It implies consistency in it. But this is about all we can say. The form of the curves is so general that practically any behaviour is covered by it, and any prediction can be derived from it.

To judge Shackle's theory by its power to furnish predictions would not, however, do justice to the author's intentions. For the theory was formulated not so much to predict any actual choices of strategies as to give an interpretation of the mental processes involved in them. The purpose was to devise a conceptual framework which would make it easier for us to communicate to other people what we experience when we make such choices and to analyse our reasons for them.

(7.3) Spreading the Risks

(7.3.1) Strategies may be regarded as comparable on the ground of the prospects of pay-offs to which they give rise only if they are identical in every other respect. Thus if the individual has a certain amount of capital which he can invest in various ways, the strategies are these various ways in which his capital can be invested, including that of leaving it wholly or partly idle. Strategy A_1, for instance, may mean that the whole capital is invested in securities, not necessarily all of them of the same kind; strategy A_2 that one-half of the individual's capital is invested in securities and the other half kept in cash as a reserve; A_3 may mean buying a shop and keeping the rest in cash; and so on. In all these cases the focus gains and losses, and in consequence the ranking of the strategies which give rise to them, correspond to different ways in which the whole capital is invested and not to those of any particular parts of it.

Originally Shackle tried to arrive at focus gains and focus losses from different ways of investing the whole capital by aggregating those from different parts of it. This, however, made his theory inconsistent with the principle of spreading the risks. As the point has become a subject of controversy and has often been referred to in the literature, a few words may also be said about it in this book.

(7.3.2) The argument was as follows.[1] Suppose that an individual has a certain capital K which he may invest in two ways. Let the standardized focus gains and focus losses corresponding to these two ways be g', l' and g'', l'', respectively. According to Shackle the relation between them and the amounts of capital invested may be treated as linear. Thus $g' = a'RK$, $l' = b'RK$,

[1] What follows is a very simplified version of Chapter IV of Shackle's *Expectation in Economics* (2nd ed.), Cambridge University Press (1952).

$g'' = a''(1 - R)K$ and $l'' = b''(1 - R)K$, where a's and b's are constants and R is the proportion of the total capital invested in the first way.

The overall focus gain and focus loss from both forms of investment taken together is equal to the sum of those from the two forms of investment taken separately. Thus

$$g = g' + g'' = [(a' - a'')R + a'']K$$

and $$1 = l' + l'' = [(b' - b'')R + b'']K$$

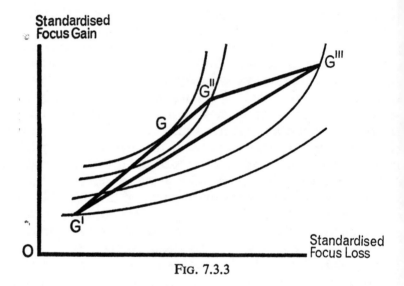

Standardised Focus Gain

Standardised Focus Loss

O

FIG. 7.3.3

Either of them is thus a linear function of R. If we eliminate R from the above equations,

$$g = \frac{a' - a''}{b' - b''} \cdot 1 + \left[a'' - \frac{a' - a''}{b' - b''} \cdot b'' \right] K$$

and one becomes also a linear function of the other.

(7.3.3) If the individual can divide his capital between the two forms of investment as he wishes, he may adjust R so as to obtain a combination of g and l which is on a higher indifference curve than any other. The opportunities which are open to him are shown by the line $G'G''$ in FIG. 7.3.3. Point G' represents the focus gain and focus loss from the strategy of investing the

214

whole capital in the first way. Proportion R is then equal to unity. Point G'' represents $g = g''$ and $l = l''$ when R is equal to zero. Focus gains and focus losses corresponding to the strategies of R less than unity and greater than zero are then shown by points on $G'G''$. As the relation between them is linear, $G'G''$ is a straight line.

If the individual had to choose between either the first or the second form of investment, he would choose the second form. For if his gambler indifference map is as in FIG. 7.3.3, G'' is on a higher indifference curve than G'. If, however, he could divide his capital between the two forms of investment, he would choose the strategy represented by G which is between the other two, that is to say he would divide his capital between the first and the second form.

(7.3.4) It may now be shown that even if more than two ways of investing one's capital were available, not more than two would be chosen. For suppose that in addition to the forms of investment which give rise to focus gains and focus losses of G' and G'', there is also a third form which gives rise to those of G'''? By combining the second and the third form, the individual may then reach any point along the line $G''G'''$; by combining the first and the third he may reach any point on $G'G'''$; and by combining the three forms of investment together he may reach any point in the triangle $G'G''G'''$. All the latter must, however, be on lower indifference curves than that which is tangential to the boundary $G'G''G'''$. Only a boundary point, therefore, corresponding to a combination of not more than two forms of investment, may be chosen.

The number of the forms of investment which the individual may choose depends in this case on the number of the focus outcomes. If the ranks of the various strategies were determined by three focus outcomes, the boundary of the points representing all possible combinations of those outcomes would be a surface, and a point on it would correspond to a combination of three forms of investment. Is not, therefore, Shackle's hypothesis of two focus outcomes disproved by the fact that people behave often in accordance with the principle of spreading the risks?

(7.3.5) The answer is in the negative. For the conclusion that with two focus outcomes not more than two forms of investment can be chosen, depends also on the assumption that the relation between focus outcomes from particular forms of investment and the amounts of capital invested in them is linear. If this relation were not linear, the relation between the overall focus gains and focus losses would not be linear either. The line $G'G''$ (a curve in that case) could then be above $G'G''G'''$. And a point corresponding to a combination of three forms of investment could be above either of them.

Furthermore, the addition of the focus gains and focus losses from particular forms of investment to obtain the overall one from all the capital at the individual's disposal implies perfect correlation between the former. The individual is supposed to concentrate his attention on the sum of all focus gains and on the sum of all focus losses. The possibility of losses from some investments being offset by gains from some others is not taken into account. In fact, however, the latter is the situation to which the principle of spreading the risks applies. The individual regards the outcome of all losses or of all gains as very unlikely and if he had to focus his attention on two outcomes only, he would choose those in which losses from some forms of investment combine with gains from the others. The overall focus gains and focus losses would not then be totals of those from all forms of investment; and a combination of a large number of the latter might give rise to a pair of them which is higher up on the individual's scale of preference than any of the pairs from a smaller number of the forms of investment.[1]

It seems, therefore, that Shackle's theory is not so much disproved by the fact that many people behave in accordance with the principle of spreading the risks, as that it is empty in this respect. In general, focus outcomes of pay-offs from the whole capital cannot be derived from those of any particular parts of it. The pairs of focus outcomes which the individual compares on his gambler indifference map may correspond to strategies of spreading the risks as well as to those of putting all eggs in one basket. The theory does not permit us to distinguish between them.

[1] The point was discussed more fully by R. A. D. Egerton in, Investment, Uncertainty and Expectations, *Review of Economic Studies*, **XXII** (2), (1954–5), pp. 143–50; and in, *Investment Decisions under Uncertainty*, Liverpool University Press (1960), pp. 18–22.

7.4) Deferred Action

7.4.1) Another attempt to arrive at focus outcomes of pay-offs from a strategy by combining those from some parts of it has been made by Shackle in connection with his analysis of the motives for holding capital resources liquid.[1] The question is his. Suppose that a number of strategies is available to an individual, which may be started right now. If confronted with those only, the individual would choose that strategy which gives rise to focus outcomes of pay-offs represented by a point on the highest indifference curve that he can reach. Suppose, however, that he may also adopt the strategy of keeping his capital in a liquid form and investing it later on, when more information will be available about possible profits from the respective projects. Is it possible for the focus outcomes from this strategy of deferred action to be on a higher indifference curve than those of an immediate action? And what is the relation between the overall focus outcomes from the strategy of deferred action and the focus outcomes from the projects which may be chosen when the time for action arrives?

(7.4.2) An obvious condition for a positive answer to the first question is that more information about profitability of various projects will really become available later on. It is by no means certain that this must be so. For although with the passage of time some expectations about the immediate future become clarified, more future becomes also relevant. It is, therefore, possible for the individual to become better informed only in such cases in which some crucial facts about the future become revealed at some known points of time. A General Election, for instance, may be held next year or a bill may be passed which will affect the level of profits from the contemplated projects quite radically and for many years to come. Even, therefore, if by waiting some distant and uncertain future is brought within the individual's horizon, the knowledge of the election results, or of the bill passed, may none the less make him better informed of what his profits will be.

(7.4.3) This is the common sense of the deferred action. To explain how the possibility of its being preferred to an immediate

[1] G. L. S. Shackle, Expectation and Liquidity, Mary Bowman (ed.), Expectations, Uncertainty, and Business Behaviour, op. cit., pp. 43–4.

action has been analysed by Shackle let us return to our
former example of the General Election being held at time t_k
and of the expected profits being earned at t_s. Suppose that the
best strategy for immediate action gives rise to standardized
focus outcomes represented by point A in FIG. 7.4.3. This would
be, therefore, the strategy which the individual would choose if
he would like to invest his resources right now. If he decides to
wait, he will be able to adjust his strategy to the result of the
General Election which will become known at t_k. Suppose that
if the Conservative Party wins the election, he would then choose
the strategy which gives rise to standardized focus outcomes

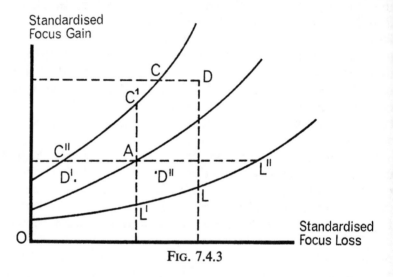

FIG. 7.4.3

represented by point C. If the Labour Party wins, he would
choose that which gives standardized focus outcomes at L.

It may happen that both C and L are on higher indifference
curves than A. For A may, for instance, correspond to a flexible
but inefficient method of production which is preferable to an
efficient one only because it is not known yet what the actual
demand for the firm's product will be; it may be either very
large or very small according to whose party's policy will be
carried out. Strategies C and L, on the other hand, may correspond to efficient methods of production and lead to expectations
of higher profits in either case. To defer action is then preferable
to A.

Suppose, however, that this is not so. The situation is as in FIG. 7.4.3. The point representing strategy C is on a higher and that representing L is on a lower indifference curve than A. What can we say of the relative merits of the immediate and of the deferred action?

(7.4.4) The answer suggested by Shackle is as follows. If strategy A is the best that the individual may choose if he wants to invest his capital now, it may be taken as a norm with respect to which the advantages and disadvantages of the deferred action are appraised. Points C and L may thus be reduced to one pair of focus outcomes by sliding them along their respective indifference curves downwards, so as to make them differ from A in one dimension only, that of their respective focus gains. The individual would be indifferent between being confronted with C and C^1, and L and L^1, respectively. By deferring action he should, therefore, concentrate his attention on a possible loss of AL^1 and a possible gain of C^1A (in relation to the standardized focus gain from A). If we plot these gains and losses on the same graph, we arrive at point D^1 which represents the strategy of deferred action. In the case on the graph it is on a higher indifference curve than A. The individual will thus keep his capital in a liquid form and adopt either C or L when the result of the General Election becomes known.

(7.4.5) It has been pointed out by Shackle himself that the procedure is arbitrary. For instead of sliding the points C and L so as to eliminate the differences in standardized focus losses, we may slide them also so as to eliminate the differences in the standardized focus gains. The points would then assume positions indicated by C'' and L'', and the focus gain and focus loss from the deferred action would be $C''A$ and AL'' respectively. The strategy of deferred action would be represented by D^2 on a a lower indifference curve than A. According, therefore, whether we derive the standardized focus gain and focus loss from the deferred action as the gain and the loss in the standardized focus gain, or in the standardized focus loss (in relation to those from the best immediate action), we arrive at different results.

We may add a more fundamental objection. The derivation of standardized focus outcomes of the deferred action as outcomes of gains and losses in standardized gains and losses themselves, is inconsistent with the general hypothesis of two focus outcomes only. For if the strategy of the deferred action may lead to C or L, the standardized focus outcomes represented by these points correspond to four possible outcomes from it. According to the hypothesis of two focus outcomes the individual should then concentrate his attention on two of those four only. As the points on the graph represent standardized outcomes, they indicate also the degree to which the individual's attention is attracted by the primary focus outcomes to which they correspond. Thus the focus gain corresponding to C will attract his attention more than that of L, and the focus loss corresponding to L will attract his attention more than that of C. The standardized focus outcomes from the strategy of deferred action are, therefore, represented quite unambiguously by point D. In the case on the graph it is on a higher indifference curve than A. The individual whose indifference system this graph represents will, therefore, not commit himself to any particular form of investment until it becomes known which party has won the election.

(7.4.6) Does this analysis increase in any sense our knowledge of what actually takes place? As a theory it does not say more than that deferred action may be preferable to an immediate one. It does not permit us to say either in what conditions it is so or how a change in conditions may affect the individual's choice. It may be argued that the more important is the event at t_k, the greater improvement in focus outcomes may be achieved by deferring action, and the more likely such deferment may be. This is, however, outside the context of the theory. For the focus outcomes of profits which the individual compares depend then also on the characteristics of the respective strategies, and these do not appear in the theory at all.

As the whole Shackle's theory, the argument about deferred action could be accepted only as an interpretation of mental processes which determine or accompany the choice of a strategy. The processes are supposed to be the same as in other applications of the theory. The argument does not seem, therefore, to add anything to what was said before.

(7.5) A Consumer Analogy

(7.5.1) In very general terms, Shackle's theory may be summarized as follows. An individual chooses that strategy which gives rise to the most desirable view of the future. The views from which he makes his choice are prospects of pay-offs from the strategies which are available to him. They are formalized as functions of potential surprise. But the attractiveness of those views is evaluated not on the ground of all outcomes in those functions but on the ground of focus gains and focus losses only as if no other outcomes existed at all.

(7.5.2) One may wonder, however, whether if this is true with respect to choices between different strategies, the same should not be true in relation to choices in general. The views of the future have as their characteristics outcomes and degrees of potential surprise attached to them. For instance, one of the characteristics of a certain view of the future may be that profits will be high if the Labour Party wins the election next year; and as no General Election is likely to be held next year, the outcome of high profits may be associated with a high degree of potential surprise. Some other view, corresponding to some other strategy, may be characterized by high profits if the Conservative Party remains in power; and this may be associated with a low degree of potential surprise. The choice of a strategy depends on the evaluation of all the characteristics of the views of the future to which all the strategies which are available give rise. The same, however, applies to choices between other alternatives. If a consumer, for instance, makes up his mind which car to buy, he evaluates all the characteristics of the available alternatives, such as maximum speed, petrol consumption, styling, etc.; and he buys that car which gives him the most satisfactory combination of them.[1]

One may raise here the objection that the argument by analogy is not valid because the characteristics of a prospect – that is to say the outcomes and the corresponding degrees of potential surprise – are alternatives; and the characteristics of a car are complements. If an individual chooses a certain strategy, he does not obtain all the pay-offs which appear in the prospect. He obtains one only, that which comes off. Whereas if he decides to buy a certain car, he obtains all its characteristics. The car is fast or sluggish, its petrol consumption is large or small, its style attractive or conventional, and so on.

[1] Compare N. Georgescu-Roegen, Choice, Expectation and Measurability, *Quarterly Journal of Economics*, **LXVIII**, November (1954), pp. 503–34.

In fact, however, this is not quite so. For at the time of the expectation, when the choice of a strategy is made, the characteristics of the prospect are not alternatives. They exist merely in the individual's mind, all of them at the same time. The same is true in the case of a car. At the moment of the decision its various characteristics are not experienced but only thought of. The individual derives pleasure from imagining only that there will be a Labour Government next year and his profits will be high, or that he will find himself on an empty road and will be able to drive fast. The characteristics of what takes place in his imagination are then not alternatives in either case. The relevant question is not whether all of them may come true, but how they are evaluated when all of them appear in the individual's mind.

(7.5.3) According to Shackle's hypothesis, an individual cannot contemplate more than two outcomes in a prospect, and he arrives at an evaluation of the strategy which gives rise to it on the ground of these two outcomes only. The same should, therefore, apply to choices between other alternatives. In the case of choosing a car he might also be expected to focus his attention on two characteristics only, on speed, for instance, and on petrol consumption. What these characteristics would be must depend on what stimulates most his imagination. More sport-minded people would concentrate on speed, more economy-minded on petrol, more beauty-minded on styling. All of them, however, would not take into account more than two characteristics because, according to the hypothesis, they are not able to concentrate their attention on more than two of them.

(7.5.4) Do we really choose in this way? No better answer can be given to this question in the case of a strategy than in that of a car. Our powers of imagination cannot be observed by anybody except ourselves. Furthermore, we are rarely fully conscious of the views which appear in our mind when we arrive at a decision. They are not facts which we could record and inspect. The question is thus not so much whether the hypothesis of two focus characteristics fits the facts, as whether such interpretation of our mental processes appeals to our intuition; whether in other words it gives us that yes-feeling which accompanies the perception of truth.

No definite answer is very likely. In science, questions of this kind are never asked. Suppose, however, that we have got an answer. Suppose that in very many cases of which we happened to think we have experienced the feeling that the hypothesis of two focus characteristics is right; that it helps us to understand the choices we make. Could this help us to understand the choices made by others?

(7.5.5) If it did, it would do it in the same sense as any other interpretation of states of mind. If we enter a grocer's shop to buy bread, we interpret our state of mind as that we are anxious not to be hungry later on during the day. If then we see other people buying bread, we understand what they are doing. They too are anxious not to be hungry later on and want to have something to eat. Understanding of our own behaviour helps us to understand the behaviour of others; we see them doing the same thing which we would do if we were in the same position.

Similarly, if we find the interpretation of our choices in terms of two focus characteristics helpful in the analysis of our own behaviour, we may understand other people better if we use the same interpretation in the analysis of their behaviour. If, for instance, we see a man choosing a different car than we would choose, his choice may be less puzzling to us if we admit that he may be focusing his attention on different characteristics than we would do. Or if we see people asking for more credit when the rate of interest is reduced, we may understand their behaviour better if we think of the focus gains in their expectations being increased and focus losses reduced.

(7.5.6) This seems to be the purpose which Shackle's theory is supposed to serve. It supplies a conceptual framework which if generally accepted might help us to understand better each other when we speak of expectations and decisions about strategies. The conditions for it to serve this purpose is that it is accepted intuitively as a correct interpretation of what is going on in our mind when we choose between alternatives with many characteristics. Shackle seems to be certain that as far as his own choices are concerned, the interpretation is correct. The condition, however, of its universal acceptance does not seem to be very easily fulfilled. Interpretation of choices in terms of sure-prospect equivalents still holds the field. We usually say that people demand more credit because they expect a greater profit from

223

their investments. To many people, an interpretation of choice in terms of two focus characteristics must be quite meaningless

(7.5.7) Experiments have been devised to show that Shackle's hypothesis of two focus outcomes leads to wrong predictions of our behaviour. The following, for instance, has been suggested by de Graaf and Baumol.[1] Suppose that the individual may choose between two strategies, A and B. In either case he has to pay £1 to have a chance of the following pay-offs. A ball will be drawn from a bag containing one red, one white, and one black ball. If the individual chooses strategy A, he will receive £10 if the red ball is drawn, £7 for the white ball, and nothing at all for the black one. Strategy B promises the same pay-off for the red and the black balls, but £3 instead of £7 for the white ball. Focus gains and focus losses are then £9 and −£1 for both strategies. But there is no doubt that most of us would choose strategy A.

Similar experiments may be devised for playing roulette, tossing coins, dies, etc. It seems to be obvious that in all these cases we do not focus our attention on two outcomes only. One may wonder, however, whether the results of these experiments disprove Shackle's theory. For the latter is supposed to apply to the conditions of uncertainty only, when no objective probability weights can be attached to possible outcomes. And in drawing balls, or tossing coins and dies, probability weights can be determined in an objective sense. It seems, therefore, that the criticism to which these experiments lead is not so much that the hypothesis of two focus outcomes is inconsistent with our actual behaviour, as that the field to which it is supposed to apply is much more restricted than it might appear at first sight.

(7.5.8) The hypothesis of two focus outcomes has also been criticized on the ground of lack of any descriptive evidence that it fits the facts. Many decisions in business and in government are taken formally and collectively. If, therefore, the hypothesis of two focus outcomes applied to them, there would have to be some evidence of this in the records of the proceedings. And none so far has ever been found.[2]

[1] R. Turvey, J. de V. Graaf and W. Baumol, and G. L. S. Shackle, Three Notes on Expectations in Economics, *Economica*, **XVI**, November (1949), p. 339.
[2] This point was made by L. Foldes, Uncertainty, Probability and Potential Surprise, *Economica*, **XXV**, August (1958), pp. 246–54.

7.6) Standardization and Measurement of Surprise

7.6.1) It has been explained in (7.1) that to each prospect, that is to say to each potential surprise function, correspond two pairs of focus gains and focus losses, the primary and the standardized ones. The primary foci are two-dimensional. They are combinations of pay-offs and of degrees of potential surprise which go with them. The standardized focus gain and focus loss are one-dimensional. The degrees of potential surprise attached to them are zero.

(7.6.2) Standardization of the primary focus gains and focus losses enables us to represent the gambler indifference system on a two-dimensional graph. The gains and the losses can be measured along the two axes, and the ranking of them can be represented by means of a system of indifference curves. Standardization, however, is even more difficult to be ascertained by introspection than the evaluation of the prospects on the ground of a pair of outcomes only. The idea that we evaluate the attractiveness of a certain view of the future on the ground of a focus gain and a focus loss, may appeal to us because it puts some order into our thinking about what we actually do. It simplifies our conception of the process of choosing by splitting it into stages: first the selection of the focus gain and the focus loss, and then the evaluation of the pair which has been selected. Standardization, however, makes this process more complicated. It puts something between the stages of selection and of evaluation for which no counterpart can be found in what we actually experience. For in the actual practice of choosing we do not standardize any characteristics of what we choose.

The question thus arises, what in the above scheme of thought standardization actually means? Is it only an analytical device introduced into the argument to make it amenable to geometrical treatment? Or is it an essential part of the theory without which the latter would be inconclusive or inconsistent? Suppose that we make the gambler indifference system four-dimensional. Standardization is then superfluous. Pairs of primary focus gains and focus losses may be represented as points in a four-dimensional space. They need not be standardized. Why has this not been done? What do we gain by standardization?

(7.6.3) To answer the first part of the question, suppose that

225

the gambler indifference system is four-dimensional. The argument is then as follows. The individual selects a primary focus gain and a primary focus loss for each view of the future, and chooses that strategy which gives him the most attractive pair. In this vague form the hypothesis may be worth considering. Difficulties, however, appear if it is made more precise. The question arises whether potential surprise is or is not measurable. If potential surprise is measurable, it does not matter whether the attractiveness of a pair of focus gains and focus losses is a function of four or of two variables. A mathematical form can be given to it in either case. If, however, potential surprise is not measurable, the attractiveness of a view of the future cannot be a function of it.

(7.6.4) To explain the point, suppose that potential surprise is measurable up to an arbitrary choice of the origin and of the unit of the scale. As soon as we choose the latter, the attractiveness of the various views of the future, that is to say the rank of the various pairs of focus gains and focus losses, may be expressed as a function of four numbers. The form of this function depends also on the origin and the unit of the scale, but when these are decided upon it is fixed too and is independent of what pairs of focus gains and focus losses happen to be compared.

The situation is similar to that of our ranking the attractiveness of the bath on the ground of the temperature of the water. Up to a certain limit the hotter is the water, the more attractive is the bath. If the temperature rises above the limit, the bath becomes less attractive. But a bath which is too hot may still be more attractive than one which is too cold if it is not too much too hot. All these rankings may be expressed in the form of a function which is independent of the temperature of the bath actually taken; although to discover what this function is, each possible temperature must have been tried some time in the past.

If potential surprise is not measurable, we cannot speak of any system of ranking of primary focus gains and focus losses as existing independently of what we actually experience. The situation is then similar to our ranking the attractiveness of the bath without having a thermometer. We cannot say that we prefer the bath of 30°C to that of 40°C. These measures do not mean anything to us. All we can do is to feel the water and to say that we prefer this to that. We can do this whenever we are confronted with a choice. But we cannot state our preferences in the form of a system of rankings which would be independent of what we at the moment compare.

(7.6.5) Can standardization help us to get rid of this difficulty? This is the question to which we must now turn. Shackle thought that standardization can help because even if the index of potential surprise is arbitrary, the standardized focus gains and focus losses are independent of what it actually is. We will argue in the next section that this is so if standardization is actually performed. If, however, standardization is only a step in the analysis, it merely conceals the difficulty without getting rid of it.

(7.7) The Nature of Standardization

(7.7.1) Suppose that the standardization is actually performed. The individual chooses first the primary focus gain and focus loss. He then looks for outcomes of pay-offs with zero degree of potential surprise which attract his attention exactly as much as the primary focus gain and focus loss do. And he evaluates them in accordance with his gambler indifference system. Selection, standardization, and evaluation are then three distinct mental acts. Selection is the focusing of one's attention on a pair of outcomes in the actual prospect. Standardization is the replacing of them in one's imagination by a pair of equally arresting outcomes but with zero degree of potential surprise. And evaluation is the comparing of the attractiveness of one pair of the standardized focus gain and focus loss with other pairs. If each step is actually performed, it implies ranking of one's experiences only. The step of selection implies ranking of our interest in various pay-offs and degrees of potential surprise attached to them as they appear in the prospect. The step of standardization implies ranking of our interest in the outcomes selected, and in those which might appear in the prospect with zero degree of potential surprise. And the step of evaluation implies ranking of the extent to which we enjoy contemplating various pairs of standardized focus gains and losses. The question of measurement does not arise in any of these steps because in each of them we compare either what we actually experience or what we would experience if we were confronted with a situation described quite unambiguously in terms of pay-offs with zero degrees of potential surprise. The stages of selection and standardization on one hand, and of evaluation on the other, are independent one from the other. For the step of standardization ends and the step of evaluation begins with a pair of pay-offs which are determined independently of their subsequent ranking and ranked independently of their previous determination.

(7.7.2) The position is different if standardization is not performed. We, the observers, must then pass along the locus of combinations of pay-offs and potential surprises which equally attract the individual's attention (from P_L and P_G in FIG. 7.1.7 to S_L and S_G). For this to be done by the observer the locus must be made available to him. The observer must be able to identify the degrees of potential surprise, not as the actual experiences, but as those experiences' formal representations. Unless, therefore, a method is found to describe the individual's experiences of potential surprise either in numbers or uniquely in words the observer cannot perform the standardization.

It has been pointed out before that such descriptions could be obtained by means of a marking or of a Jevonsian operation.[1] The individual must only be able to identify the intensity or to rank the differences in the intensity of what he experiences. Thus if this condition would be satisfied standardization could be an analytical device. Otherwise, standardization may be a mental act, but not a step in analysis. For no system of rankings can be derived from variables which themselves can be only ranked.[2]

(7.7.3) Shackle thought that the condition is not necessary because the value of the standardized focus gain and focus loss is independent of the actual measure of potential surprise. If, for instance, the measure of potential surprise attached to the

---

[1] Shackle has ultimately decided in favour of the latter. (See G. L. S. Shackle, Expectation and Cardinality, *Economic Journal*, **LXVI**, June (1956), pp. 211–19.)

[2] 'Suppose, for instance, that we represent the stimulus by multiplying the money-outcome by an index of degree of belief (or of potential surprise, if that is preferred). Let the outcomes £100, £300, £400 carry degree of belief indices 1, $\frac{1}{2}$, $\frac{1}{4}$; so that the stimuli are 100, 150, 100. Then by changing the degree of belief indices (without altering their order) to 1, $\frac{1}{3}$, $\frac{5}{16}$ we can make the stimuli 100, 100, 125 and shift the greatest one from the second to the third position'. (C. F. Carter, A Revised Theory of Expectations, *Uncertainty and Business Decisions*, C. F. Carter, G. P. Meredith and G. L. S. Shackle (eds.), Liverpool University Press (1957), p. 56.)

primary focus gain in Fig. 7.1.7 were twice as large as it is at present, the respective point would be twice as high up on the scale. But so would be also the standardization locus $S_G P_G$. The standardized focus gain would thus remain unchanged.

The conclusion that the numerical value of the standardized focus gain and focus loss is independent of the measure of potential surprise is undoubtedly correct. But this does not mean that the standardization could be performed by an observer if there were no such measure at all. Measurability – as distinct from ranking – implies that what is measured can be identified by the measure. If a number of ten is accepted as a measure of a particular intensity of potential surprise, surprise of that intensity can be always identified by that number. If, however, the degrees of potential surprise can only be ranked, the numbers attached to them indicate merely how they compare with other degrees. No intensity of surprise can be identified by them. In Shackle's argument, the numerical measures of surprise are arbitrary, but they are measures not ranks.[2] To all points on the graph correspond certain intensities of surprise which can be identified by them. Locus $S_G P_G$ exists, therefore, independently of what surprises are at the moment experienced or imagined by the individual.

(7.7.4) This has the following consequences. If standardization is merely an analytical device, it must not have any effect on the ranking of the alternatives. In other words if a particular strategy is chosen on the ground of the evaluation of primary focus gains and focus losses, it must be also on the highest gambler indifference curve. This means that in the course of the movement along the loci $S_L P_L$ and $S_G P_G$, the individual remains on the same hyper-surface of his four-dimensional gambler indifference system. The locus must, therefore, be on that surface, and standardization consists in our moving along the latter towards a point of zero degree of potential surprise. The point is on a plane cutting through the four-dimensional space along the axes of the pay-offs of primary focus gains and primary focus losses. The gambler indifference curves are the curves along which the four-dimensional indifference surfaces intersect that

[2] This is how they also seem to be interpreted by Gorman in his criticism of Carter's point. W. M. Gorman, A Note on A Revised Theory of Expectations, *Economic Journal*, **LXVII**, September (1957), pp. 549–51.

plane, and the loci $S_L P_L$ and $S_G P_G$ are paths on those surfaces along which we move.

Why, however, should these paths be unique? If they were not, we could move along the indifference surfaces to any point on Shackle's indifference curve according to which paths we choose. The different views of the future could then be identified with particular indifference curves only, the views identified with the same curve being indistinguishable one from another. In Shackle's presentation of the theory this is not so. The views of the future are identified with points on gambler indifference curves and can be distinguished one from another even if they happen to be on the same curve.

(7.7.5) The reason why this is so is that the paths of standardization are supposed to be independent one of the other. The form of $S_L P_L$ is independent of that of $S_G P_G$, and *vice versa*. This means that the four-dimensional indifference system has the form

$$r = F[f_g(p_g, h_g), f_i(p_i, h_i)]$$

where r is the rank of the view of the future represented by a pair of primary focus gains and focus losses, p_i and p_g are the payoffs of those focus gains and focus losses, and h_i and h_g are the degrees of potential surprise attached to them. The two functions in the bracket, $f_g(p_g, h_g)$ and $f_i(p_i, h_i)$, are the indices of the degree to which the particular pairs of primary focus gains and focus losses attract the individual's attention. If s_g, 0 and s_i, 0 are the standardized focus gain and focus loss, $f_g(p_g, h_g) = f_g(s_g, 0)$ and $f_i(p_i, h_i) = f_i(s_i, 0)$. Thus standardization leaves the ranking of the respective views of the future unchanged.

The condition for the individual's indifference system to be of this form is that not only the degrees of potential surprise but also f_g and f_i are measurable. For otherwise Carter's objection, that it does not make sense to speak of a system of ranking of combinations of variables which themselves can only be ranked, would apply to this case as well. The degrees to which focus gains and focus losses attract the individual's attention can, however, be made measurable by putting $f_g(s_g, 0) = s_g$ and $f_i(s_i, 0) = s_i$. The pay-offs of the standardized focus gains and losses may simply be taken as the measures of the degree to which they attract the individual's attention. The gambler indifference system may take then the form $r = F(s_g, s_l)$, the same as in Shackle's theory.

(7.7.6) We may now answer more fully the question which was asked in (7.6.2). By means of standardization we make the degree to which various focus gains and focus losses attract the individual's attention measurable and we reduce the gambler indifference system to the form of a function of these two measures. This enables us to split the process of choosing into the stages of selection and evaluation so that no arbitrary measures of potential surprise appear either at the end of the former or at the beginning of the latter.

The procedure imposes, however, certain restrictions on the form of the indifference system. For if standardization of the focus gain and of the focus loss is to be independent one of the other, the form of the gambler indifference system must be such that a movement along the standardization locus corresponding to the focus gain does not affect the form of the standardization locus corresponding to the focus loss, and *vice versa*. Furthermore, if standardization is an analytical device, the distinction between the function which determines the degree to which the various focus gains and focus losses attract the individual's attention, and the gambler indifference system which determines the rank of the standardized foci, is only semantic. In fact, both determine the same thing. For if a movement along a standardization locus would not correspond to a movement along a four-dimensional indifference surface, standardization would affect the rank of the respective view of the future, and it would lead to a wrong interpretation of the individual's behaviour.

(7.8) A Neutral Tax

(7.8.1) At the end of this chapter it may be useful to have an example of how Shackle's theory could be applied to a definite problem. Suppose that we have been asked to devise a profit tax which would yield revenue but not discourage investment. The example is taken from Shackle's book and is reproduced here to give the reader an idea of the purpose which his theory was supposed to serve.

(7.8.2) Only those investment projects are undertaken by an entrepreneur, which lead to standardized focus outcomes of pay-offs on higher gambler indifference curves than that which passe: through the point corresponding to not undertaking any projec at all. In the original version of the argument, the latter poin was at the origin of the diagram because not doing anythin; was supposed to lead neither to any gains nor to any losses. The possibility of changes in the price level was explicitly excluded The focus gain and the focus loss from not doing anything wa: thus equal to zero, and those investment projects only could be undertaken by the entrepreneur which gave rise to prospects of pay-offs on higher indifference curves than that which passe: rough the origin.

If now a tax is imposed on profits, the right-hand side of the potential surprise curve moves to the left; the standardized focus gain becomes smaller; and as the left-hand side of the curve and the standardized focus loss are not affected by the tax (there is no loss offset), the point representing the prospect of pay-offs on the gambler indifference map moves downwards. If it falls below the curve passing through the origin, the particular project will not be undertaken. If the tax is so high that this applies to every possible project, the entrepreneur may decide not to invest his capital at all.

(7.8.3) This unfavourable effect on investment could, however, be avoided if the profit tax were so constructed that it would not affect the primary focus gain. Suppose, for instance, that no tax is imposed on profits if they happen to be equal to the primary focus gain. If they turn out to be different, the tax has to be paid at a greater and greater rate the more the actual profits differ upwards or downwards from that gain. The focus gain would not then be affected by the tax. The other pay-offs would become smaller. The outcomes of them coming off would, therefore, attract the entrepreneur's attention even less than they did before. The project would, therefore, remain represented by the same focus gain and the same focus loss, and it would remain on the same gambler indifference curve.

(7.8.4) To impose a tax of this kind, the authorities would have to determine the primary focus gain in the case of every project and of every entrepreneur. This could be done by explaining to the taxpayer the rules of the tax and asking him to suggest in advance the amount of profits from which he would like not to pay any tax if it really comes off. The taxpayer would then uggest in his own interest the amount of his primary focus gain. For if he chose some other figure, he would make the project ess attractive to him. To make the project as attractive as possible to himself the taxpayer would thus make the system work.

(7.8.5) If the theory behind this scheme is correct, the tax should not have any effect on investment. It could, therefore, be recommended on the ground that it would be a tax either on timidity, if the actual profits happen to be higher than those of the focus gain; or on wishful thinking, if they happen to be lower than that. True enterprise would not be affected by it.

But is the theory behind this scheme correct? We have in this example the whole problem reduced to a single question. Suppose that a profit tax of this kind has been introduced. Would we, as entrepreneurs, regard each particular project as as attractive with the tax as it would be without it; with very high rates of the tax as well as with very low rates? This is, in fact, another plausibility test of the theory. For those who give a negative answer reject in fact the whole theory.

8

Theory of Games

THEORY of games deals with situations which are different from
those discussed in the other chapters of this book in one very
important respect. So far the prospects of the states of the world
were supposed to be independent of the individual's strategy.
The fact that the individual had taken the umbrella had no
effect on the weather. The pay-off which he ultimately received
was determined by both the state of the world and by
the strategy. The former, however, was independent of the
latter.

In the theory of games the situation is different. The state of
the world is determined not only by the forces of nature which an
individual endeavours to exploit to his advantage by choosing a
suitable strategy, but also by other individuals who are the
former's opponents and try to turn the state of the world to his
disadvantage. The situation cannot be exploited by taking the
prospect of what the actual state of the world is going to be and
choosing a strategy which gives the greatest pay-off from it. The
individual must also take into account the possibility that his
opponents will find out or guess what his strategy is going to be,
and adjust the state of the world accordingly. What state of the
world will ultimately come off may, therefore, depend on the
individual's strategy. The situation is more complicated than
that which was discussed before, and a different theory is needed
to deal with it.

The theory of games is also a branch of mathematics. In the
present study, however, the mathematical side of it will be neglected. Our objective will be to consider it as a part of economic
theory, and to elucidate the hypotheses about expectations
which it implies. To stress the fact that the theory applies to
situations which can be compared to a game we will often call

the individuals concerned *players*, and we will refer to their strategies as being *played* by them.

(8.1) Classification of Games

(8.1.1) The state of the world may depend on the individual's strategy in a variety of situations which are in many respects different one from another. Games are, therefore, usually classified into groups. The relevant criteria are (i) how many individuals take part in them, (ii) what is the relation between the pay-offs which they may receive in all the possible states of the world, and (iii) whether they have to choose their strategies individually or are allowed to form coalitions.

The criteria are very formal. It will be shown, however, that the classes which they describe contain situations in which specific problems arise, different in different classes. The chapters of the theory of games which deal with different classes may, therefore, be treated as different theories, explaining different forms of behaviour.

(8.1.2) With respect to the number of participants, games are usually classified into *two-person* and *more-than-two-person games*. The class of more-than-two-person games is not quite homogeneous because the problems which arise in four- or five-person games are not necessarily the same as those which arise in three-person games. Their mathematics may not be the same either. For the purpose of the analysis given in this book, however, these differences are not important. They do not correspond to any significant differences in the form of possible behaviour.

The distinction between two-person and more-than-two-person games is important because the latter allow for coalitions to be formed by some individuals against the others. In two-person games the individuals are facing each other alone. Both may sometimes be better off if they form a coalition against the rest of the world. But there cannot be any coalition against other participants.

In more-than-two-person games the number of individuals taking part in the game is sufficient for coalitions being formed and yet some participants remaining outside them. For even if three individuals only take part in the game, two may form a coalition against the third. The choice of a strategy implies then a choice of a coalition to which one wants to belong. The greater is the number of players, the greater is the scope for the formation of coalitions of this kind, and the more difficult the choice.

(8.1.3) With respect to whether the individuals have to play the game alone or may join each other in coalitions, games are classified into *cooperative* and *non-cooperative games*. Cooperative games are those in which the individuals may form coalitions against other participants or against the rest of the world. Non-cooperative games are those in which the formation of coalitions is prohibited. The classification of games into cooperative and non-cooperative is independent of the number of individuals who take part in them. For even if the game is a two-person game, it may be cooperative if the conditions allow for some advantage to be derived from a coalition against the rest of the world.

In the mathematical theory of games, the criterion of co-operation or non-cooperation is strictly formal. Non-cooperative games are those in which the possibility of cooperation is not taken into account. If the criterion is applied to a real situation, interpreted only as a game, it must be stated in terms of the characteristics of the situation to which it applies. In some cases the condition of non-cooperation may be identified with that of cooperation being prohibited by law or virtually impossible owing to lack of communication. There are, however, also cases in which this is not so. Cooperation may be informal, established by custom, without any agreement or previous communication. The condition of non-cooperation cannot then be stated in terms of the characteristics of the situation in which the individuals behave. It is rather about how they behave. It is then, not so much a criterion of classification of the situations to which the theory applies, as a part of a hypothesis in terms of which the behaviour which takes place is explained.

(8.1.4) With respect to how the possible pay-offs of different individuals are related one to another games are classified into *zero-sum* and *non-zero-sum* games. Zero-sum games are those in which the pay-offs of all the individuals who take part in the game add up to the same figure in all possible combinations of strategies and states of the world. The game is then about how a certain total amount of pay-offs, either in possession of the individuals already or to be given to them in the course of the

236

game, is to be divided between them. Non-zero-sum games are those in which the total amount of pay-offs is not fixed but depends on the individuals' strategies. The game is then not only about how a certain amount of pay-offs is to be divided, but also about what it is going to be.

The term zero-sum game implies that the total of pay-offs which is divided between the individuals in the course of the game must be zero. This, however, is not a significant restriction, for in a formal treatment of the theory the pay-offs are usually expressed in utilities, subject to an arbitrary choice of the unit and of the origin of the scale. It is, therefore, always possible to adjust this unit and the origin so as to make the total of pay-offs in terms of utility equal to zero, quite irrespective of whether the total of monetary pay-offs is greater or less than zero. The unit and the origin of the scale may also be adjusted so that the sum of pay-offs in terms of utility is equal to some positive or negative figure. Zero-sum games might, therefore, also be called constant-sum games.

(8.1.5) The utility measure may, however, be a cause of trouble even in this simple problem of classification. For if marginal utility is not constant, a transfer of a certain sum of money from one individual to another does not leave the sum of utility pay-offs unaffected. The utility lost by the former is not necessarily equal to that gained by the latter. Thus a game which is a zero-sum game in terms of money may not be a zero-sum game in terms of utility; and *vice versa*, to be zero-sum in terms of utility it may have to be a non-zero-sum game in terms of money.

From the point of view of economic theory, classification in terms of monetary pay-offs is much more important than that in term of utility. For the conditions in which the different forms of games arise can then be described in objective terms, independent of individuals' 'tastes'. Take, for instance, the case of bilateral monopoly. It is a perfect example of a situation in which a zero-sum game may arise. The condition may be easily identified if it is stated in terms of monetary pay-offs. A seller may, for instance, bargain with a buyer for the price of a product which the former values much lower than the latter. If, however, the condition is stated in utility pay-offs, a zero-sum game need not correspond to any market situation with which economic theory might be concerned. On the contrary. It may impose

237

quite arbitrary conditions on it. For the possible monetary pay-offs would not then be determined by factors which are independent of how and by whom the game is actually played. They would have to satisfy the condition that their utility measures add up to zero.

The difficulty does not arise if marginal utility of money is constant. For if the scale of utility is so adjusted that a particular pay-off in money represents the same pay-off in utility for every individual in the game, the condition that the game is a zero-sum one in terms of utility implies that it is also a zero-sum one in terms of money. Alternatively, if in the context of the theory the behaviour of the individuals is supposed to be determined not by utility but by monetary pay-offs, the question of utility pay-offs does not arise at all, and a zero-sum game is only another name for a constant-sum game in terms of money.

(8.1.6) The hypothesis of constant marginal utility of money contradicts both our intuition and Friedman's, Savage's, and Markowitz's hypotheses in their theories of behaviour in the condition of risk. It might, however, be accepted on the ground that it is a useful approximation to the actual conditions in those cases to which the theory of game applies. For it will be shown in the next section that although mean values of pay-offs play an important part in the determination of an optimum strategy, the hypothesis of the theory of games is not that of moral expectation. It requires ranking of pay-offs only; not their numerical evaluation. Although, therefore, the hypothesis of constant marginal utility of income cannot explain the phenomena of gambling and insurance, it is not inconsistent with the individuals playing a game. Games could be played in accordance with the hypotheses formulated to analyse them even if the marginal utility of income were constant.

(8.1.7) In the literature the problem of what is the actual relation between utility and monetary pay-offs has been usually neglected. We will follow here a similar line. Little attention will be paid in this chapter to the actual measures of pay-offs, except in those cases in which they might affect the solution and could, therefore, be important for the appraisal of the theory. Classification of games into zero-sum and non-zero-sum ones will be regarded as purely formal. The relevant criterion will be whether all the pay-offs add up or do not add up to the same figure in money or in utility according to what the context of the theory requires.

(8.2) The Maximin Hypothesis

(8.2.1) The main hypothesis of the theory of two-person zero-sum games is that in the prospect of the future state of the world a full weight is attached to the outcome which gives the greatest pay-off to the opponent and the smallest pay-off to the player himself. The individual is supposed to choose his strategy so as to maximize this minimum pay-off. Hence the hypothesis is usually called the maximin hypothesis. The minimum pay-off which the individual maximizes is called his *security level*. By choosing the respective strategy he makes himself secure against anything worse than that.

(8.2.2) Consider this hypothesis in more detail. In a two-person zero-sum game the pay-offs of the two individuals who take part in it add up to zero. They may be interpreted as payments which one individual makes to the other. What one pays is then equal to what the other receives, and the pay-offs cancel out. It is not necessary, therefore, to specify the pay-offs for both individuals. If they are specified for one of them, those of the other are specified as well. For they are numerically the same, only of an opposite sign.

Suppose now that the possible pay-offs of one individual, to be called Individual I, are as in Table 8.2.2. The rows in it represent different strategies, and the columns different states of the world. Which of these states of the world will come off depends on what strategy the other individual, Individual II, will choose. Individual I's expectations are in this respect quite definite. Individual II will choose that strategy (that is to say that column in the table) which gives Individual I the smallest possible pay-off from the strategy he himself has chosen. If thus Individual I chooses strategy S_{30}, he expects that Individual II will choose S_{03}.

The maximin strategy of Individual I is that which maximizes this minimum pay-off. In our example it is S_{20} because in all other rows the minimum pay-offs are smaller than that in the second row. According to the maximin hypothesis, Individual I will thus choose strategy S_{20}.

239

Table 8.2.2

	S_{01}	S_{02}	S_{03}
S_{10}	1	2	9
S_{20}	7	6	8
S_{30}	4	5	3

(8.2.3) The same argument may be applied to Individual II He too is facing the problem of choosing a strategy so as to obtain the greatest possible pay-off for himself in conditions in which the state of the world on which it depends is determined by the strategy of Individual I. He expects that the latter will choose a strategy which minimizes that pay-off. According to the maximin hypothesis he too will, therefore, choose a strategy which maximizes this minimum pay-off.

Table 8.2.2 may be used to illustrate Individual II's problem if the columns in it are interpreted as Individual II's strategies and the rows as the states of the world determined by the strategies of Individual I. According to the maximin hypothesis, Individual II will choose strategy S_{02} because the minimum pay-off which he can then obtain is greater (that is to say the maximum pay-off of Individual I is smaller) than in any other column in the table.

(8.2.4) In the above example the maximin strategy of Individual I is that which minimizes Individual II's pay-off from his maximin strategy, and the maximin strategy of Individual II is that which minimizes Individual I's pay-off from his maximin strategy. It is by no means necessary for this to be always the case. It may, however, be convenient to stop at this point to see what are the implications of the maximin hypothesis if this particular arrangement of pay-offs does obtain. In technical language the condition is usually described as that the game has a *saddle point*. The pay-off at which the two maximin strategies intersect is a saddle because on a three-dimensional diagram the relation between the strategies of the two individuals and the pay-offs corresponding to them would be represented by a surface which bends downwards in both directions along the axis of the first individual's strategies and upwards along that of the second individual's strategies.

240

If this condition is satisfied, the maximin strategy is an optimum one for the individual who believes that his opponent will also choose a maximin strategy. For if Individual I in the above example chooses S_{20}, Individual II cannot do better than choose S_{02}. Any other strategy would give him a smaller pay-off. And if Individual II chooses S_{02}, Individual I cannot do better than choose S_{20}. In this case, the maximin strategies represent, therefore, an equilibrium of a sort. Any deviation from them makes the respective individual's position worse and can be corrected only by him retreating back to equilibrium.

For these reasons the maximin strategies in a two-person zero-sum game are usually regarded as the solution of the game. They describe the behaviour which the theory would predict. Some difficulties arise if the game has several saddle points and in consequence several maximin solutions. For one may then wonder which of them is relevant. But we need not go into these difficulties here. In a zero-sum game it does not matter much which maximin strategies are actually chosen because all possible pairs of them result in the same pay-offs and all are equilibrium pairs. Although, therefore, the solution of the game is undetermined in terms of strategies, it is determined in terms of pay-offs.

(8.2.5) Is the maximin hypothesis acceptable on plausibility grounds? Suppose that we are one of the individuals in a two-person zero-sum game. Would we behave as the hypothesis says that we should? The answer may depend on whether the game is played only once or many times.

Take first the case of its being played only once. Suppose that in Table 8.2.2 Individual I chooses strategy S_{10} but somehow makes the second individual believe that he has chosen S_{30}. Individual II will then respond by choosing S_{03}. And the result is that Individual I's pay-off is much greater and Individual II's pay-off much smaller than the latter expected. The outcome is even worse for him than that of the saddle point. If, therefore, Individual I can mislead his opponent about his proper intentions, he has every reason to choose a strategy which is not a maximin one.

Similar considerations apply to the other individual. He too may choose a strategy which is different from the maximin one, hoping that Individual I in turn may be misled about his

241

intentions and induced to choose a strategy which will give him a smaller pay-off. Thus in fact the maximin strategies are not a better solution of the game than any others. For if the individuals tend to outwit each other in their choice of strategies, they may end up with a pair of them which has nothing to do with the maximin pair. They have then no reason to expect that their opponents will choose maximin strategies, and no reason, therefore, to choose them themselves.[1]

(8.2.6) It may be argued that such outwitting of the opponent is not possible if the game is played many times. For it would then become apparent that the individuals do not actually choose the strategies which they appear to choose, and their opponents no longer would let themselves be misled. In fact, however, the matter is not as simple as that. For even if it becomes known that apparent and actual strategies do not agree, it is by no means certain that the individuals tend to correct their mistakes in a way which leads them to an equilibrium solution. To be able to say to what position such mutual adjustments would ultimately lead we would need a dynamic theory of games, which would tell us how step by step strategies change in response to mistakes discovered. No such theory has so far been invented.

It may, however, be also argued that if there are ways of misleading the opponent, they are a part of the game and should be explicitly taken into account in the matrix of possible pay-offs. To say, for instance, 'no bid' with a smile is a different strategy than to say it with one's eyes cast down. This is in fact what we have to accept. The maximin hypothesis implies that the individuals in the game expect their respective opponents always to make the best for themselves of every situation that may arise. The possibility of them being outwitted is not taken into account. If the opponent makes a mistake, our pay-off may be higher than we expected. This, however, is only a windfall profit which does not affect the individual's behaviour. There is no way of leading the opponent up to a mistake. The only sensible strategy is to play safe, to maximize the minimum pay-off that can be obtained.

(8.2.7) The theory of games could be a positive theory if the

[1] Compare D. Ellsberg, Theory of the Reluctant Duelist, *The American Economic Review*, **XLVI**, December (1956), pp. 909–23.

actual behaviour in games were consistent with that which it predicts. How useful it could then be would depend on how well its predictions fit the facts. What these facts actually are is not quite clear. The theory of games was invented to explain actual behaviour and to lay down rules of rational behaviour in games proper. The possibility of its being applied to economics and to social sciences in general was considered for the first time by Von Neumann and Morgenstern in their *Theory of Games and Economic Behaviour* in 1944. This was the starting point of a rapid and spectacular development of what may now be regarded as a new branch of economics. If, however, even at this advanced stage the question is raised what the theory actually predicts, nothing definite can be said even by way of an example. Our interest in it derives more from the fact that economic behaviour takes place in conditions which in many respects resemble those of a game and that for this reason the theory may become useful when it is more developed, than from our appreciation of its present state.

(8.3) Mixed Strategies

(8.3.1) The hypothesis that a pair of maximin strategies is a solution of a game applies to those games only which have a saddle point. If a game has no saddle point, the argument that a maximin strategy is the best response to a maximin strategy of the opponent is no longer valid. For if we knew that the opponent will choose his maximin strategy, we could obtain a greater pay-off if we chose not a maximin one.

That this is so can be seen from the matrix of pay-offs in Table 8.3.1. It has no saddle point. The maximin strategy of Individual I is S_{20}; that of Individual II is S_{03}; and the pay-off

Table 8.3.1

	S_{01}	S_{02}	S_{03}
S_{10}	−24	0	8
S_{20}	18	−6	2
S_{30}	9	9	−7

of 2 at which these two strategies intersect is not a saddle point. For S_{03} does not maximize the second individual's pay-off if the first chooses S_{20}. Individual II would do better if he chose S_{02}. Similarly, S_{20} is not the best response of Individual I to Individual II's S_{03}. It would be better to choose S_{10}.

Thus in this case there seems to be no equilibrium solution. For if an individual believes that his opponent will choose his maximin strategy, he will not choose a maximin strategy himself. And if his opponent thinks the same, he will not choose the maximin strategy either. The condition that the individuals cannot mislead each other is not sufficient in this case for the maximin strategies to be an equilibrium solution. For even if it is satisfied, the maximin strategies are not the best answers to themselves and cannot, therefore, be expected to be actually played.

(8.3.2) To be able to deal with this case in the same way as with those in which saddle points exist, Von Neumann and Morgenstern introduced the concept of mixed strategies. These are simply decisions to leave the choice of strategy to chance. Instead of choosing a strategy himself, the Individual is supposed to set up a mechanism with certain probability weights attached to strategies as outcomes and to play that strategy which comes off. Individual I may, for instance, decide that he will play either S_{10} or S_{20} according to whether heads or tails come off in a toss with a coin. The tossing of the coin is then the mechanism which determines the ultimate choice of the strategy. If the coin is fair, the probability weights of the prospects of the two strategies are $\frac{1}{2}$ and $\frac{1}{2}$. Different probability weights could obtain if the coin were tossed several times. Strategy S_{10} might then be played if one from a number of sequences of heads and tails came out, and S_{20} if the result was some other sequence. If the number of tosses were sufficiently large, any probability distribution of weights could be approached as closely as the individual might wish.

A mixed strategy does not mean that the game is repetitive. It presupposes only that there is a set of strategies from which the mechanism is expected to select that which will ultimately be played. It will be shown in the subsequent paragraphs that if certain conditions are satisfied, mixed strategies may give the individual a higher security level than he could obtain if he played pure strategies only. The individuals might, therefore, be expected to use mixed strategies whenever this is the case. It will also be shown that if all possible mixed strategies are included into the set of those which the individuals can play, every two-person zero-sum game must have a saddle point.

(8.3.3) Consider first the conditions which must be satisfied for this to be the case. They are simply that the pay-offs from mixed strategies are evaluated on the ground of their mean values. In other words if an individual decides to play a mixed strategy and sets up a mechanism with certain probability weights, the sure-prospect equivalent of the pay-offs from it is equal to the mean value of those pay-offs. If the pay-offs are in utility, the moral expectation is relevant. If they are in money, the sure-prospect equivalent is the mean value of the monetary pay-offs.

Suppose, for instance, that in Table 8.3.1 Individual I decides to set up a mechanism in which strategies S_{10} and S_{20} appear with probability weights $\frac{1}{3}$ and $\frac{2}{3}$ respectively. If his opponent chooses S_{03}, the mean value of Individual I's pay-offs is 4. If Individual II chooses S_{02}, it is -4. These are, therefore, the sure-prospect equivalents to which Individual I is supposed to adjust himself.

Similar considerations apply to Individual II. He too may play a mixed strategy. He may, for instance, set up a mechanism in which S_{02} and S_{03} appear with probability weights $\frac{1}{2}$ and $\frac{1}{2}$. The sure-prospect equivalent of pay-offs is then -2 if he has reasons to believe that Individual I will choose S_{20}, 4 if the latter will choose S_{10}, and so on.

(8.3.4) It can now be shown that if this is so, the individuals concerned may achieve higher security levels by mixing their strategies than by playing the pure ones. For consider again S_{10} and S_{20} in Table 8.3.1. The security level of S_{10} is -24, and that of S_{20} is -6. As the latter is higher than the former, Individual I will choose S_{20}. This is what the maximin hypothesis says if it is applied to pure strategies only.

Suppose, however, that Individual I chooses a mixed strategy in which S_{10} and S_{20} appear with probability weights $\frac{1}{3}$ and $\frac{2}{3}$. The mean values of pay-offs corresponding to the three strategies of his opponent are then 4, -4, 4, and the security level which the mixed strategy offers is -4. It is higher than either that of S_{10} or that of S_{20}. Furthermore, if the probability weights with

245

which the latter appear in the mixed strategy are not $\frac{1}{3}$ and $\frac{2}{3}$ but $\frac{1}{2}$ and $\frac{1}{2}$, the mean values of pay-offs are -3, -3, 5, and the security level increases still further. It becomes equal to -3.

(8.3.5) It is not difficult to see why this is so. The security level of a pure strategy is the lowest number in the corresponding row of the matrix of pay-offs (-6, for instance, for S_{20}). If there is another pure strategy which offers a greater pay-off for the same strategy of the opponent (as S_{10} does for S_{02}), some combination of the two must offer a mean value of pay-offs which is greater than the security level of the former (greater than -6 of S_{20}). The mean values of pay-offs corresponding to other strategies of the opponent may become smaller, but as they were greater than the security level, there is always some scope for the latter to be increased.

The condition for this to be the case, is that there is some other strategy which offers a greater pay-off for the same strategy of the opponent than the security level does. It would not be satisfied if the game had a saddle point and the security level were just at that point. For it would represent then not only the lowest pay-off in its row, but also the highest in its column. In a game with a saddle point no advantage can, therefore, be derived from mixed strategies. The highest security levels which the players can achieve are those of the pure maximin ones. If, however, a game has no saddle point, mixed strategies are preferable.

(8.4) The Saddle Point Theorem

(8.4.1) It has been already mentioned in the preceding section that if mixed strategies are included into the set of all those which can be played, every two-person zero-sum game has an equilibrium solution. The proof of this proposition has been given by Von Neumann and Morgenstern and is a very spectacular piece of mathematics. No attempt is made here to reproduce its formal steps. The example given below may help, however, to see the sense of it.

(8.4.2) Suppose that the game has no saddle point as in Table 8.3.1. With what probability weights must the pure strategies appear in a mixed strategy if the security level of the latter is to be maximized? To answer this question consider two strategies of Individual I, his maximin strategy S_{20} and some other, for instance S_{10}. The security level of the former is -6 and appears in the second column of the matrix; that of the latter is -24 and appears in the first column. As S_{20} is a maximin strategy, its security level is higher than that of S_{10}.

If these two strategies are mixed together, the mean value of pay-offs in the first column is smaller and the mean value of pay-offs in the second column is greater, the greater is the probability weight of S_{10} and the smaller is that of S_{20}. To maximize his security level, Individual I must thus adjust the mechanism so that S_{10} and S_{20} appear in the mixed strategy with probability weights which make the mean values of pay-offs the same in the first and the second column. For any deviation from this position would reduce either one or the other. In our example, this condition is satisfied if the mechanism is so adjusted that the probability weights are $\frac{1}{2}$ and $\frac{1}{2}$, and the required security level is -3.

(8.4.3) The same argument may be applied to other strategies. The first may, for instance, be combined with the third, and the third with the second. The optimum probability weights and the mean values of pay-offs are then as in the first three rows of Table 8.4.3. The security level which can be achieved by mixing

Table 8.4.3

	S_{01}	S_{02}	S_{03}	$(\frac{1}{8}S_{01} + \frac{3}{8}S_{02} + \frac{1}{2}S_{03})$
$(\frac{1}{2}S_{10} + \frac{1}{2}S_{20})$	-3	-3	5	1
$(\frac{1}{3}S_{10} + \frac{2}{3}S_{30})$	-2	6	-2	1
$(\frac{2}{3}S_{20} + \frac{1}{3}S_{30})$	15	-1	-1	1
$(\frac{1}{3}S_{10} + \frac{1}{3}S_{20} + \frac{1}{3}S_{30})$	1	1	1	1

together two strategies is higher than that of either of them in Table 8.3.1. It can be increased still further if all the three strategies are mixed together. For if they are given probability weights of $\frac{1}{3}$ each, the security level becomes equal to 1.

If the other individual maximizes his own security level (that is to say if he minimizes his opponents maximum pay-off) he too will resort to mixed strategies. The details of the security levels which he could achieve by mixing together two pure strategies have been omitted from the table. It can be seen, however, that if he uses all his three pure strategies with probabilities $\frac{1}{6}$ for S_{01}, $\frac{2}{3}$ for S_{02} and $\frac{1}{2}$ for S_{03}, he can reduce his opponent's pay-off also to 1 (that is to say to the highest security level which the latter can achieve by mixing his own strategies).

(8.4.4) The numerical relations between the pay-offs from various strategies and the probabilities with which they can be mixed together are what in fact the mathematical theory of two-person zero-sum games is about. The mathematics of our numerical example is very simple. But this is only because the number of pure strategies in it is very small and the pay-offs from them have been so chosen that no difficulties arise. In general this is not so. It is not known in advance which (nor even how many) pure strategies would appear in the solution. Furthermore the solution is subject to the condition that the probability weights with which the pure strategies appear in it cannot be negative. It cannot, therefore, be obtained by solving a linear system of simultaneous equations as in the example above. Quite new mathematical procedures must be applied to arrive at it.

Very little, therefore, can be said about the mathematical side of the theory on the ground of a numerical example. One point, however, comes out quite clearly even now. If both individuals use mixed strategies so as to maximize their security levels, they arrive both of them at the same result. A numerical example cannot be taken as a proof that this is always so. It is, however, a useful illustration of what the mathematics of the theory has established as true.

It follows that if mixed strategies are admitted, every two-person zero-sum game must have an equilibrium solution. For if the maximin pay-offs of both individuals are equal one to the other, they are a saddle point of the game. And if a game has a saddle point, it has also a solution.

(8.4.5) The result is quite an achievement from a formal point of view. One may wonder, however, in what sense it may help to establish the maximin hypothesis as a part of a positive theory of our behaviour. The theory may easily acquire a normative sense. For it shows that if an individual uses a mixed strategy, he can achieve a higher security level than he could do if he used pure strategies only. If, therefore, he really wants to maximize his security level (and accepts the mean values of pay-offs as

;ure-prospect equivalents of his prospects of pay-offs from mixed strategies), he is well advised not to choose a pure strategy himself but to toss a coin and do what the coin says.[1] To give the theory a positive sense one might also argue that if this is so, many people should be tossing coins whenever they happen to be confronted with situations in which the element of a game is present. The prediction, therefore, which we could derive from the theory would be that people set up various mechanisms to decide what strategies to choose if such situations arise. This can hardly be regarded as being the case.

(8.4.6) It can be shown that if both players were using mixed strategies to maximize the mean values of pay-offs, they would arrive at a solution which maximizes also their security levels. For the pay-off of unity in Table 8.4.3 represents not only the mean value of pay-offs if both individuals play their mixed strategies so as to maximize their security levels, but it is also a maximum mean value from the point of view of either of them. For if one player wanted to change it in his favour by changing the mix of his strategy, his opponent would either not respond, and the pay-off would remain the same; or the opponent would adjust his mix so as to maximize the mean value of his pay-offs and reduce that of the individual who made the change first. It may thus be argued that in this case the hypothesis of a maximum security level and that of a maximum mean value of pay-offs come to one and the same thing. The argument is quite independent of whether the game is repetitive or is played only once. For the notions of the security level and of the mean value of pay-offs apply equally well to both of them.

(8.5) Two-Person Non-Zero-Sum Games

(8.5.1) Non-zero-sum games are those in which the pay-offs of the individuals who take part in them do not add up to the same figure for all strategies which the individuals may choose. Thus in a two-person game, the pay-offs of the two individuals differ one from the other not only in sign but also in their numerical value. Each entry in the matrix of pay-offs consists, therefore, of a pair of figures, one of them representing the pay-off of one

[1] On the nature of a mixed strategy see also L. D. Luce and H. Raiffa, *Games and Decisions*, John Wiley (New York, 1958),'pp. 74–6.

of the individual and the other that of the other. This does not affect the conclusion that if mixed strategies are admitted every two-person game must have an equilibrium solution. The respective theorem applies to all non-cooperative games. The point is only that if a game is not a zero-sum one, the equilibrium strategies may not be the maximin ones.

The following example may be considered as an illustration. Suppose that the matrix of Individual I's pay-offs is as in Table 8.3.1. It is reproduced in the first three rows and columns of Table 8.5.1a below. The other two rows and columns represent pay-offs from mixed strategies. Individual II's pay-offs are shown in Table 8.5.1b. As the game is not a zero-sum one, the numerical values of the latter differ from those of the former.

Table 8.5.1a

	S_{01}	S_{02}	S_{03}	$(\frac{1}{8}S_{01} + \frac{3}{8}S_{02} + \frac{1}{2}S_{03})$	$(\frac{1}{4}S_{01} + \frac{1}{4}S_{02} + \frac{1}{2}S_{03})$
S_{10}	-24	0	8	1	-2
S_{20}	18	-6	2	1	4
S_{30}	9	9	-7	1	1
$(\frac{1}{3}S_{10} + \frac{1}{3}S_{20} + \frac{1}{3}S_{30})$	1	1	1	1	1
$(\frac{1}{2}S_{10} + \frac{1}{2}S_{30})$	$-7\frac{1}{2}$	$4\frac{1}{2}$	$\frac{1}{2}$	1	$-\frac{1}{2}$

Table 8.5.1b

	S_{01}	S_{02}	S_{03}	$(\frac{1}{8}S_{01} + \frac{3}{8}S_{02} + \frac{1}{2}S_{03})$	$(\frac{1}{4}S_{01} + \frac{1}{4}S_{02} + \frac{1}{2}S_{03})$
S_{10}	12	6	-6	$\frac{3}{4}$	$1\frac{1}{2}$
S_{20}	-15	15	3	$5\frac{1}{4}$	$1\frac{1}{2}$
S_{30}	-9	-3	9	$2\frac{1}{4}$	$1\frac{1}{2}$
$(\frac{1}{3}S_{10} + \frac{1}{3}S_{20} + \frac{1}{3}S_{30})$	-4	6	2	$2\frac{3}{4}$	$1\frac{1}{2}$
$(\frac{1}{2}S_{10} + \frac{1}{2}S_{30})$	$1\frac{1}{2}$	$1\frac{1}{2}$	$1\frac{1}{2}$	$1\frac{1}{2}$	$1\frac{1}{2}$

The maximin strategies are $(\frac{1}{3}S_{10} + \frac{1}{3}S_{20} + \frac{1}{3}S_{30})$ and $(\frac{1}{4}S_{01} + \frac{1}{4}S_{02} + \frac{1}{2}S_{03})$ for Individual I and II respectively. They are not in equilibrium one with the other. For if Individual I knew that his opponent was going to choose his maximin strategy, he himself would choose S_{20}; and if Individual II knew that Individual I was going to choose ($\frac{1}{3}S_{10} + \frac{1}{3}S_{20} + \frac{1}{3}S_{30}$), he would choose S_{02}. The equilibrium strategies are ($\frac{1}{2}S_{10} + \frac{1}{2}S_{30}$) and ($\frac{1}{8}S_{01} + \frac{3}{8}S_{02} + \frac{1}{2}S_{03}$). Neither of the two individuals has then any incentive to change his strategy even if he knew for certain that his opponent was going to play his.

(8.5.2) The fact that an equilibrium pair of strategies may not be a maximin one raises the question what is the rationale of the individuals choosing the equilibrium pair. In a zero-sum game an equilibrium strategy maximizes the respective individual's security level. The rationale of choosing it is thus that the worst that he may expect to happen is then the least bad that may happen. Whatever the opponent does, whether he turns the state of the world completely to his advantage or makes a mistake and chooses a strategy which is less advantageous to him, the worst that the individual whom he opposes may expect is less bad if he himself chooses an equilibrium strategy than it would be if he chose some other.

In a non-zero-sum game this is not so. If an individual chooses an equilibrium strategy, he may obtain a lower than equilibrium pay-off. For the equilibrium pay-off may then not be the lowest in the respective column or row. It is that pay-off to which corresponds the greatest pay-off of the opponent. It is, therefore, only if the latter is always supreme, in the sense that he always turns the state of the world completely to his advantage, that the individual whom he opposes may be certain that his pay-off will not fall below the equilibrium level. If the opponent is not supreme, the respective pay-off may be smaller. For the opponent may then choose a strategy which does not give him the greatest pay-off; and so the individual whom he opposes may also obtain a smaller pay-off.

It seems, therefore, that in zero-sum and in non-zero-sum games, the rationale of choosing an equilibrium strategy is not quite the same. In zero-sum games the equilibrium pay-off is a security level in an absolute sense, both against the opponent being supreme and against one's own bad luck. In the case of non-zero-sum games it is a security level against the opponent being supreme only. For if an individual is unlucky, his opponent may make a mistake and choose a strategy which gives him a lower than equilibrium pay-off. Thus it is only if an individual

251

wishes to make himself secure against his opponent being supreme that he may be supposed to choose an equilibrium strategy. If he wished to make himself secure against his bad luck, he would choose a maximin one.

(8.5.3) It follows that the hypothesis which is implied in the equilibrium solution of a non-zero-sum game, is that the individuals behave as if they knew that their opponents would win the game. They do not take into account the possibility that they may lose more because of the opponent's mistake. This is not the same thing as being timid or cautious in general, as in the case of the maximin hypothesis. One may wonder, therefore, if there are any other reasons for the hypothesis of a maximin strategy to be discarded in favour of that of an equilibrium one, other than that the latter hypothesis is consistent with equilibrium and the former may not be consistent with it.

(8.5.4) If the game is played only once, it is difficult to say how we would in fact behave if we were playing it. We might try to mislead the opponent to induce him to play a strategy which is more advantageous to us. Or if this was not possible, we might play the equilibrium strategy and tell the opponent what it was to avoid him making a mistake which would give us a smaller than the equilibrium pay-off. We might not tell him which strategy we have chosen, hoping that he would make a mistake and give us a greater than the equilibrium pay-off. If we decided not to disclose our strategy, we might also play a maximin strategy to make ourselves secure against mistakes which are bad to us, but hoping that the one which the opponent makes will be good. As long as the behaviour of the opponent is uncertain, there are no special reasons for our choosing our equilibrium strategy rather than some other.

(8.5.5) If the game is played several times, equilibrium strategies may be interpreted as positions which the individuals approach as they adjust themselves to those of their opponents so as to maximize their pay-offs from them. This point has been discussed already with reference to zero-sum games. We argued then that such interpretation of the equilibrium solution implied a hypothesis that at each step of the process the players regarded the opponents' strategies as independent of what they themselves did, and that the interpretation required a dynamic theory of games which so far was not available.

Now it must be added that further complications may arise if the game is not a zero-sum one. For if a game has several equilibrium solutions, they may be different one from another both in terms of strategies and in those of pay-offs. In a zero-sum game the equilibrium solutions may be different in terms of strategies only; the pay-offs must be the same. We could argue, therefore, that whichever equilibrium pair of strategies the individuals would ultimately choose, they would be always in the same position with respect to their pay-offs. In a non-zero-sum game this is not so. According to how the individuals approach their equilibrium, they may arrive at a different position with respect to both the strategies and the pay-offs.

The question, therefore, arises what happens if an individual arrives at an equilibrium position which gives him a smaller pay-off than some other equilibrium position would do. Can the position at which he arrives be regarded as an equilibrium position? If he knows the matrix of the possible pay-offs, he must be aware of the existence of the other position as well. He may, therefore, try to upset the equilibrium at which he has arrived, by choosing a strategy which gives him a smaller pay-off, hoping that this will start a process of adjustment which will lead ultimately to a different and more satisfactory equilibrium position. This more satisfactory position, however, may then be upset by the opponent. And so the game may go on without any permanent equilibrium being attained. For an equilibrium position would then be acceptable to both individuals, only if it gave either of them a not smaller pay-off than any of the others. And in a non-zero-sum game such a position may not exist.

(8.6) Cooperation against the Rest of the World

(8.6.1) The possibility of cooperation against the rest of the world raises some further questions. The notion of equilibrium strategies does not then apply at all. The very reason for the formation of a coalition against the rest of the world is that if the individuals choose non-equilibrium strategies they may obtain, both of them, greater pay-offs. Furthermore, irrespective of whether a particular pair of strategies is or is not an equilibrium solution in the non-cooperative sense, it is not a cooperative solution if some other pair of strategies leads to greater pay-offs.

253

For if the individuals formed a coalition, they would always choose that other pair. The condition for a pair of strategies to be a solution of a cooperative game is that it is not dominated by any other pair, in the sense that it does not offer both individuals smaller pay-offs than that other pair does.

This is how the solution of a cooperative two-person game was defined by Von Neumann and Morgenstern. The hypothesis it implies is that if the individuals form a coalition, they always discard a pair of strategies if there is another pair which offers them greater pay-offs. This need not be the case if the evaluations of the pay-offs are interdependent. If, for instance, an increase in the pay-off of one of the individuals makes the other miserable even if his own pay-off increased as well, the latter may prefer a solution which gives both of them smaller pay-offs. Such interdependence is, however, usually neglected. The hypothesis is then acceptable on plausibility grounds.

(8.6.2) The difficulty is of a different kind. The theory of which the hypothesis is a part is incomplete. For in every game there is always not one, but several pairs of strategies which are not dominated by any others. The hypothesis singles out not one, but a whole set of possible solutions, and the theory of which it is a part does not say which of them is relevant. Some of them are better for one, others for the other individual. Which pair of strategies will, therefore, be ultimately chosen depends on whose interest will ultimately prevail. The bargaining skill, the relative strength of the bargaining positions, ethical standards and social restraints are the factors which determine the outcome. The formal theory of games stops, however, before they come into play. It singles out a set of strategies only, the so-called *negotiation set*. The pair to be actually played remains undetermined.

(8.6.3) There is further the complication that if the coalition is formed, the pay-offs which the individuals actually receive may depend not only on the strategies which they choose, but also on how they decide to distribute between themselves the pay-offs which these strategies offer. Formal theory distinguishes, therefore, between games with and without side payments. In games without side payments the division of the spoils is determined by the choice of the strategies. The bargain about the division may thus affect the total. For the only way to increase one's pay-off is then to force upon the other player a different pair of not dominated strategies, and this may result in a smaller joint pay-off. In games with side payments there is the possibility of the individuals redistributing between themselves the pay-offs from whatever strategies they choose. They have, therefore, to solve not one but two problems. One is to choose a suitable undominated pair of strategies; the other is to redistribute the pay-offs from them.

If no restrictions are imposed by the rules of the game on the redistribution of pay-offs, the solution of the problem of choice may be quite trivial. For both individuals are then interested in the greatest joint pay-off. The pair of strategies which maximizes this joint pay-off is, therefore, the solution of the game. If the distribution of pay-offs has to be agreed upon and laid down in a formula before the strategies are chosen, or if the individuals are not indifferent between receiving their pay-offs through redistribution and directly from outside because this might affect their strategic positions when the coalition is dissolved, the possibility of a pair of strategies being chosen which does not maximize joint pay-offs must again be taken into account. Unless, therefore, the theory provides for a solution of the problem of distribution, it cannot do more than select a number of pairs of strategies as possible solutions of the problem of choice.

(8.6.4) The formal theory of games has very little to offer in the case of two-person cooperative games. No hypotheses have been formulated so far to explain even the most general features of our behaviour. A theory of arbitration schemes has been developed to deal with special cases of the side-payments problem. But it is more of a normative character. It lays down rules for arbitration which lead to a 'fair' decision, consistent with value judgments which most people accept. No claim is made in it that the decisions are those which people actually make.

In its present state the theory of two-person non-zero-sum games cannot, therefore, be expected to play any useful part in economic theory. The hypotheses which its solutions imply are not more plausible than any others, and the theories in which they appear are incomplete. The plausibility test is not decisive. Incompleteness makes the theory so inconclusive in its predictions that very little could also be said about it on the ground of an empirical test. The very division of games into cooperative and non-cooperative ones, with and without side payments, is an admission that several types of solutions may arise, and several predictions can be made.

(8.7) Many-Person Games without Side Payments [1]

(8.7.1) Many-person games differ from two-person games not only in the degree of complexity of the problem of choosing individual strategies, but also in the character of the coalitions. In two-person games coalitions can be formed solely against the rest of the world. The individuals concerned may have, therefore, an incentive to form them only if the game is a non-zero-sum one. In many-person games coalitions may be also against the other players, and they may appear in zero-sum games as well.

A pattern of possible coalitions is usually called a *coalition structure*. The greater is the number of players the greater is also the number of such structures. In a three-person game, no coalitions at all may be formed, three coalitions of two players may be formed against the third, and one of three players against the rest of the world if the game is not a zero-sum one. In a four-person game, the number of possible coalitions of two increases from three to six, that of three increases from one to four, and there is also the possibility of a coalition of four against the rest of the world. Furthermore, if a coalition of two is formed, the other two players may either play the game each of them alone, or they too may form a coalition. Thus as the number of players increases, the number of possible coalition structures increases too, and very rapidly indeed.

(8.7.2) As in the case of two-person cooperative games, the main problem of the theory of many-person games is what to regard as their solution. In two-person zero-sum games the solution is a pair of maximin strategies which in that case are always in equilibrium one with the other. They may have to be mixed if the pure strategies in the game have no saddle point. If the possibility of mixing is taken into account, a solution always exists. In two-person non-zero-sum and non-cooperative games the solution is the equilibrium pair of strategies. If mixed strategies are admitted at least one such pair exists in this case as well. But it need not be a maximin pair. Finally in two-person non-zero-sum cooperative games the solution is the set of strat-

[1] For the points discussed in this and the following section, see also L. D. Luce and H. Raiffa, *Games and Decisions*, op. cit. Chapters 8 and 9.

·gies which are not dominated by any others. If the number of individuals is greater than two and the game is not a cooperative ·ne, the concept of the solution as a set of equilibrium strategies nay still apply. The theorem that there is always an equilibrium et of non-cooperative strategies is valid for all games, irres-·ective of the number of players. It may be even argued that if ·he game is played several times, the hypothesis that the players ·hoose equilibrium strategies is the more plausible the greater ·s the number of players. For it is then less likely that a large ·roportion of them would start to experiment with their strat-·gies at the same time, and more reasonable for them to adjust ·heir strategies to those of the others as if the latter were to ·emain unchanged.

(8.7.3) The concept of the solution as a set of undominated ·trategies does not apply if more than two individuals take part ·n a cooperative game. The reason is that there may then be no undominated strategies at all. Consider, for instance, the follow-ing game. Let there be three players in it; *A*, *B*, and *C*. Suppose that the game is a zero-sum one without side payments and that the players have no choice of strategy if they play it alone. They either have to play it in one particular way or form a coalition.

Table 8.7.3

| | Pay-offs of | | |
	A	*B*	*C*
No Coalition	4	4	4
Coalition of *B* and *C*	0	5	7
Coalition of *A* and *B*	5	7	0
Coalition of *A* and *C*	7	0	5
Coalition of *A*, *B*, and *C*	4	4	4

The conditions are summarized in Table 8.7.3. If no coalition is formed, all the individuals receive the same pay-off of 4. If all of them form a coalition against the rest of the world, they also receive 4 each. But if two of them form a coalition against the third, they may improve their pay-offs at the cost of the latter.

If no coalitions were permitted the solution would be trivial. The individuals would play the strategies which can be played,

257

and they would receive the pay-offs of 4 each. If, however, the players are allowed to form coalitions, no equilibrium solution can emerge from the data. For as soon as a coalition is formed, it tends to be disrupted in favour of some other. If, for instance, A and B form a coalition, their pay-offs become 5 and 7 respectively. C may then easily persuade A to form a coalition with him. For this would increase A's pay-off from 5 to 7. Then, however, B may persuade C to form a coalition with B. A may in turn win B back to a coalition with A. And so on, every coalition tends to be broken up and replaced by some other which is then also broken up and replaced.

(8.7.4) This is due to the fact that the relation of domination need not be transitive in this case. In cooperative two-person games one pair of strategies is said to dominate some other pair if the pay-offs which both players receive from the former are greater than those which they would receive from the latter. This is thought to be a sufficient reason for the latter to be discarded in favour of the former. The solution of the game is the set of strategies which are not dominated in this sense by any others. In many-person games, one coalition may be replaced by another. For this to be the case it is enough that one member of the former is offered a greater pay-off in the latter. For the other members cannot prevent him from leaving. There is, therefore, a tendency for one coalition to be replaced by another if it is dominated by it with respect to those players who become members of the new coalition. And as the same coalition may both dominate some others with respect to some players and be dominated by still others with respect to other players, the relation of domination need not be transitive, and there may be no coalition which would not be dominated at all.

(8.7.5) Not all many-person games need be like that. If there are more strategies to choose from and mixed strategies can be played jointly by members of the coalitions, a set of coalition structures and corresponding strategies may be found which are not dominated by any others, with respect to any players. Furthermore, the rules of the game may impose restrictions on changes in the structure of the coalitions. For instance, not more than one member of a coalition may be allowed to negotiate other coalitions. These restrictions may be due to various institutional, social, and psychological factors which affect the

258

formation of coalitions. If stated in a definite form, they could be accepted as hypotheses of a theory. So far, however, very little work has been done along these lines.

(8.8) Side Payments

(8.8.1) If side payments are permitted, we must distinguish between pay-offs before and after they have been made. The choice of the strategy is then determined by the latter only. They must, however, satisfy certain conditions if the particular structure of coalitions is to arise. In the first place (i) no player will take part in a coalition which offers him a smaller pay-off than the minimum which he could obtain if he played the game alone. Furthermore, if the joint pay-off from a coalition of all the players against the rest of the world were greater than the sum of their pay-offs from some other coalition structure, it could be redistributed between them so that every player would receive more than from that other coalition structure. The latter would then be abandoned in favour of the former. Those coalition structures may, therefore, be regarded as a solution which satisfies the condition that (ii) the pay-offs from them add up to not less than the total of pay-offs from a coalition against the rest of the world. Finally this last condition may be extended so as to cover not only the coalition of all players against the rest of the world, but also other coalition structures which the rules of the game permit. Thus a third condition may be added. If a coalition structure and the corresponding set of strategies is to be accepted as a solution, (iii) there must be no other coalition in the game which, even if opposed by a coalition of all the other players, would give its members a greater joint pay-off than what they receive in the solution. This third condition implies the other two as special cases.

(8.8.2) In the formal theory of games coalition structures and strategies which satisfy the first two of the above conditions are called *imputations*, and the structures and strategies which satisfy the third condition are called the *core of the game*. There is no generally accepted notion of a solution. It is sometimes defined as those imputations only which are in the core. At other times it includes also some of those which are outside it. The difficulty with the former definition is that in most cases the core is empty.

There is often no coalition structure which would satisfy condition (iii). The difficulty with the latter definition is that if condition (iii) is rejected, it is not easy to justify condition (ii). For if we do not take into account the possibility of a coalition being disrupted by some of its members forming an alternative coalition against other players, why should we take into account the possibility of its being disrupted by all its members forming a coalition against the rest of the world?

Table 8.7.3 may help to put these notions in a more definite form. The rows of pay-offs in it are imputations. The respective pay-offs are not smaller than the minimum which each individual could obtain if he played the game alone against a coalition of the other two, and they add up to not less than what the individuals could obtain jointly from a coalition of all of them against the rest of the world. But none of these imputations belongs to the core. For there is always another imputation in the table which dominates it with respect to the corresponding coalition. The core is empty in this case. For whatever imputation we might take, there would be always another imputation which dominates it with respect to some other coalition.

(8.8.3) Von Neumann and Morgenstern's definition is that the solution of a many-person game with side payments is the set of imputations which satisfy the following conditions: (i) none of the imputations in the solution must dominate any other in the solution with respect to any coalition, and (ii) any imputation outside the solution must be dominated by an imputation in the solution with respect to at least one coalition. Thus whatever coalition is formed and whatever side payments agreed upon outside the solution, the agreement may always be disrupted by a coalition and side payments in the solution. But no coalition and side payments in the solution can be disrupted by another coalition and side payments in the solution.

It is not difficult to see that Von Neumann and Morgenstern's solution of the game summarized in Table 8.7.3, may consist of those imputations in which the pay-offs in the three possible coalitions are so redistributed through side payments between their members, that either of them receives 6. Any other imputation is then dominated and may be disrupted by one of those three; and none of the imputations in that solution is dominated and can be disrupted by any other in it.

This, however, is not the only solution. For the members of a coalition may also allow side payments to the player who remains outside it. Thus a set of imputations which give a certain fixed pay-off not greater than 6 to one of the players, and variable pay-offs adding up to what remains from 12 to the other two, is also a Von Neumann and Morgenstern solution. And there are three such solutions, each corresponding to a different player's pay-off being fixed. The indeterminacy in this case is even greater than in that of games without side payments. For not only we do not know which result from those in the solution will actually occur, but we do not know from which solution it will come.

(8.8.4) The remarks made in this chapter do not do justice to the amount and importance of work which has been done in the field of the theory of games as a whole. They refer to those aspects of the theory only which are relevant to the purpose in hand. One point, however, seems to emerge from them which is important for the appraisal of the theory. If a game is in its simplest form, a two-person zero-sum one with a saddle point, the theory may be interpreted as a descriptive one. The maximin hypothesis is then both plausible and sufficient to determine the outcome. The further away, however, we move from this simplest form, the less satisfactory is the result. If the game has no saddle point, mixed strategies have to be introduced to obtain an equilibrium solution. If the game is not a zero-sum one, the possibility of a coalition against the rest of the world must be taken into account, and the solution becomes a set of possibilities, a negotiation set. The actual result is supposed to be an element of this set. Which element will actually occur depends on institutional, sociological, and psychological factors which do their work outside the field of the theory of games. Finally, if the game is a many-person game, the scope for the formation of coalitions is so wide that it is difficult to determine even a single set of possibilities as a solution.

As a descriptive theory of our behaviour, the theory of games does not seem, therefore, to have reached the stage yet at which definite hypotheses could be assessed as plausible or tested empirically. It is in fact not very clear what hypotheses about our behaviour the particular solutions imply or what aspects of that behaviour they are meant to explain. The most obvious field for the application of the theory to economics is that of oligopoly and bilateral monopoly. Even in this case, however, little more has been achieved so far than the presentation of some parts of the existing theory in game-theoretic terms.[1]

[1] Compare, for instance, the relevant paragraphs in Von Neumann and Morgenstern's, *Theory of Games and Economic Behaviour, op. cit.*; M. Shubik, *Strategy and Market Structure*, John Wiley (New York, 1959); J. P. Mayberry, J. F. Nash and M. Shubik, A Comparison of Treatments of a Duopoly Situation, *Econometrica*, **21**, January (1953), pp. 141-54; H. Neisser, Oligopoly as a Non-Zero-Sum Game, *Review of Economic Studies*, XXV (1), October (1957). An interesting attempt to apply game theory to the problem of the selection of crops was made by Sidney Moglever, A Game Theory Model for Agricultural Crop Selection, *Econometrica*, **30**, April (1962), pp. 253-66.

9

Other Hypotheses

SHACKLE'S theory of expectations and the theory of games relate the behaviour of individuals to some extreme outcomes in the expectations to which this behaviour gives rise. The difference is in the provisions which the respective theories make for the selection of these outcomes. In Shackle's theory the focus gain and focus loss are determined by the individuals' subjective attitudes towards the possible pay-offs and degrees of potential surprise. They are those possible outcomes which attract most the individuals' attention. In the theory of games, the outcomes are selected by a formula. They correspond to those strategies of the opponent which belong to the solution.

In the theories discussed in this chapter, the behaviour is also related to some selected outcomes. The provision for their selection contains, however, both the subjective element and that of a formula. This is probably the only feature that they have in common. In other respects they differ one from another. But as none of them requires a whole chapter to be explained and appraised, this mixture of subjective and rational elements may be a sufficient ground for grouping them together.

The theories are those of Savage's minimum subjective loss, Hurwicz's index of pessimism and optimism, Fellner's theory of safety margins, and Roy's theory of a minimum chance of disaster. None of them has ever been put forward as a general theory. They have been devised *ad hoc* to deal with some problems in which expectations become involved. But all of them could be interpreted as a general theory, and it is in this extended form that they will be considered here.

263

(9.1) Maximin and Maximax

(9.1.1) The *maximin hypothesis* of the theory of games may also be applied to non-game situations. Suppose, for instance, that S_{01}, S_{02} and S_{03} in Tables 8.2.2 or 8.3.1 are not strategies of the opponent, but states of the world independent of the behaviour of the individual who plays the game. In other words (as in the second part of this book) the choice of the row of the matrix has no effect on which of the columns will come off. The strategies represented by the rows may then be ranked according to what is the smallest pay-off that can be obtained from them, and the individual may be choosing that strategy which gives him the greatest from those smallest pay-offs.

To be accepted as plausible in a non-game situation, the maximin hypothesis requires a different justification than it does in the theory of games. In this latter case the opponent wants to make our pay-off as small as possible. It is, therefore, by no means implausible that if we find ourselves in a situation of this kind, we behave so as to be always prepared for the worst. If, however, the situation is not one of a game, the laws which govern the behaviour of the world are not those of minimizing our pay-off. The maximin hypothesis could, therefore, be plausible only if either (i) we felt certain that the state of the world with the smallest pay-off would ultimately come off, or if (ii) we were so frightened or distressed by the possibility of this smallest pay-off coming off that we would not be able to think of any other.

(9.1.2) The first alternative is inconsistent with the condition that the state of the world is independent of the strategy we choose. For if the minimum pay-offs in different rows of the matrix are also in different columns, we cannot expect the minimum pay-offs to come off unless we think that the coming off of the column depends on the choice of the row. Only if all minimum pay-offs happened to be in the same column and we thought that the state of the world represented by that column would actually come off, only then would our belief that the actual state of the world will be that of the lowest pay-off not be inconsistent with the condition that it is independent of our strategy.

The alternative that we feel so distressed by the possibility of the lowest pay-off that we cannot think of any other is not inconsistent with any of the conditions to which the hypothesis is supposed to apply. It does not seem, however, to be very plausible either. For if we imagine ourselves in a situation in which the pay-off from every strategy that we may choose is uncertain, we are not likely to be so distressed by the possibility of the lowest pay-off as not to take into account any others. In some cases such extreme caution might be justified. But as a general rule it does not seem to be acceptable.

(9.1.3) The maximin hypothesis is disproved by the fact that people gamble. For if they were always behaving so as to make as good as possible the worse that may happen to them, they would never buy any lottery tickets. They would be so distressed by the prospect of losing, that they would not pay any attention to that of winning.

(9.1.4) The opposite of the maximin is the *maximax hypothesis*. It says that people behave so as to maximize the greatest pay-off that the respective strategies permit. This means that they are so pleased with the prospect of the greatest pay-off that they do not pay any attention to the possibility of its being smaller than that. They choose, therefore, their strategies so as to make this greatest pay-off the greatest possible.

The reservations which have been made above with respect to the maximin hypothesis apply to this case as well. We might be so optimistic or reckless in our behaviour as to neglect the possibility of all others except the maximum pay-off in very special circumstances only. In general the maximax behaviour is not plausible. And it is inconsistent with the fact that people insure themselves against possible losses. For if only the greatest pay-offs were taken by them into account, the possibility of losses would be irrelevant to their decisions.

(9.1.5) The other two combinations of min and max of pay-offs may be dismissed straightaway. A minimax and a minimin hypothesis would imply that the individual chooses his strategies so as to minimize either the maximum or the minimum pay-off. This is so much at variance with what we intuitively perceive as true, that it need not be considered.

(9.2) The Minimax Hypothesis of Subjective Loss

(9.2.1) Another hypothesis of one extreme is that of a minimum maximum loss. It has been originally formulated as a part of the theory of statistical decisions[1] but may also be turned into a positive theory of behaviour. The idea is as follows. Suppose that a certain state of the world will come off. If the individual knew what state of the world this would be, he would choose the strategy which gives him the greatest pay-off from it. If, for instance, he knew that state D in Table 9.2.1 would come off, he would choose strategy B. In fact, however, he does not know

Table 9.2.1

	F	D	O
C	9	1	−7
B	5	3	−2
U	2	2	2

which state of the world will come off, and he may choose strategy C. His pay-off would then be 1 instead of 3. The difference between what he could get and what he actually gets may be accepted as a measure of his subjective loss from having chosen C instead of B. If the actual state of the world were F and he chose B, the measure of his loss would be 4 (because he would get 9 instead of 5 if he chose C).

(9.2.2) An optimum strategy is supposed to be that which minimizes the maximum loss. To determine it we must transform the matrix of pay-offs into one of losses. To the highest pay-off in a particular column corresponds zero subjective loss. For the individual cannot do better than to choose the strategy from which this highest pay-off can be obtained; and so if he chooses it, he cannot feel any loss. The measures corresponding to other strategies are the differences between the pay-offs from them and the highest pay-off in the same columns. Table 9.2.2 has

Table 9.2.2

	F	D	O
C	0	2	9
B	4	0	4
U	7	1	0

[1] See L. J. SAVAGE, The Theory of Statistical Decisions, *Journal of the American Statistical Association*, **46**, (1951), pp. 55-67.

been derived in this way from Table 9.2.1. According to the minimax hypothesis of subjective loss the individual will choose strategy B. For B exposes him to the possibility of loss of up to 4, and C and U up to 9 and 7 respectively.

(9.2.3) The minimax hypothesis of subjective loss is subject to the same objections as all other hypotheses of one extreme. The individual is supposed to concentrate his attention on the highest figure of possible losses to the exclusion of all the others. In the example given above, he prefers B to U because the greatest loss to which he exposes himself is 4 if he chooses B, and 7 if he chooses U. The intermediate pay-offs and losses are supposed to be quite irrelevant to how he ranks the strategies. As in the case of other extremes he must, therefore, either regard the state of the world as not independent of his own strategy, or he must be so distressed by the possibility of a loss that he is not able to see any other outcomes than those which would give him the most of it. The first alternative is equivalent to the situation being seen by the individual as one of a game and has been discussed in Chapter 8. The second is acceptable on logical grounds. It is, however, not very plausible as a description of the mental processes which actually take place.

This is the more so, the more states of the world there are with intermediate measures of subjective losses. If, for instance, there are not three but ten states of the world, there must be not one but eight such intermediate measures. If then the greatest possible loss from one strategy is only a little lower than that from some other, the former is supposed to be chosen even if the latter leads to a much lower loss than the former from all the other states of the world. It is by no means clear why this should be so.

(9.2.4) The 'extremeness' of the minimum loss hypothesis is smaller than that of the maximin one of pay-offs. For if the behaviour of the individual is determined by the former, it depends not on one pay-off from each strategy but on how this pay-off differs from some others. In Table 8.3.1, for instance, S_{20} is a maximin strategy because the lowest pay-off from it is greater than the lowest pay-offs from S_{10} and from S_{30}. The pay-offs which are not the lowest are irrelevant. In the minimax hypothesis of subjective loss, some of these other pay-offs are relevant. For the maximum possible loss from C in Table 9.2.2

267

depends on the pay-off from C and O in Table 9.2.1 being -7 and on the pay-off from U and O being 2; and the maximum loss from U depends on the pay-offs from C and F and from U and F being 9 and 2 respectively.

Table 9.2.4

	F	D	O
B	0	0	4
U	3	1	0

This reduction of the 'extremeness' of the maximin hypothesis gives rise, however, to the following difficulty. Suppose that an individual behaves in accordance with the minimax hypothesis of subjective loss, and chooses B in Tables 9.2.1 and 9.2.2. The least satisfactory strategy is C because it exposes the individual to the greatest possible loss. It seems, therefore, that whether or not C is available, this should not have any effect on the individual's behaviour. It would not be chosen in either case. In fact, however, this is not so. If C is not available, the loss matrix becomes as in Table 9.2.4, and not B but U minimizes the individual's maximum loss.

(9.2.5) What is involved in this argument will probably be seen better if a more topical interpretation is given to the matrices in the tables. Suppose that the pay-offs in Table 9.2.1 are subjective utilities which we derive from using three types of transport in different traffic conditions. The strategies C, B and U mean going by car, by bus, and by underground; and the states of the world F, D and O mean that traffic is moving freely, with difficulty, and that it is obstructed. The utility pay-offs from C and B are greater the better are the traffic conditions. Those from U are independent of them. The numerical measures of these pay-offs reflect our ranking of the alternatives.

It follows from the argument in the preceding paragraph that if all the three means of transport are available, we will go to town by bus. If, however, we have not got a car, we will go by underground. Does this make sense? The following rationalisation might be put forward as a justification. If we have got a car, we may not use it to go to town because we cannot face the prospect of being caught in a jam if the roads happen to be obstructed; and we do not use the underground because we would be angry with ourselves that we have not taken the car if the roads happen to be free. So the bus is the answer. If, however, we have not got a car, we do not miss much if we take the underground and the roads happen to be free; and we avoid also the displeasure of a long journey in a bus if they happen to be obstructed. Thus the underground is the answer.

Do we behave in this way? An affirmative answer is very unlikely. But it is not impossible. Plausibility considerations do not lead to any conclusive result. The argument points also towards an empirical test. For if people were really changing their means of transport as indicated above, the hypothesis would in a sense be confirmed by facts. No evidence, however, seems to be available that this is so.

(9.3) *Index of Pessimism-Optimism*

(9.3.1) Hurwicz's[1] index of pessimism-optimism is an example of a hypothesis of two extremes. It has been devised as an element in a normative theory. To give it the status of a hypothesis means, therefore, to deal with its incidental aspects only. Every normative theory may, however, be turned into a descriptive one if it is supplemented with a hypothesis that people behave as they should. Treated in this way, Hurwicz's hypothesis belongs to the same class as the hypothesis of focus gain and focus loss in Shackle's theory of expectation. For in both cases, the individual is supposed to concentrate his attention on two outcomes – the best and worst. Only the criteria of what is the best and the worst are different.

In Shackle's theory, the best and the worst outcomes are those which attract most the individual's attention because they offer large or small pay-offs without much potential surprise. The selection is subjective. According to how the individual's imagination is stimulated by the respective pay-offs and degrees of potential surprise one rather than some other pair of focus

---

[1] L. Hurwicz, *Optimality Criteria for Decision Making Under Ignorance.* The paper was mimeographed (in 1951) as Cowles Commission Discussion Paper, *Statistics*, No. 370. The present section follows the summary given by R. D. Luce and H. Raiffa in their *Games and Decisions, op. cit.*, pp. 282–4.

gain and focus loss is selected as a basis for the appraisal of the strategy.

In Hurwicz's theory, the best and the worst outcomes are simply those which offer the greatest and the smallest pay-off. Subjective elements may affect the selection only through the appraisal of these pay-offs. If two individuals differ in the latter, they may select different outcomes. The selection itself is completely objective. The outcomes selected are always those of the greatest and the smallest pay-offs.

(9.3.2) The evaluation of the prospects to which different strategies give rise is subjective in both theories. Hurwicz's theory is, however, much more definite in this respect than Shackle's theory. For in this latter case, nothing is said about the evaluation of strategies except that the pairs of the best and the worst outcomes are ranked by the individual so that the ranking satisfies the conditions of consistency and transitivity, and can be represented by a system of upward sloping indifference curves. The knowledge of the exact form of the latter is essential to the prediction of choices in any actual situations. In Hurwicz's theory, the subjective attitudes of the individual towards the best and the worst outcomes are summarized in a numerical coefficient, a pessimism-optimism index, which reduces to a common denominator all possible pairs of pay-offs.

The idea is as follows. Suppose that the smallest pay-off which the individual may expect from a certain strategy is m and the greatest pay-off is M. Hurwicz's formula is that the respective strategy is ranked higher or lower according to what is the numerical value of the expression

$$am + (1 - a)M$$

in which a is the respective individual's index of pessimism-optimism. The greater is that index the more is the individual influenced in the evaluation of the strategy by the worst outcome and the less by the best outcome in the prospect of pay-offs to which it gives rise. In the extreme cases in which a is unity or zero, the strategies are ranked according to what are the smallest or the greatest pay-offs, and Hurwicz's hypothesis is equivalent to the maximin or the maximax hypotheses respectively.

(9.3.3) The pessimism-optimism index plays the same rôle in Hurwicz's theory as the gambler indifference system does in that of Shackle. If we know the index, we can predict the individual's choices of strategies on the ground of the matrices of pay-offs to which they give rise. The ranking of the strategies could then be also represented on an indifference map. To be summarized as an index, however, the map would have to be of a very special form. All indifference curves with respect to m's and M's would have to be straight lines sloping downwards at an angle whose tangent is $(1/a - 1)$.

This arbitrary restriction on the form of the indifference curves is the price which has to be paid for them to be ascertainable by observation. Shackle's gambler indifference curves could be ascertained point by point only by introspection. For they refer to combinations of pay-offs and degrees of potential surprise which exist only in the individual's imagination. They could not predict, therefore, any other choices except those which in the individual's imagination have been already made. Hurwicz's index of pessimism-optimism can be derived from the individual's choices by observation, and it can be applied to the prediction of other choices, other than those from which it has been derived.

(9.3.4) The procedure is the same as in Von Neumann and Morgenstern's utility index or in Ramsey's and Savage's subjective probability measure. Consider the following operation. Suppose that the individual is confronted with two strategies to choose from. One is simply to take a certain sum of money, say c, whatever state of the world comes off. The other is to expose oneself to uncertainty what the actual pay-off will be, subject only to the restriction that it will not be smaller than m and not greater than M. According to Hurwicz's hypothesis, the individual will choose the second strategy if $am + (1 - a)M$ is greater than c and the first strategy if the opposite is true. Suppose, however, that c is so adjusted that the individual is indifferent which strategy he chooses. We have then $am + (1 - a)M = c$, and the index of pessimism-optimism can be determined by solving this equation for a.

The index may then be used to predict the individual's choices in other situations. If he is confronted with strategies to which correspond some other smallest and greatest pay-offs, the ranking of the strategies may be predicted by calculating $am + (1 - a)M$ for each of them. The value of the index a is the only

271

information about the individual which we need to make the prediction.

(9.3.5) If there are two outcomes only, Hurwicz's index of pessimism-optimism cannot be distinguished from Ramsey's and Savage's measure of subjective probability. For if we accept that what is measured is also defined in terms of the operation by means of which it is measured, both Hurwicz's a and Ramsey's p come to one and the same thing. The names by which they are called are only interpretations of the individual's states of mind which they formalize. Probability conveys the idea that the states of the world in which the particular pay-offs would occur represent a certain proportion of all possible states of the world which in virtue of the available evidence are thought to be equally likely. It is outward looking. Even if interpreted as subjective probability, it summarizes certain properties of the world as seen by the respective individual. The index of pessimism-optimism is inward looking. It summarizes the individual's emotional attitudes towards what this world may be like. Formally they are, however, defined in terms of the same operation, and they are therefore undistinguishable one from the other in the formal scheme of the theory.

If more than two outcomes of pay-offs appear in the prospect, Hurwicz's index of pessimism-optimism cannot be identified with probability. For this would amount to the same thing as that zero probability weights are attached arbitrarily to the outcomes of all intermediate pay-offs. More than that. If different strategies were compared, zero probability weights would have to be attached to outcomes of different states of the world. Thus to be consistent in his pessimism-optimism, the individual would have to be inconsistent in the prospect of the future state of the world.

(9.4) Some Further Comments

(9.4.1) Is Hurwicz's hypothesis plausible? The reduction of a multi-outcome prospect to two extreme outcomes only is subject to the same objections as Shackle's focus gains and focus losses. The outcomes which offer less than the maximum and more than the minimum pay-offs are not irrelevant to our decisions. For suppose that in one strategy all of them are very close to the maximum, and in some other they are very close to the minimum. Would we regard the two strategies as equally satisfactory if they offered the same maximum and the same minimum pay-offs? Most people would say that they would not.

We might rule out this objection on the ground that those who say that they would not regard the two strategies as equally satisfactory would be thinking in terms of probability weights; and Hurwicz's theory applies to those cases only in which weights of outcomes cannot be formalized as probability weights. If, however, we argued in this way, we would have to say clearly to what cases the theory does and to what cases it does not apply. Uniqueness of the events on which the pay-offs depend is not the relevant criterion, because subjective probability weights may be attached to outcomes in prospects of unique events as well. Nor could it be our ignorance of the weights. For ignorance may mean equal probability weights. If, therefore, we are not to think in terms of probability weights, there must be something else that prevents us from doing so. So far, however, no satisfactory explanation has been given of what this actually is.

(9.4.2) Hurwicz's theory of pessimism-optimism could be tested empirically. For it provides for an operation by means of which the index can be ascertained and the individual's choices predicted. But no such tests seem to have ever been made. The theory was put forward as a normative criterion of rational behaviour. Rational grounds only have therefore been given for its acceptance. In view of the difficulties mentioned in the preceding paragraph, one might even wonder if any test could disprove the hypothesis. For a negative result might always be interpreted as not that the theory was wrong but that the condition of not thinking in terms of probability weights was not satisfied in the test.

(9.4.3) Luce and Raiffa[1] criticised Hurwicz's index on the ground that it may lead to inconsistency in the individual's choices of mixed strategies. Take the following example. Suppose that there are three possible states of the world and two strategies. Let the respective pay-offs be as in Table 9.4.3. Suppose that the index of pessimism-optimism is $\frac{3}{4}$. Both S_{10} and S_{20} have then the same rank on the individual's scale of preference. For the worst and the best pay-offs are the same in either case;

(1) R. Duncan Luce and Howard Raiffa, *Games and Decisions*, op. cit., p. 283.

273

Table 9.4.3

	S_{01}	S_{02}	S_{03}
S_{10}	1	0	0
S_{20}	0	1	0
$(\frac{1}{2}S_{10} + \frac{1}{2}S_{20})$	$\frac{1}{2}$	$\frac{1}{2}$	0

and $\frac{3}{4}.0 + \frac{1}{4}.1 = \frac{1}{4}$. If the two strategies are mixed together with probability weights $\frac{1}{2}$ and $\frac{1}{2}$, the respective pay-offs are as in the last row of the table. The best pay-off is then $\frac{1}{2}$, and the rank of the mixed strategy is $\frac{3}{4}.0 + \frac{1}{4}.\frac{1}{2} = \frac{1}{8}$, lower than that of S_{10} and S_{20}. Thus although the individual is indifferent between S_{10} and S_{20}, he is not prepared to leave the choice to chance.

(9.4.4) The criticism applies not so much to Hurwicz's hypothesis of the index of pessimism-optimism as to the individual ranking strategies in accordance with Hurwicz's hypothesis but evaluating the prospects of pay-offs in different states of the world according to their mean values.

It is possible to argue that the behaviour of the world is so uncertain that no probability weights can be attached to different outcomes of what it may be; and in a mixed strategy special mechanism is set up to determine the probability weights of the two pure strategies in it. The prospects of pay-offs from the mixed strategies can, therefore, be evaluated on the ground of their mean values; but the states of the world which give rise to them have to be taken into account in accordance with some other theory.

It has, however, been shown in (4.4.6) that the derivation of sure-prospect equivalents from conditional expectations may easily lead to arbitrary results even if the hypothesis of the mean value is applied throughout. One might expect, therefore, this to be even more so if different hypotheses are used side by side. In Luce and Raiffa's case the rank of the mixed strategy is derived from sure-prospect equivalents of pay-offs for each possible state of the world. The result depends then on whether we calculate first the mean values of pay-offs for each possible state of the world and use Hurwicz's hypothesis to evaluate the mixed strategy next; or whether we evaluate first the pure strategies on the ground of Hurwicz's hypothesis and calculate the mean values next. In the first case the result is $\frac{3}{4}.0 + \frac{1}{4}(\frac{1}{2}.0 + \frac{1}{2}.1) =$ $\frac{1}{8}$; in the second case it is $\frac{1}{2}(\frac{3}{4}.0 + \frac{1}{4}.1) + \frac{1}{2}(\frac{3}{4}.0 + \frac{1}{4}.1) = \frac{1}{4}$. Thus if the mean values come first, and Hurwicz's pessimism-optimism index second, the rank of the mixed strategy is below that of the two pure ones; and if Hurwicz's index comes first and the mean values second, all the three strategies have the same rank. Which procedure has to be chosen is the matter for the theory to decide. In Hurwicz's theory, mixed strategies were not considered at all. Nothing, therefore, could have been said in it about how they would be ranked.

(9.4.5) It may be further argued that Luce and Raiffa's objection applies not only to Hurwicz's index of pessimism-optimism but also to the maximin hypothesis in the theory of games. For suppose that two strategies in a game offer the individual the same security levels. According to the maximin hypothesis the individual is then indifferent whether he chooses one or the other. By combining them into a mixed strategy he may, however, increase his security level. He prefers, therefore, the mixed strategy to either of the two pure ones. The situation is then similar to that discussed above. The individual is indifferent between two pure strategies and none the less he is not indifferent whether to choose one of them himself or leave the matter to chance. The difference is only that in the case of the maximin hypothesis the lowest pay-offs only count. The mixed strategy cannot, therefore, be ranked lower than the pure strategies which are mixed in it. In Hurwicz's theory both the lowest and the highest pay-offs count. The rank of the mixed strategy may, therefore, be higher as well as lower than that of the pure ones.

(9.4.6) It can be also shown that Hurwicz's theory of pessimism-optimism can explain gambling without introducing the notion of increasing marginal utility of income over any range of the utility curve. For suppose that the utility curve is as in FIG. 9.4.6. Marginal utility diminishes over its whole length. Suppose further that the worst pay-off is OW, the best is OB, and that Hurwicz's index of pessimism-optimism is VB/WB. The rank of the strategy which gives rise to these pay-offs is indicated by VP. If then H satisfies the condition that $MH = VP$, a sure-prospect pay-off which the individual would prefer to a gamble for pay-offs in the range between OW and OB cannot be smaller than OH.

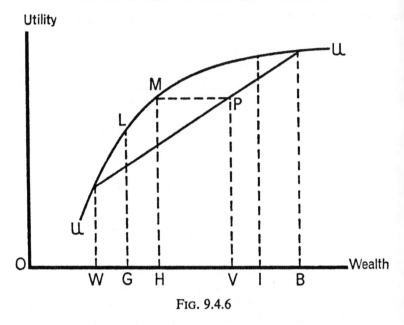

FIG. 9.4.6

Suppose now that the present wealth of the individual is at *G*, somewhere between *W* and *H*, and that the strategy which he contemplates is a gamble in which he would have to pay *WG* in order to have a chance of winning at most *WB*. The utility of *OG* is *GL*, lower than that of the gamble. Thus the individual will choose the gamble. If his present wealth were at *B*, and the strategy which he contemplated were to pay *IB* to insure himself against losses up to *WB*, he would choose the insurance.

For these conclusions to be valid *WG* in the gamble must not exceed *WH*, and *IB* in the insurance must not exceed *HB*. Within these limits, however, the actual amount of the stake and of the premium are irrelevant. Thus the argument holds also for 'unfair' gambles and insurances. The stakes and the premiums may cover profits and costs of those who organise them. It leads also to the prediction that most popular gambles are for large prizes at small stakes, and that the most popular insurances are against large losses at small premiums.

(9.4.7) In spite of it not being readily acceptable on plausibility grounds, Hurwicz's theory does not seem to be doing very badly as an explanation of our behaviour in some typical situations. Those who subscribe to the Marshallian law of satiable wants

276

and insist on marginal utility of income to be always diminishing, might even derive some satisfaction from the fact that Friedman-Savage-Markowitz's hypothesis that marginal utility of income may be increasing, is not the only explanation of gambling we have. Hurwicz's index of pessimism-optimism might do the trick as well.

(9.5) Theory of Safety Margins

(9.5.1) The theory of safety margins was invented by Fellner to account for certain aspects of the behaviour of firms in pricing their products and in holding cash reserves. It attracted some attention after the last war. Now the questions which it attempted to answer are less topical than they were then. The theory, however, contains hypotheses about the behaviour of firms which are worth considering for their own sake, quite apart from the purpose for which they were originally formulated.

(9.5.2) Take first Fellner's theory of pricing.[1] Its general outline is as follows. Firms accept as a basis for their decisions 'best-guess' curves of demand and of costs. But they take also into account the possibility of these best guesses being wrong. The demand curve may turn out to be lower or the cost curve higher than was originally thought because there may be an unexpected change in the conditions of demand for the product or in the prices of the factors.

This uncertainty about the actual position of the demand and of the cost curves may have the following consequences for the firm's price-output decisions. Suppose that the best-guess demand curve and the best-guess average cost curve of the firm are as DD, AC, and MC in Fig. 9.5.2. The best-guess maximum profit output is then OQ_m. It is determined by the condition that the best-guess marginal revenue is equal to the marginal costs. If it then turns out that the actual demand curve is further down, as D^1D^1 for instance, output OQ_m must be sold at a loss. For the price which can be obtained for it is below the average costs. If, however, the firm decided to produce OQ, it could still have some profits. Similarly, if the actual cost curve happened

[1] W. Fellner, Average-Cost Pricing and the Theory of Uncertainty, *Journal of Political Economy*, LVI, June (1948), pp. 149–52 ; and *Competition Among the Few*, Kelley (New York, 1960), pp. 146–56.

to be AC^1, the firm would have some profits from OQ, but losses only from OQ_m. To make itself secure against as much of such losses as possible the firm would have to fix its output at that point at which the distance between DD and AC is the greatest.

Fellner's hypothesis is that firms either maximize safety margins, or at least compromise between safety and profit requirements. The compromise takes usually the form of a certain mark up for safety margins being added to average variable costs and of the output being fixed so that best-guess profits are

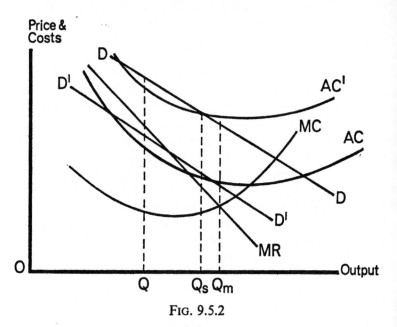

FIG. 9.5.2

maximized subject to the condition that even if the cost and demand curves shift by the whole extent of the safety margin, profits will not fall below zero. If in FIG. 9.5.2, the curve of best-guess average variable costs plus safety margin were AC^1, the firm's output would be OQ_s.

(9.5.3) The result is the same as if the firms were adjusting their outputs to prices fixed at the level of the average variable costs plus a mark up for overheads and profits. The theory is thus an explanation of the pricing procedures which have been found prevalent in the actual world. Businessmen's assertion that the mark-up is for overheads and profits may be only their

278

own rationalization of what they are doing. In fact the mark-up is a safety margin.

(9.5.4) Fellner's analysis of demand for cash reserves[1] follows a similar line. Suppose that the curve AY in FIG. 9.5.4 represents the relation between best-guess average yield and the amount of investment. The average yield is measured along the vertical axis and the amount of investment along the horizontal axis. Suppose also that capital for investment can be obtained in unlimited quantities at a constant rate of interest OR. If the firm maximizes best-guess profits, the optimum amount of investment is OI_m. The marginal best-guess yield is then equal to

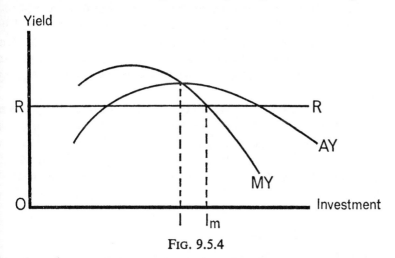

FIG. 9.5.4

the rate of interest. If the firm maximizes safety margins, the optimum amount of investment is OI. It corresponds to the point at which the distance between AY and RR is the greatest.

Losses are usually cumulative. For if they occur, the firm may be compelled to sell some of its assets in unfavourable market conditions; it may find it more difficult to obtain credit; or it may even be forced into liquidation in spite of the fact that given time it might easily recover from what is only a temporary setback. To prevent this happening, firms usually hold contingency balances, reserves of cash which enable them to overcome the difficulties due to unexpected losses. The smaller the safety

[1] W. Fellner, Monetary Policies and Hoarding in Periods of Stagnation, *Journal of Political Economy*, **LI**, June (1943), pp. 191–205.

margin, the easier such unexpected losses may occur, and the greater is the need for the balances. The amount of contingency balances is thus inversely related to the safety margins which the particular investment can offer.

(9.5.5) Suppose now that at the rate of interest and with the best-guess average yield curve as in FIG. 9.5.4, the amount of investment which the firm contemplates is OI; then, owing to some unfavourable trends in the industry to which the firm belongs, the curve of best-guess average yields shifts downwards. The result is a decline in safety margins. The particular project may then be abandoned altogether. But it is also possible that the firm will go on with the project, increasing only its contingency balances to compensate the decline in safety margins. The same may happen if the rate of interest is increased. This too leads to smaller safety margins, and the firms which want to go on with their investment plans must have greater contingency balances.

This is the proposition which the theory of safety margins was expected to establish. Such perverse reactions of demand for cash balances to changes in the best guess yields and in the rate of interest, did in fact occur in the United States of America in the interwar period. Fellner's theory was an attempt to account for them.

(9.6) Fellner's Hypothesis

(9.6.1) Without going into the merits of Fellner's theory as an explanation of full cost pricing and of perverse reactions in demand for money, let us disentangle from it the precise form of the hypothesis from which its conclusions derive. If the data in FIG. 9.5.2 were segregated into a finite number of classes, they might be summarized in a table. Consider, for instance, a matrix of pay-offs as in Table 9.6.1. The rows of the matrix correspond to different outputs of the firm; the columns to different, unspecified states of the world; and the figures of pay-offs are total profits. In Fellner's theory, no numerical weights are attached to the outcomes of different states of the world. One of them, however, the best-guess state of the world, has a special status. It represents 'zero' of a sort from which 'distance' of the other states of the world is measured.

Table 9.6.1

	S_{01}	S_{02}	S_{03}	S_{04}	S_{05}
S_{10}	5	3	1	−1	−3
S_{20}	12	8	4	0	−4
S_{30}	15	9	3	−3	−9
S_{40}	16	8	0	−8	−16
S_{50}	15	5	−5	−15	−25

To obtain the measure of that distance, the strategies and the states of the world are arranged in the following way. The strategies of output are arranged in an ascending or a descending order. The states of the world are arranged so that in each row the pay-offs decrease as we move from left to right. As different states of the world correspond to different positions of cost and demand curves either higher up or further down along the whole length of them, such arrangement is both possible and unique. The distance of any particular state of the world from the zero one can then be measured by the number of columns in the matrix the former is away from the latter.

(9.6.2) The hypothesis that the individual maximizes his safety margins means that he chooses that strategy which offers him positive pay-offs from the most distant state of the world. In Table 9.6.1 he chooses S_{20}. If safety margins were a constraint only, he might choose S_{30}. In the first case no numerical measure of the distance is required. For to select the strategy which offers a positive pay-off from the most distant state of the world, it is enough to know that the states of the world further to the right are more distant than those further to the left. In the case of a constraint, a clear meaning must be given to the margin beyond which the individual does not wish to go.

(9.6.3) The difficulty in Fellner's theory is that in fact there are no discrete states of the world. The distance function of safety margins cannot, therefore, be defined in terms of the number of the columns which would represent those states of the world. If the range of what is possible is partitioned into a number of states of the world which correspond, each of them, to a different position of the cost and demand curves, the arrangement of these states of the world in a descending order of pay-offs is unique. So is the distance function of safety margins. The partitioning, however, to which this function applies is not unique. As the range of possible positions of the cost and demand curves is continuous, it may be partitioned in a variety of ways. To each way corresponds then a different matrix of pay-offs and a different measure of safety margins.

In Fellner's formulation of the theory, the partitioning of the states of the world is in accordance with the best-guess estimates of the difference between the average revenue and the average costs. The greater is that difference, the more states of the world are supposed to be between the best-guess state and the most distant one with zero profits, the greater the distance between them and the greater the safety margin. The latter is thus proportional to the difference between the average revenue and average costs. But this is not the only way in which the range of possible positions of the respective curves can be partitioned. For instance, it may also be partitioned in accordance with the difference between the best-guess estimates not of average but of total revenues and costs. The greatest number of the states of the world with positive pay-offs corresponds then to the strategy which gives the best-guess estimate of the greatest difference between the total revenue and total costs, and the hypothesis of maximum safety margins comes to one and the same thing as that of maximum best-guess profits.

Furthermore, the range of possible states of the world may be so partitioned, and the distance function of the safety margins so defined, that maximum safety margins correspond to that strategy at which not the absolute difference between revenue and costs is at a maximum, but to that at which this difference bears the greatest proportion to the former or to the latter. And this again may apply to either the average or the total revenue and costs. It is also possible that the individual does not think of the relation between output and price as one between a hypothetical output and a guess of the price at which it could be sold, but as one between a hypothetical price and a guess of the output which can be sold at that price. His strategies are then the different prices he might choose. To maximize safety margins, he has to choose that price at which the horizontal distance between the revenue and the cost curves is the greatest, or at which it bears the greatest proportion to the former or to the latter.

(9.6.4) Are there any reasons for one of these hypotheses to be accepted as more plausible than another? With respect to some of them, the choice may have to be made on grounds of their applicability. If, for instance, the institutional and technical conditions of production are such that output of the firm must be planned some time in advance and sold at the price which it can fetch on the market, output is the firm's strategy, and the safety margins have to be measured by the differences between revenues and costs at those different outputs. The alternative mentioned at the end of the preceding paragraph cannot then apply. If on the other hand the institutional and technical conditions are such that the price must be fixed in advance and the output adjusted later on according to what the market can take, the price is the firm's strategy, and the measure of safety margins is the difference between revenues and the costs at different prices.

It is also possible that if a businessman makes a guess of what revenue he can obtain from the sale of a particular output, he thinks first of the price which he can obtain for it; and only then, as a second step in his calculation, he multiplies the price by the quantity of the product. Similarly, when he estimates his costs, he thinks first of the prices of raw materials and of the wages of labour which he will have to pay per unit of output. His original mistakes are in average rather than in total revenues and costs. He is, therefore, more inclined to identify safety margins with the difference between the former than with that between the latter. The fact that a particular absolute mistake appears bigger if it is made in relation to a smaller than to a bigger value, may be further an argument in favour of the relative differences between the best-guess revenues and costs. All these considerations, however, are far from conclusive. The actual procedures of guessing are too vague and uncertain to be a basis for the selection of a hypothesis about them.

(9.6.5) The theory of safety margins might also be appraised on the ground of how well the predictions which can be derived from it would pass an empirical test. But also in this respect the evidence is not very clear. The theory was invented to account for the practise of full cost pricing and for perverse reactions on the side of the demand for money. This is about all that it can do. No other predictions have been derived from it which would be confirmed by facts. If applied to gambling or insurance, it does not give any explanation of what actually takes place. For an individual who maximizes safety margins would not gamble; he would always insure himself, even at premiums which are not much less than the maximum loss for which the insurance provides a cover.

(9.7) Roy's Safety First

(9.7.1) If the future is partitioned into equally likely states of the world, the hypothesis of maximizing safety margins is equivalent to that of minimizing the chance of suffering a loss. For if the individual chooses a strategy which permits him to obtain a positive pay-off from the most distant state of the world, the strategy he chooses minimizes also the number of the states of the world from which he would obtain a negative pay-off. Thus if all the states of the world are equally likely, the strategy minimizes the chance of having a loss.

That an individual may behave in this way is the main hypothesis of Roy's theory of safety first.[1] Its actual form is more general and at the same time more precise than that of maximum safety margins. It follows, however, the same track and derives from similar considerations with respect to the objectives which the individual is supposed to pursue.

(9.7.2) The objectives are to avoid disaster. In Fellner's theory, the disaster is to have losses. For losses are likely to become cumulative and may easily lead to bankruptcy. In Roy's theory the level of pay-offs at which the disaster begins is left open.[2] It may be different for different individuals and in different circumstances. Not all losses become cumulative. They must reach a certain level if the danger of bankruptcy is to arise. And if the prospects of profits are very good, even a profit may be accepted as a disaster if it fails to reach a certain level. Thus the

[1] A. D. Roy, Safety First and the Holding of Assets, *Econometrica*, **20**, July (1952), pp. 431–49.

[2] In, On Choosing between Probability Distributions, *Review of Economic Studies*, **XXII** (3), (1954–5), pp. 194–202 ; and in, Risk and Rank or Safety First Generalised, *Economica*, **XXIII**, August (1956), pp. 214–28, Roy introduced the hypothesis that people want to avoid their incomes falling below those of the people they meet. The disaster level may then be identified with the income per head or per family in the relevant group of people. We will, however, neglect this point.

hypothesis is that the individual sets himself a limit below which he does not want his pay-off to fall.

(9.7.3) Large parts of Roy's argument are in mathematical form and will not be reproduced here. The sense of it is as follows. Let us go back to FIG. 5.2.2 in Chapter 5. The indifference curves represent there the individual's scale of preference with respect to what we have called lucrativity and risk. Lucrativity (plotted along the horizontal axis) is a measure of the general level of expected pay-offs; risk (plotted along the vertical axis) is a measure of uncertainty as to what the actual pay-off will be. A strategy is supposed to be more attractive the greater is its lucrativity and the smaller the risk. Hence the upward sloping form of the indifference curves.

An opportunity line may also be drawn as a boundary of points which represent lucrativity and risk of all strategies which are available. As more lucrative and less risky strategies are preferable to less lucrative and more risky ones, strategies represented by points above the boundary may be discarded straight away as inefficient. The individual will choose that strategy on the boundary which is on the highest indifference curve.

(9.7.4) This is the logic of choice in the conditions in which different strategies give rise to expectations of pay-offs of different lucrativity and risk. It applies to all possible measures of lucrativity and of risk, and to all possible forms of the indifference curves and of the opportunity line. The technique may be used to show what restrictions are imposed on the individual's scale of preference by various hypotheses about his behaviour. For instance, the hypothesis of the mean value implies that the mean value of pay-offs is the measure of lucrativity and that all indifference curves are vertical. The hypothesis that the individual chooses always the safest strategy presupposes that the indifference curves are horizontal. And so on, every hypothesis about our behaviour may be represented by a suitable system of indifference curves drawn with respect to suitable measures of lucrativity and risk.

(9.7.5) In Roy's theory the measure of lucrativity of strategies is the mean value of pay-offs, and the measure of risk is the standard error. Both are arbitrary. As long, however, as no other meaning is attached to them than that they are the result of certain arithmetical manipulations of the outcomes of pay-offs and of the probability weights attached to them, their choice is quite legitimate.

The mean value of pay-offs, and the standard error, are data which the individual is supposed to know. Probability weights of the possible states of the world are not known to him. The individual is not even able to describe the states of the world which he regards as possible. But he has some idea (derived from past experience) of the mean value of pay-offs and of the standard error.

(9.7.6) It can be shown by Tchebycheff's theorem[1] that the probability of a pay-off equal to or smaller than some arbitrary value d cannot exceed

$$p = \frac{s^2}{(m-d)^2}$$

where s is the standard error and m is the mean value of pay-offs. Thus Roy's hypothesis that the individual behaves so as to minimize the chance of a disaster, means that he chooses a strategy for which $s/(m-d)$ is the smallest.

This imposes the following restrictions on the form of the individual's indifference curves. In Fig. 9.7.6 the mean values of pay-offs from different strategies are plotted along the horizontal axis, the standard errors along the vertical axis, and the disaster

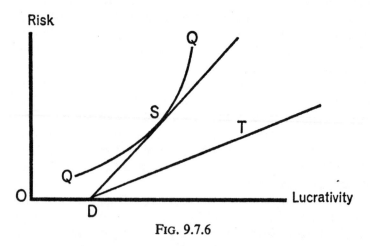

Fig. 9.7.6

[1] See H. Cramér, *Mathematical Methods of Statistics* (Princeton, 1946), pp. 182–3 (quoted by Roy).

value d is equal to OD. The fraction $s/(m - d)$ is the slope of a line drawn from D to the point representing the particular combination of the mean value of pay-offs and of the standard error. If, for instance, m and s are as at the point T, the fraction $s/(m - d)$ is equal to the slope of the line DT.

It follows that to minimize the chance of disaster, the individual must choose a strategy with such m and s that the corresponding point is on the least steep line drawn from D. The actual position of that point on the line is irrelevant. It is the slope that matters. The line may thus be interpreted as the individual's indifference curve. The steeper the line the more satisfactory are the respective combinations of m and s. If thus QQ is the opportunity line, the most satisfactory strategy is at S.

(9.7.7) What do we gain if we accept Roy's hypothesis and the restrictions with respect to the form of the indifference curves which it implies? One possible gain is that it may be applied as a normative theory. If our objective is to minimize the chance of disaster, the strategies which are available to us may be ranked by means of a formula. It is possible, for instance, that the mean values of pay-offs from particular types of investment and the respective standard errors, can be derived from the records of past experience. The investments which minimize the chance of disaster can then be selected by taking the smallest $s/(m - d)$.

(9.7.8) The other gain, the only gain in fact that is relevant to our purpose here, is that by means of Roy's hypothesis it is possible to explain the phenomenon of spreading risks. The argument is as follows. Suppose that there are n types of investment which all of them give rise to the same mean values of pay-offs per unit of investment and to the same standard error. Suppose further that there is no correlation between the possible deviations of pay-offs from their mean values in different investments. The strategies are the various ways in which the individual may distribute his resources between those investments. Let these resources be denoted by k. We may then argue that if the individual puts all of them into one type of investment, the mean value of pay-offs from them is km, and the standard error is ks. The disaster level d is also per unit of resources invested, and the slope of the respective indifference curve is $s/(m - d)$.

287

If, however, the individual distributes his resources evenly bet ween all types of investment, the standard error becomes $(k/n)s$ and the slope of the respective indifference curve is $s/n(m - d)$ As n is greater than unity, the latter strategy is preferable to the former.

The result is more complicated if the mean values of pay-off and the standard errors are different in different types of invest ment, and if the possible deviations of pay-offs are correlated one with another. Even then, however, the slope of the indiffer ence curve corresponding to a combination of different types of investment is generally less steep than that which corresponds to one type only. In the extreme case in which the deviations of pay-offs are completely correlated, the slopes of the two indiffer ence curves may be the same. Also the differences in the standard errors and in the mean values of pay-offs from different forms of investment may be such that one particular form is preferable to any combination of them. This, however, may be true in special cases only. In general spreading of risks is preferable to putting all the eggs in one basket.

(9.7.9) The advantage of having an explanation of the prin ciple of spreading risks is bought in this case at a very high price. For the restrictions imposed on Roy's hypothesis on the form of the indifference curves make the individual's scale of prefer ence intransitive. Point D in Fig. 9.7.6 represents a sure prospect of disaster. If, therefore, all indifference curves start there, all of them might be thought to correspond to the same place on the scale of preference, the same in fact as that of the sure prospect of disaster. Different slopes of the curves indicate, however, different places on that scale.

Furthermore, diversification can also be explained by other hypotheses. It has been shown by Markowitz[1] that if lucrativity and risk of a combination of assets are formalized as the mean value and the variance of the possible outcomes of returns from it, efficient combinations (that is to say those which lead to the greatest mean values of pay-offs at the respective levels of risk) imply diversification. Whatever, therefore, the exact form of the indifference curves, a diversified combination of assets is always preferable. The only condition is that lucrativity is a positive

[1] H. Markowitz, Portfolio Selection, *Journal of Finance*, VII, March (1952) pp. 77–91.

element and risk a negative element in the prospect of pay-offs to which the assets give rise.[1]

9.8) Inconclusive Descriptions

9.8.1) Most of the hypotheses discussed in this book lead to determinate predictions of behaviour. Those strategies are supposed to be chosen which maximize the mean value or the moral expectation of pay-offs, minimize subjective loss, are on the highest indifference curve, or satisfy some other but equally restrictive condition. In each case the data which the theory accepts as given are sufficient to determine what the chosen strategy will be. The only exception is the theory of games. It leads often to whole sets of strategies as a solution and does not enable us to say what the individual will actually do. The selection of the strategy he may adopt depends then on factors which are outside the context of the theory. In this last section we will deal briefly with two more theories which are incomplete in this sense.

(9.8.2) The following argument was put forward by Carter[2] as a modification of Shackle's theory. When contemplating a prospect, the individual is supposed to attach some weight to various outcomes in it by intuition. Quite irrespective, however, of whether the weights are subjective probabilities or degrees of potential surprise, he is not able to arrive at a very fine classification of them. All he can do is to distinguish between such steps as absolutely possible, likely, unlikely, etc. There may be several outcomes on each step. In that case, however, only the greatest gain on the side of gains and the greatest loss on the side of losses will attract the individual's attention.

[1] In his analysis of hedging, L. G. Telser (Safety First and Hedging, *Review of Economic Studies*, XXIII (1), (1955-6), pp. 1–16), made use of Roy's hypothesis as a constraint. He accepted the strategies which offer a smaller chance of disaster than an arbitrary limit as admissible, and introduced the hypothesis of the mean value of pay-offs to determine the strategy which was ultimately chosen. R. A. D. Egerton (The Holding of Assets: 'Gambler Preference' or 'Safety First', *Oxford Economic Papers*, 8, February (1956), pp. 51–9) suggested a way in which Roy's hypothesis of safety first might be translated into a special case of Shackle's theory.

[2] C. F. Carter, A Revised Theory of Expectations, *Economic Journal*, LXIII, December (1953), pp. 811–20; and in C. F. Carter, G. P. Meredith and G. L. S. Shackle (ed.), *Uncertainty and Business Decisions*, Liverpool University Press, (1957).

The result is the elimination of a number of outcomes from the original prospect. Only as many of them remain as there are steps in the weights on the side of losses and on the side of gains. Shackle would go further and select two outcomes only, one focus gain and one focus loss. Carter's hypothesis does not go as far as that. The individual is supposed to be capable of contemplating as many outcomes as there are steps in the weights. The strategies must, therefore, be compared one with another on the ground of prospects of pay-offs in which several outcomes appear.

As the number of steps is small, it may easily happen that at every level of the weight the outcome of gain is greater and the outcome of loss is smaller in one prospect than in some other. The strategy which gives rise to the former is then quite unambiguously preferable to that which gives rise to the latter. It may, however, also happen that at some steps of the weight one prospect is preferable to some other, and at other steps the latter is preferable to the former. In that case the theory offers no solution. The choice of the strategy is determined by factors which are outside its context. Or, the individual thinks up some third strategy which is unambiguously preferable to either of the former two.

(9.8.3) As a description of mental processes which lead to the choice of a strategy, Carter's theory may appeal to our intuition. As a scientific theory, it does not go further than common sense would go. For the only prediction which can be derived from it is that if within the limits imposed by our ability to see various characteristics of the alternatives, one alternative promises more than some other in every respect, it will be chosen. A case like this does not present any problem. A problem arises only if one alternative is preferable to the other in some respects, and the latter to the former in some others. In this case, however, the theory does not enable us to make any predictions at all.

(9.8.4) The theory might be developed along the following lines. When we are confronted with a number of alternatives, we usually have a very limited information about what the payoffs from them are likely to be. Even in the case of buying a good, a car for instance, the information we have about its characteristics and about the opportunities which we may have to use it is very limited. In the case of a strategy we know even less than we do in the case of a good. Our choices cannot, therefore, be regarded as the result of a process of maximization of pay-offs. For we do not know exactly what are the pay-offs which we would like to maximize.

The situation is rather that we classify all the alternatives as satisfactory or not satisfactory. A satisfactory alternative may, for instance, be that which is better in every respect than our present position or which promises a higher pay-off than some arbitrary aspiration level; an investment, for instance, which promises greater outcomes of pay-offs at every step of the weight, or an offer of a higher price for a house than the minimum which we would be prepared to accept. If we were confronted with a complete set of alternatives, we would probably find many elements in it which satisfy this condition. The hypothesis would then be incomplete. It would not enable us to predict the choice which the individual actually makes. The point, however, is that we are never confronted with a complete set of alternatives. The latter appear sporadically, and we do not know whether if we miss one of them, anything better will turn up. As soon, therefore, as an alternative becomes available which we regard as satisfactory, we accept it and do not bother about the others.

(9.8.5) A theory of choice has been developed along these lines by Simon.[1] Its basic hypothesis is that people are not maximizers but satisfiers. Their behaviour cannot be interpreted as a solution of a maximum problem. For they are never in possession of all the data which would make that solution determined. They move from one alternative to another as the latter becomes available. In the course of this process the aspiration levels may change as well. It is, therefore, by no means impossible that the ultimate choice will coincide with the solution of the maximum problem. Even then, however, the behaviour which leads to it is in the nature of a dynamic process and cannot be explained by any static hypothesis of the maximization of pay-offs.

Simon's theory of choice may again appeal to us as a description of what we actually do. It may also help to explain various

[1] H. A. Simon, A Behavioural Model of Rational Choice, *Quarterly Journal of Economics*, **LXIX**, February (1955), pp. 99–118 ; and the same author's, The Role of Expectations in an Adaptive and Behaviouristic Model, in Mary Jean Bowman (ed.), *Expectations, Uncertainty and Business Behaviour, op. cit.*, p. 56.

instances of behaviour in given initial and environmental conditions. But it does not lead to any amplifications of economic theory. Although, therefore, the comments made in these paragraphs do not do any justice to the elegance of the form in which the theory was presented and to the attention which it has then attracted, little more can be said about it within the context of this book.

A POSTSCRIPT ON
PURPOSE AND RESULTS

WHAT conclusions can be drawn from the analysis of the theories which have been discussed in this book? The theories cover a very wide range of problems in the behaviour of firms, in investment, gambling, liquidity preference, and choice in general. The questions asked, the hypotheses suggested, and the techniques used, differ from one case to another. All of them, however, treat of expectations. Our analysis should, therefore, throw some light on the purpose which the latter may serve.

Expectations are often identified with plans and all sorts of other anticipatory data. The purpose of the theory is then to derive from these data predictions of future behaviour. Much interesting work has been done in this field by the Bureau of Economic and Business Research of the University of Illinois. In the present book, however, this aspect of the theory has been completely neglected. It was explained at the beginning that we would be concerned here with expectations proper, and that anticipatory data are forecasts or programmes. The analysis of how the latter can be used in making predictions of other data is, therefore, outside the scope of the book. Our question is what purpose expectations proper may serve in economic theory.

To be complete, a theory which contains the element of expectations must also contain some hypotheses about how prospects can be derived from the evidence and about how behaviour can be derived from the prospects. An example of the former is that the same events are expected to take place in the future, the same prices, or the same outputs of competing firms, as those which take place at the time of the expectation. An example of the latter is that firms behave so as to maximize expected profits, or that they maximize expected sales subject to some minimum rate of profits.

In economic theory, expectations appear usually as sure pros pects. But this need not always be so. A theory may contain hypotheses about how multi-outcome prospects are related to the evidence and how behaviour is related to multi-outcome prospects. The evidence may be not about single events but about frequency distributions in repetitive events, and the theory may provide for a formula by means of which multi-outcome prospects are reduced to their sure-prospect equivalents. The mean value of pay-offs is an example of the required formula and if it is combined with the hypothesis of maximization of profits, the theory may permit us to make predictions of beha viour. In Roy's theory of safety first, for instance, the character istics of the multi-outcome prospects are identified with those of the frequency distributions which have been observed; and predictions about the individual's behaviour are derived from them by means of Tchebycheff's theorem.

In all these cases the element of expectations is formally redundant. For instead of deriving prospects from the evidence and the behaviour from the prospects, we might derive behaviour directly from the evidence by putting both formulae together. For instance, instead of saying that firms maximize profits with respect to prices which they expect and that they expect prices ruling at the time of the expectation to be also ruling at the time of the subject, we might simply say that firms maximize profits with respect to prices which are actually ruling at the time of the expectation. Or, instead of saying that multi-outcome prospects of prices have the same characteristics as the frequency distributions which have been observed in the past, and that firms adjust their positions to the mean values of the possible outcomes, we might simply say that firms adjust their positions to the mean values of prices which have been observed in the past. The element of expectations would then disappear from the theory. Its predictive value would, however, remain the same.

The reason why this is not usually done is that the element of expectations turns a causal theory into a teleological one, and that the latter appeals more to our intuition as an explanation of our behaviour than the former. We believe that our behaviour is determined by the objectives which we want to achieve. We do not work and do not buy goods because we respond in this way to some impulses which emanate from the environment.

We do so because we want to earn money and to consume goods which we buy. We know also that if the consequences of what we do now depend on what is going to happen in the future, a purposeful behaviour implies adjustment to expectations of what is going to happen. If profits, for instance, depend on prices at which our product will be sold in the future, maximization of profits implies adjustment to expectations of those prices. If, therefore, a theory says that we expect prices to be the same as those which are ruling now and that we adjust ourselves to the prices which we expect, we may have doubts about the actual content of the hypothesis, but we do not object to its general sense. As the prices on which our profits depend are those which will be ruling in the future, an adjustment to the expectations of those prices is what we must actually be doing.

If the hypothesis were that in spite of the fact that the consequences of our present behaviour depend on what happens in the future we adjust ourselves to what is taking place now, we would not see much sense in it. For the belief in the purposefulness of our behaviour is so deeply ingrained in the view which we take of ourselves, that a theory which does not respect this belief seems puzzling and incomplete. A teleological explanation implies the hypothesis that our behaviour is purposeful; and this is much more general than any of the hypotheses which we could formulate within the context of a causal theory. It explains, therefore, the particular forms of behaviour also in the sense of bringing them within the fold of a wider and more familiar class.

The element of expectations permits us also to split the connection between the behaviour and the environment on which the behaviour depends into two parts, and to subject the relevant hypotheses to a more conclusive plausibility test than this would be possible without the split. We may, for instance, regard the hypothesis that we expect the current prices to be ruling in the future as not generally valid, but none the less we may find it not implausible as an approximation. The hypothesis that in general we expect future prices to be 10% above their current level would seem implausible even as an approximation. If, however, we were asked to decide whether a hypothesis that we behave *as if* we were adjusting ourselves to current prices plus 10% is or is not a plausible description of the behaviour at which we ultimately arrive, we might find it difficult to give a definite answer on the ground of our general knowledge of the world. We would have to make a test. And if this turned out to be impossible or inconclusive, we would not be able to give an answer at all.

These considerations have undoubtedly played an important part in the formulation and appraisal of various chapters of economic theory. They help us to rule out hypotheses which otherwise would require an empirical test, difficult to perform, and probably not very conclusive in results. The ground on which these hypotheses are ruled out may be of doubtful value from methodological point of view. But the practice of subjecting hypotheses to a test of this kind is quite general. Whether those which have passed the test are then accepted or rejected is quite a different matter. As many plausible hypotheses can usually be formulated to explain the same facts, an empirical test may be required to decide which of them to accept and which to reject.

The fact that the practice is general does not mean that it is satisfactory. To give preference to a teleological theory because of its form and to rule out hypotheses by intuition are procedures to which many a scientist would object. If, therefore, expectations were introduced into economic theory merely to enable us to persist in those practices, their usefulness would derive solely from our inability to treat economics as a science.

We would be on much firmer ground if we could show that expectations permit us to explain behaviour which without them could not be explained. Hart's point about inefficient methods of production belongs to this class. It refers to situations in which no frequency distributions of outputs have been observed in the past. The behaviour of firms cannot, therefore, be related to any data about such distributions as the evidence. On the other hand, no inefficiency could arise if the methods of production were adjusted to sure prospects of outputs. Multi-outcome expectations are thus an indispensable element in the explanation of the fact that inefficient methods are often preferred to the efficient ones. The same applies to the hypothesis of the reduction of prospects by choice. The element of expectations interposed between the environment and the behaviour, permits us to account for some otherwise unexplained changes in investment, for liquidity preference, spreading risks, etc. In all these cases behaviour depends ultimately on the individual's tastes, and the element of expectations is indispensable for it to be accounted for. Gambling and insurance could not be explained either if the outcomes of both gains and losses were not taken into account.

It seems, therefore, that besides giving economic theory a teleological and intuitively more acceptable form, expectations also serve the purpose of making it more effective in explaining some special forms of behaviour. If the notion of expectations were removed from it, gambling, insurance, inefficient methods of production, etc. could not be explained by it. A more careful analysis of the attempts which have been made so far makes one wonder, however, if explanation is the right word in this case. For although very often the hypotheses about expectations fit very well the facts which the theory is supposed to explain, they do not necessarily fit any other facts. They are like formulae which fit a particular sequence of the registration numbers of the cars which we have already met, but do not tell us anything about those which we are going to meet.

The crucial point is that the operations in terms of which expectations are defined, cannot usually be performed. If, for instance, we could determine the probability weights and the utility measures of different pay-offs, we could derive from the moral expectation theory predictions of how the respective individual would choose his strategy. The hypothesis might then fit not only some of his choices but also others, any others in fact with which he might be confronted. Each individual choice would then be explained in the sense of being accepted as a member of some wider and already familiar class. If, however, expectations cannot be ascertained, the theory is only about some general features of our behaviour and contains hypotheses about general features of expectations. The features of behaviour may be, for instance, that we often gamble or insure ourselves. The hypotheses which the theory contains may then be that over the range which is relevant to the former marginal utility of income is increasing and over the range which is relevant to the latter marginal utility is diminishing. These hypotheses fit the facts of gambling and insurance. But they do not explain them in the sense of bringing them within the fold of a wider and more familiar class.

299

This comment applies probably less to the moral expectation theory than to any of the others which have been discussed here. For the hypothesis of increasing and diminishing marginal utility has been used by Friedman and Savage to explain also other facts; that lotteries offer usually more than one prize, that returns from more risky forms of investment are higher than those from less risky ones, etc. But these are only exceptions which confirm the rule. In general, the hypotheses about expectations fit the facts rather than explain any of them.

Furthermore, the facts which these hypotheses fit are so general that they may be fitted in various ways. Liquidity preference, for instance, may be accounted for by the reduction of prospects by choice as well as by Shackle's hypothesis of two focus outcomes. Gambling and insurance may be fitted by the moral expectation theory, by Hurwicz's index of pessimism-optimism, and by the reduction of prospects by choice. Inefficient methods of production may be derived from any form of aggregation of possible outcomes. And as usually the implications of these theories do not go outside the class of the phenomena which they fit, it is difficult to discriminate between them on any empirical grounds.

The conclusions do not seem, therefore, to be very encouraging. To a large extent, expectations have been introduced into economic theory to give it a teleological form and to make its hypotheses intuitively more acceptable. In some cases they help also to account for such facts as gambling, insurance, liquidity preference, etc. The more scientific, however, is the view which we take of them the less in fact they seem to explain.

Index

301

303